IMAGES
of America

San Antonio Cemeteries Historic District

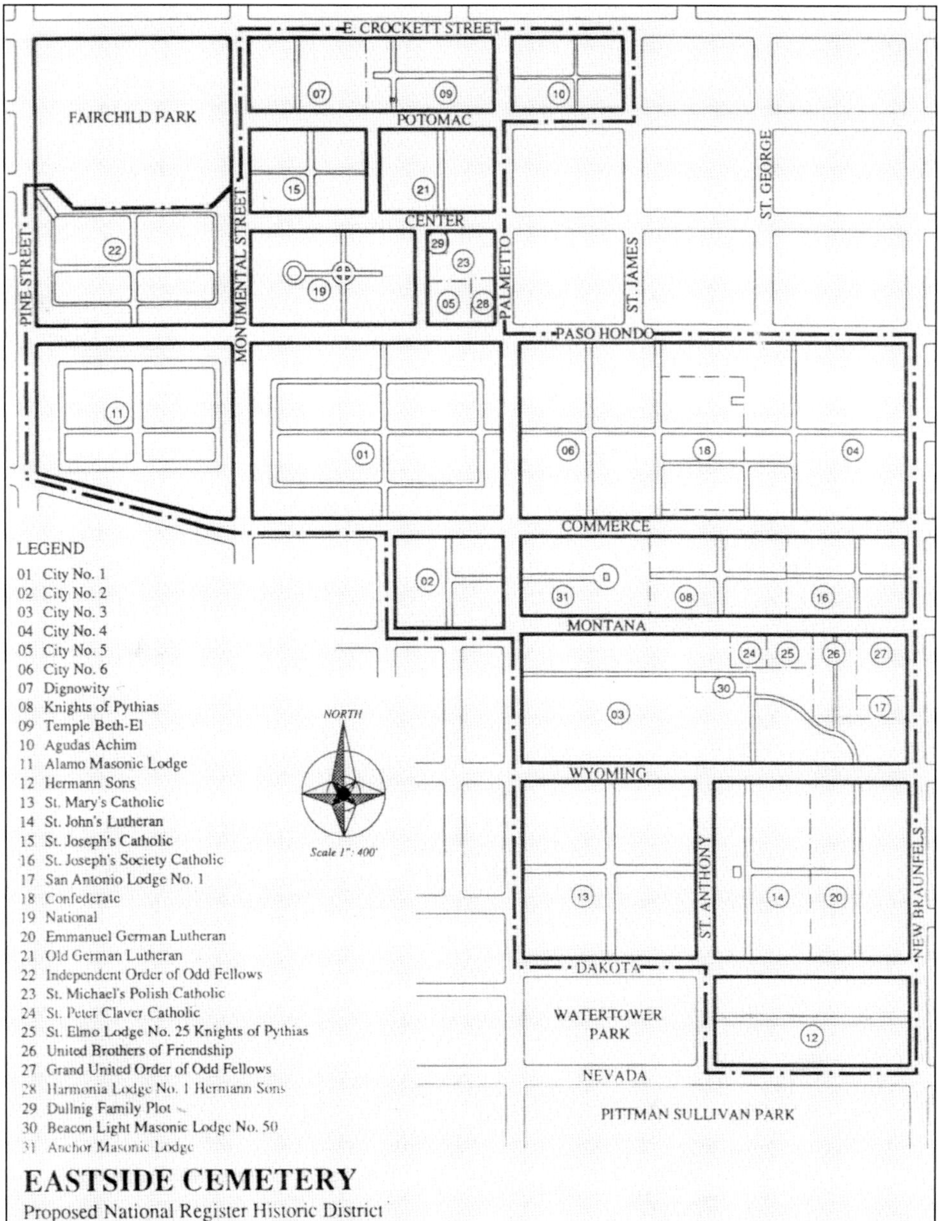

This map shows the locations of the 31 cemeteries in the Old San Antonio City Cemeteries Historic District. Each is numbered. After each caption, a bracketed number has been placed to indicate that cemetery's location. The map is from *The Eastside Cemetery District: Where San Antonio History Lives.* (Courtesy of the Texana and Genealogy Department of the San Antonio Public Library.)

ON THE COVER: The boy angel in the center represents Raoul Violland, born in 1902 and died in 1914, the only child of Maj. Hardie A. and Aurora P. Violland. The graves on either side are of Major Violland and his wife. Major Violland was born in Brownsville, Texas, and served in the Spanish-American War and in France during World War I. He was director of the finance department at Fort Sam Houston the two years before he retired and died in 1925. (Authors' collection.)

IMAGES
of America

San Antonio Cemeteries Historic District

Frank and Linda Faulkner

ARCADIA
PUBLISHING

Copyright © 2014 by Frank and Linda Faulkner
ISBN 978-1-4671-3186-5

Published by Arcadia Publishing
Charleston, South Carolina

Printed in the United States of America

Library of Congress Control Number: 2014941061

For all general information, please contact Arcadia Publishing:
Telephone 843-853-2070
Fax 843-853-0044
E-mail sales@arcadiapublishing.com
For customer service and orders:
Toll-Free 1-888-313-2665

Visit us on the Internet at www.arcadiapublishing.com

This book is dedicated to our children and grandchildren,
Nicholas, Colin, Kyle, Angela, Sierra, Charles,
Knight Raven, Daniel, Glorie, and Lakota.

Contents

ACKNOWLEDGMENTS

We would like to thank our son Colin and granddaughter Knight Raven who accompanied us on some of our photography trips to the cemeteries and took some of the photographs. We also offer thanks to all the librarians and researchers who compiled information we used, whether census, obituaries, biographies, military records, clipping files, or earlier published works, and indices to these and other sources. Without those devoted to maintaining these types of records, our lives would be like *Groundhog Day*, constantly starting over and accomplishing little. I must thank my staff at the Texana and Genealogy Department of the San Antonio Public Library for all their work over the years, and continuing the work as I took leave to work on this book. Finally, we would like to thank our editor at Arcadia Publishing, Stacia Bannerman, for her guidance as well as all the staff there.

All photographs of the gravestones and cemeteries are those of the authors. All other images are courtesy of the Texana and Genealogy Department of the San Antonio Public Library.

Introduction

San Antonio's Eastside Cemetery District is located on approximately 103 acres about one and a half miles east of city hall. Boundaries are Crockett Street on the north, Nevada on the south, New Braunfels Avenue on the east, and Pine Street on the west. It consists of 31 burial grounds that range in size from .06 to 10.6 acres. An average of 70 percent of the burials are pre-1949. With its multifaceted ethnic and cultural complex, the Eastside Cemetery District truly represents the history of San Antonio.

Early cemeteries had been around San Fernando church and the missions in the traditional Catholic style. During the early 1800s, burials took place in the Campo Santo (now the corner of Santa Rosa and Houston Streets), including what is now Milam Park.

On April 3, 1848, at the request of the parish priest, the city set aside eight acres, approximately half for a Catholic cemetery and half for a city cemetery.

On October 2, 1850, city alderman Onesimus Evans asked for a committee to investigate creating a new cemetery for the city near the old powder house. Powder House Hill was the site of some buildings used for storage of powder and munitions by the Spanish. It was mentioned by Berlandier in 1828, sketched by Seth Eastman in 1848, and considered for use by the Confederates later. It is believed to be adjacent to City Cemetery No. 2, on or near the site of the Lucas Monument Works at 1906 East Commerce Street.

The 1848 expansion stood the city well until January 24, 1853, when city council called for a survey of 20 acres near the powder house. On May 30 of that year, the first lots were sold to the Alamo Masonic Lodge. In the years to follow, other fraternal, religious, and ethnic organizations purchased or were given lots. By the time lot sales ceased in 1902, the complex had grown to its current 103 acres. The old Catholic and city cemeteries of 1848 were leveled and cleaned up, with most of the bodies being moved. However, there is no documentation as to the actual disposition of the burials of either cemetery.

Another point of interest that some readers will be aware of is that there was once a 32nd cemetery in the area—City Cemetery No. 7. At some time, the area just south of Hermann Sons Cemetery at Dakota Street and New Braunfels Avenue became a paupers' cemetery. In 1915, city council had been negotiating with the Catholic Church to sell the property. Because of complaints from people in the neighborhood that burials were only three feet deep and the area was unkempt and overcrowded, the city ceased burials there as of March 1, 1923. The bodies in City Cemetery No. 7 were moved to San Jose Burial Park in 1944. At the time, San Jose was bigger than it is now and part of it had been leased to the US War Department in 1941. As the war progressed and the military used the property, the location of the burials was lost. Only about 20 or 25 are known today.

The Eastside Cemetery District was one of the first west of the Mississippi to follow the pattern of the Rural Cemetery Movement of the early 1800s. Prior to the late 1700s, most cemeteries, like San Fernando, were beside local churches. As communities grew, the smell and health-related concerns caused towns to move their cemeteries away from the inhabited areas, generally to higher locations for better drainage and where they were not likely to be damaged by flooding. The Eastside complex is on a slight rise between Salado Creek and the San Antonio River valley. The southern part was the site of a soft rock quarry. It is relatively flat with little vegetation. There is a thin layer of soil over soft limestone. There are a few natural trees, mostly live oak. Others have been introduced by human or animal intervention.

The purpose of the authors is to make people aware of the community's history through those buried in these cemeteries and the history of the cemeteries themselves. In the limited space we have, we will introduce the reader to people of various occupations and social strata, different kinds of gravestones, the iconography of these stones, and the mixture of people from all over the United States and elsewhere who came together in this community.

There are a couple of things to know that make this not a totally accurate portrayal of the community as a whole. First, the community has always been heavily Hispanic, which is not reflected in these cemeteries. Hispanics have traditionally been Roman Catholic and have been buried in San Fernando Nos. 1 and 2 cemeteries, which are not part of the Eastside cemeteries. Second, the African American population has always been less than 10 percent. There are six African American cemeteries in the complex, but they are small. The primary cemetery for this group for many years has been Eastview Cemetery or Southern Memorial Park, again not part of the group. In regard to both ethnic groups, they have generally been omitted from the public record and are more difficult and time consuming to research.

At present, there is no published history for the general reader on San Antonio's Eastside cemeteries. Between June 1989 and January 1991, a study of the Eastside cemeteries was conducted for the Eastside San Antonio Economic Development Council. Sally S. Victor, project director, and her team did an excellent job of general historic research on the project area. The result was *The Eastside Cemetery District: Where San Antonio History Lives*. The City of San Antonio and other groups contracted and received *Old San Antonio City Cemeteries Historic District—Eastside Cemetery Complex Master Plan*, published in 1990. This too presented some history and made proposals to improve the area so it could be listed in the National Register of Historic Places. The final piece of background research appears in the nomination papers presented to list the cemeteries in the National Register.

These were a starting point for our own investigations of the history of the cemeteries and a selection of who and what to highlight. Research sources for the captions came from a variety of sources including federal census records, death certificates, local newspapers, various books, clipping files, and more. The notes compiled for this work will be filed in the Texana and Genealogy Department of the San Antonio Public Library.

One

City Cemetery No. 1

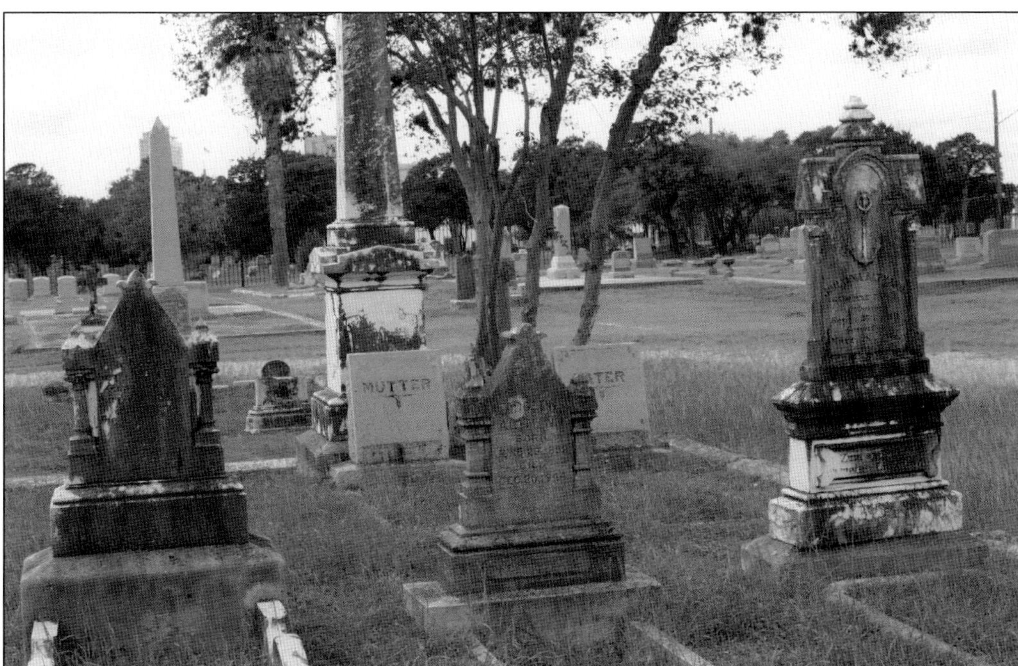

It is appropriate that the first photograph is that of the Altmann family. Brothers Anton and Adolph both worked as stonecutters. By age 30 in 1870, Anton was working as a stonemason. By 1879, Anton had worked with Frank Zeven at 212 East Commerce Street. In 1882, he committed suicide, possibly because of physical ailments. After his death, his brother Adolph worked with Zeven. The firm disappeared by 1908.

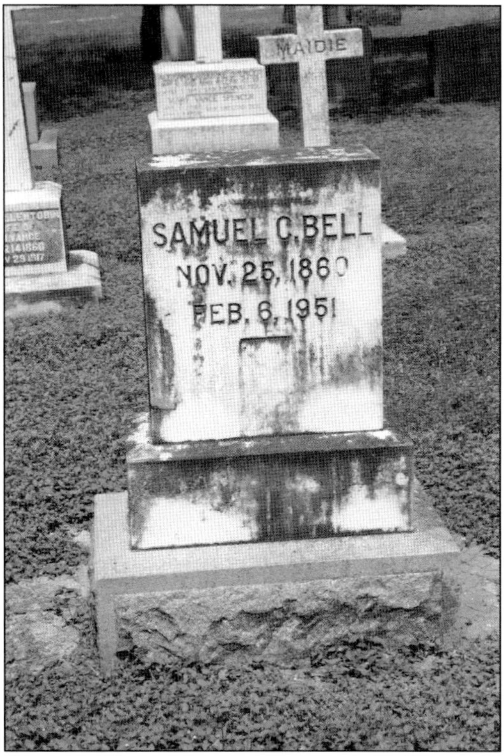

Samuel Bell began his career as a jeweler and engraver with his father and grandfather. In his thirties, he built a herd of Jersey cattle and pioneered irrigation. In his forties, he began a real estate business specializing in farms. He was elected mayor in 1917 and served until defeated in 1921 by Ku Klux Klan forces. He served as Bexar County treasurer from 1935 until his death in 1951.

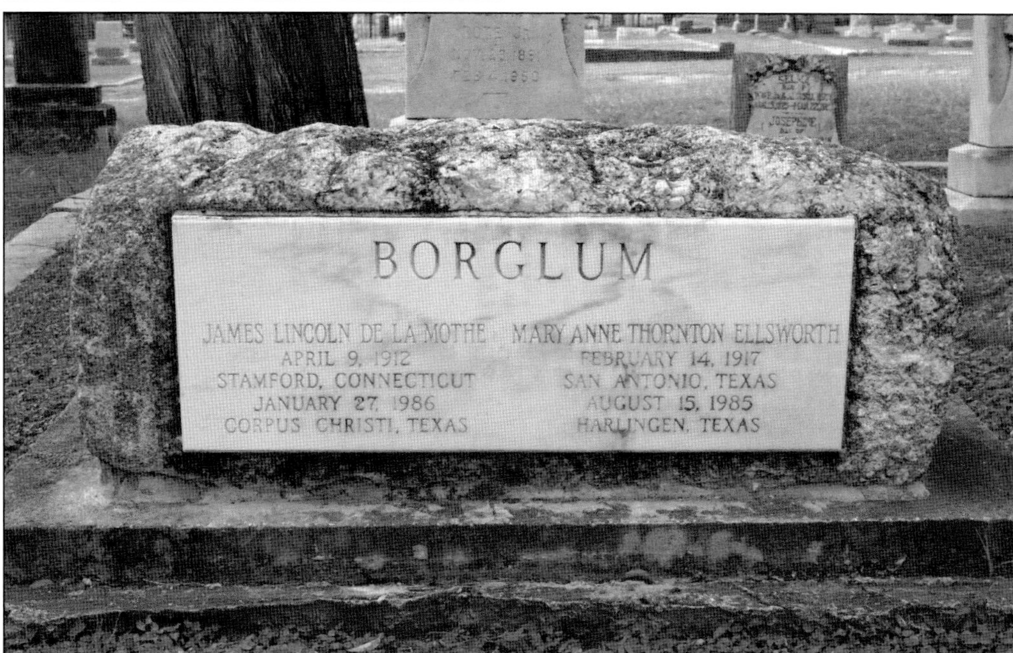

James Lincoln de la Mothe Borglum was the first child of Mount Rushmore sculptor Gutzon Borglum's second marriage. Lincoln periodically assisted his father at Mount Rushmore until Gutzon's death. In the early 1940s, Lincoln served as superintendent of Mount Rushmore National Memorial. Afterward, he returned to Texas as a sculptor in his own right.

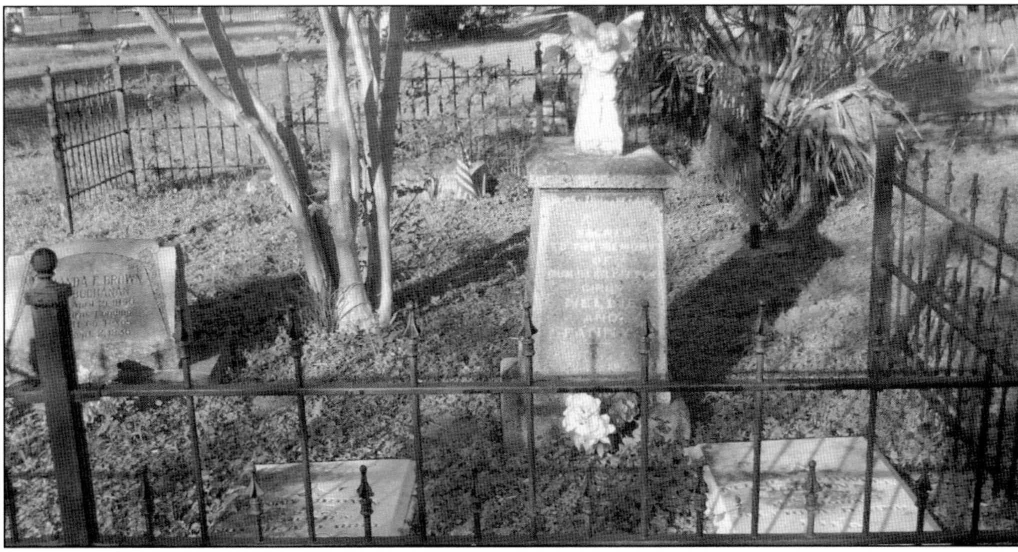

Inside this partially enclosed lot is the Brown family. Most of the family's life was on its ranch in McMullen County. The two graves with flat stones are for Nellie and Fanny, neither of whom survived to her second birthday. An angel memorial watches over the two girls. Their mother, Amanda Brown, rests beside them.

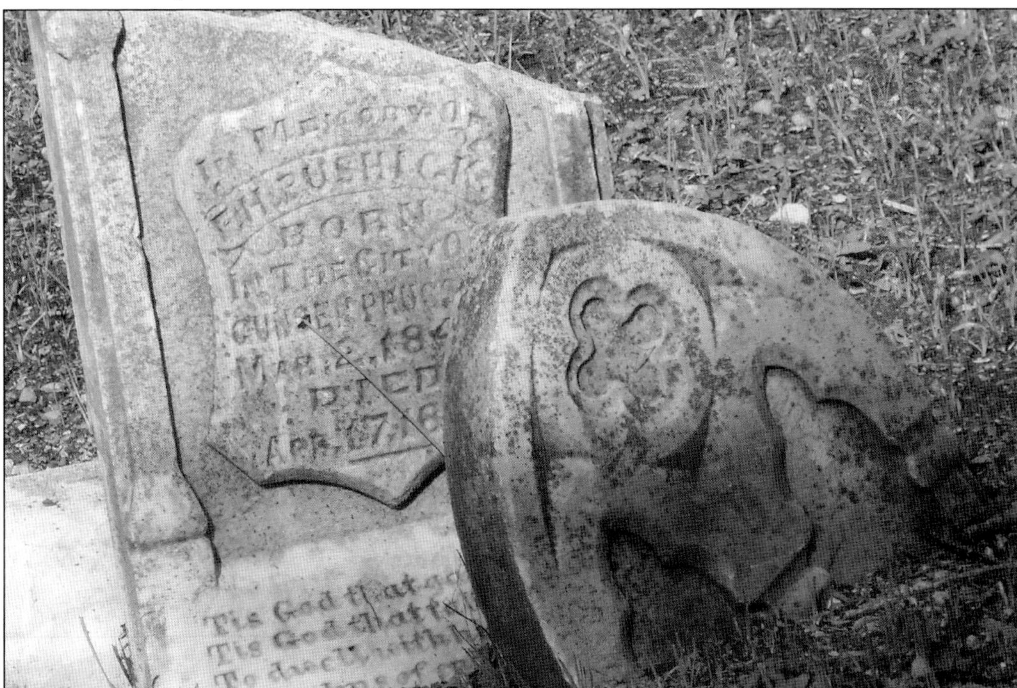

While still a child, Frank Bushick began his career as a printer and reporter for the *San Antonio Light*. In 1891, he became city editor and then managing editor of the *San Antonio Express*. For several years, he worked in the Congressional Press Gallery in Washington. He worked for several state and national Democratic campaigns. Bushick helped bring the State Tuberculosis Hospital here. In 1923, he was elected tax commissioner.

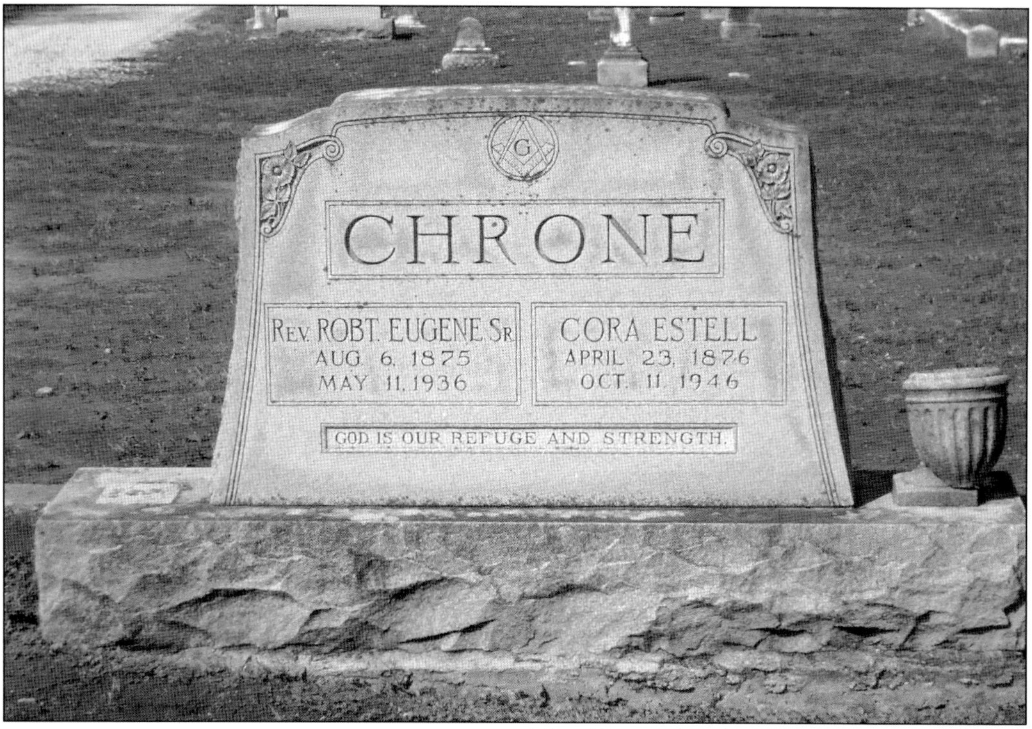

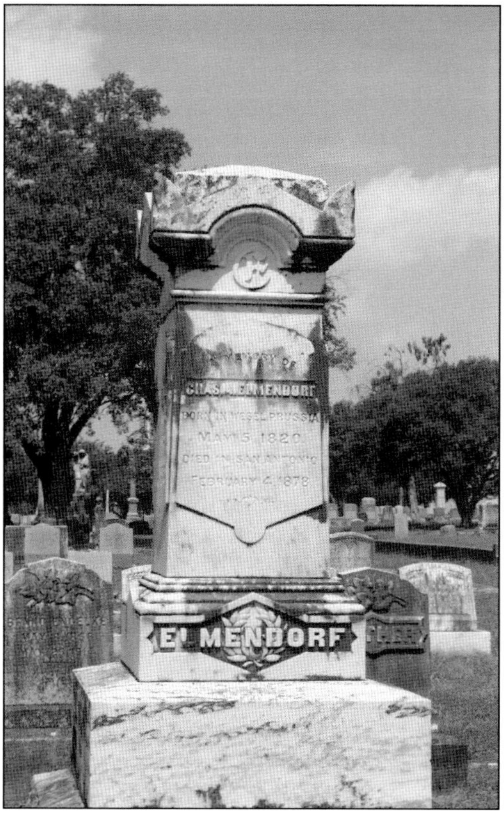

The Chrone family is typical of many in San Antonio. Robert was born in Indiana, and Cora, whose parents were from Louisiana, was born in Texas. Shortly after their son, Robert Jr., was born in California, they settled permanently in San Antonio. By 1930, he was a publisher and minister as well as an active member in the Masons, Alzafar Shrine, Alamo Lodge No. 44, and Eugene Hernandez Camp of Spanish-American War veterans.

A native of Prussia, Charles Elmendorf Sr. settled in New Braunfels in 1844. He later came to San Antonio, establishing one of the first hardware stores in the city at the corner of Military Plaza and Presidio (now West Commerce Street). In 1877, he opened a branch on the west side of Alamo Plaza. While Charles served on the city council, his son Henry was later mayor and was also the namesake of Elmendorf, Texas.

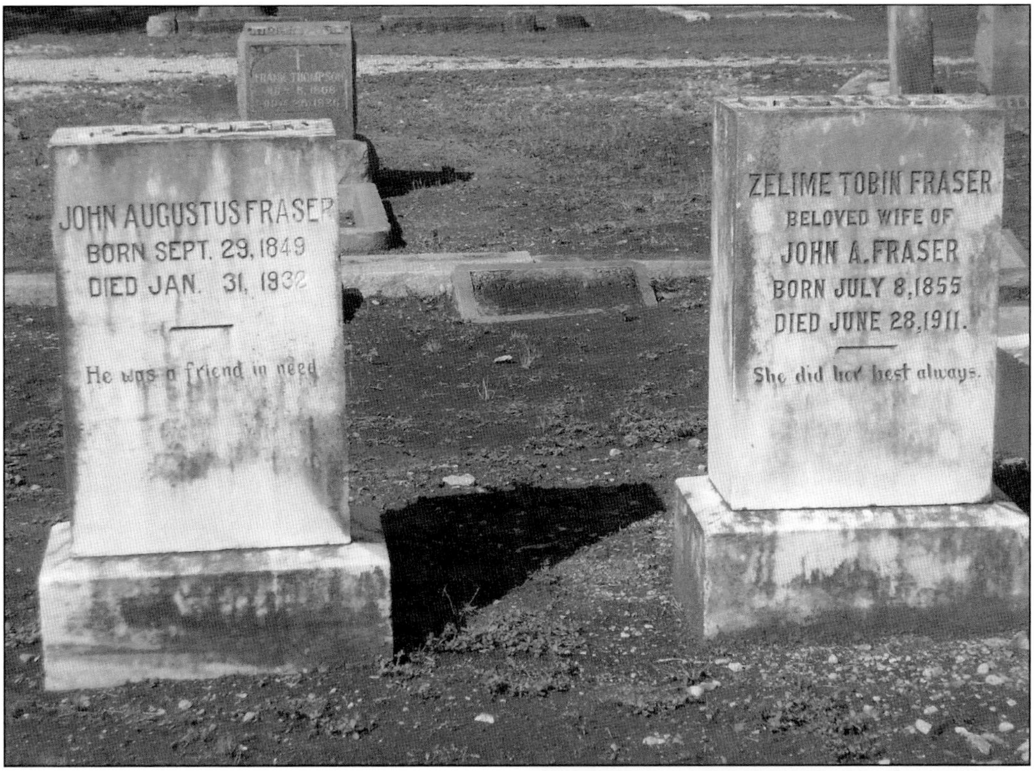

John Fraser Jr. arrived in San Antonio in the mid-1850s, later attending Bastrop Military Academy and Kentucky Military Institute as a young man. Over the years, he worked for George Brackenridge's First National Bank, San Antonio National Bank, and the bank of Sullivan and O'Connor. He married Zelime Tobin at St. Mark's Episcopal Church in 1877. He acquired, subdivided, and sold lots in Tobin Hill.

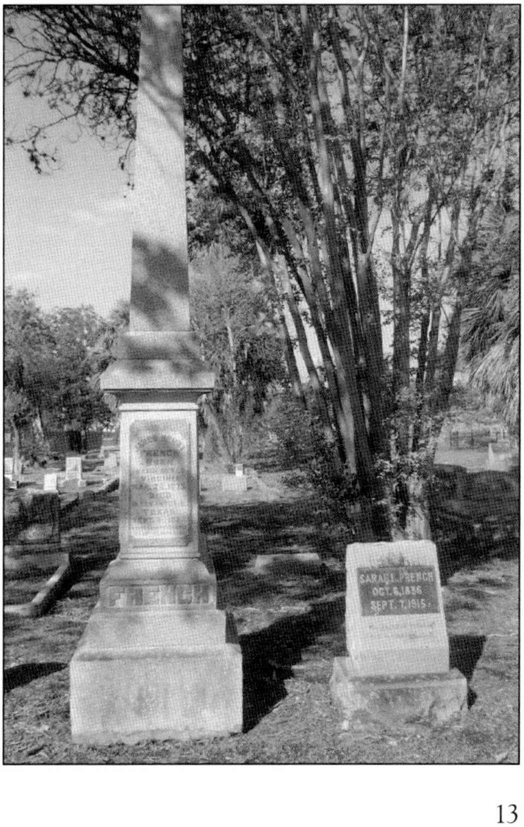

It was under Mayor James H. French's administration (1875–1885) that San Antonio ceased to be "a frontier town." The Civil War and Reconstruction resulted in fracturing local politics, which was only overcome by a non-partisan group led by French. He was the first to establish an annual budget for the city, and created a uniform street naming and numbering system, which allowed for home delivery of mail, and more.

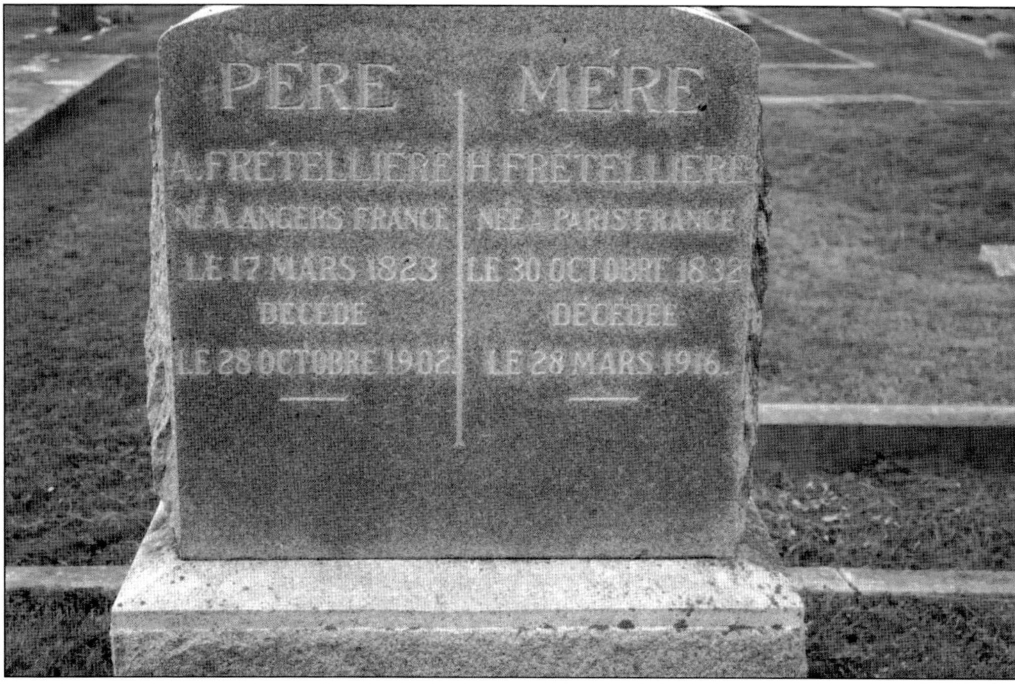

August Fretelliere and his wife, Henrietta, were both immigrants from France, along with the Grenet, Giraud, Guilbeau, and Armaud families. He was a member of the French Mutual Aid Society and a local merchant. Henrietta was a sister of Theodore Gentilz, the artist. As with many first-generation immigrants, their gravestone is in their native language, French.

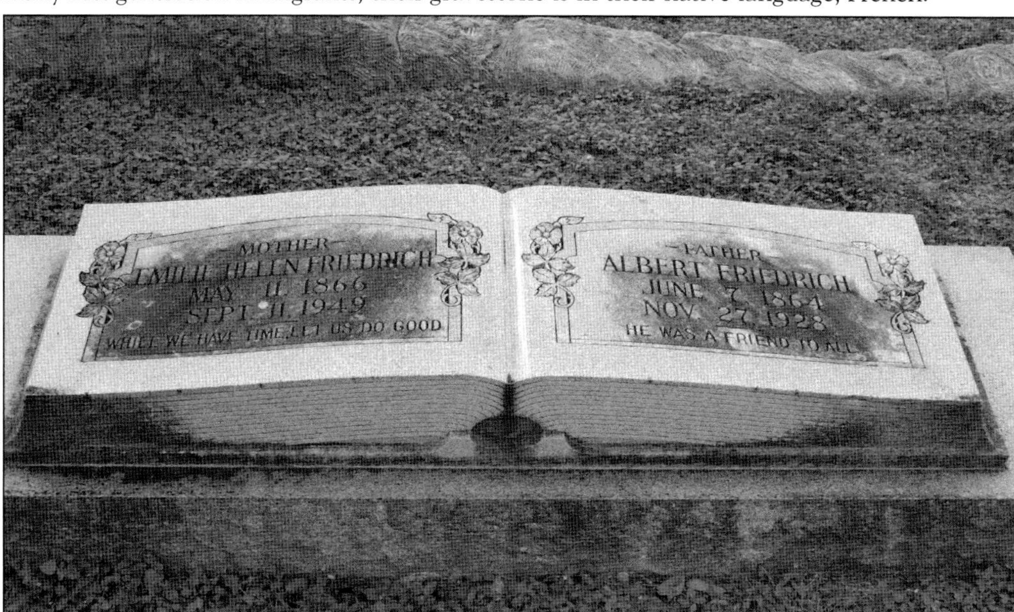

Albert Friedrich's name is synonymous with the Buckhorn Saloon. As an avid hunter, he brought trophies to the bar at the Southern Hotel. Eventually, he opened his own establishment and displayed them. His customers began to bring theirs as well. Emilie, his wife, created artwork from rattlesnake buttons. The Buckhorn continues today.

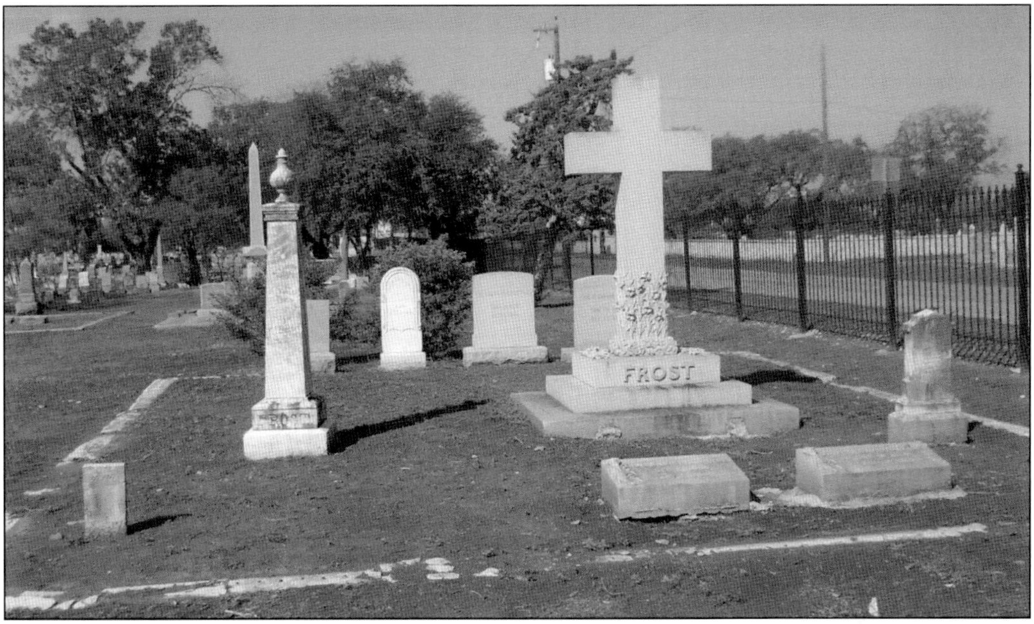

The Frost family is one of the major business families in town and has been since 1868, when Thomas C. Frost and his brother John left their Alabama farm and began as merchants and freighters. They built warehouses for wool, cotton, pecans, and other items. In 1899, they took out a national bank charter. Thomas was a delegate to Texas's Secession Convention, and he and John fought as Confederate soldiers.

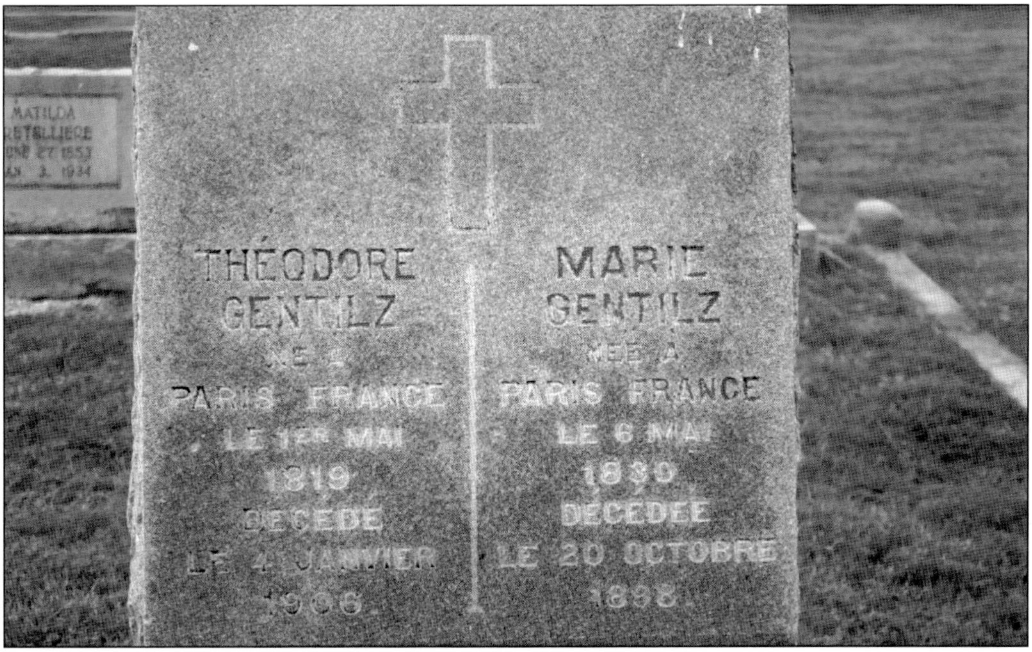

Jean Louis Theodore Gentilz, born in Paris in 1819, trained as a painter, draftsman, and engineer. In 1844, Henri Castro hired him to serve as surveyor, artist, and promotional agent for his colony in Texas. His artwork produced a valuable and accurate record of the life he saw in Texas. Also, he was a founding member of the French Mutual Relief Society.

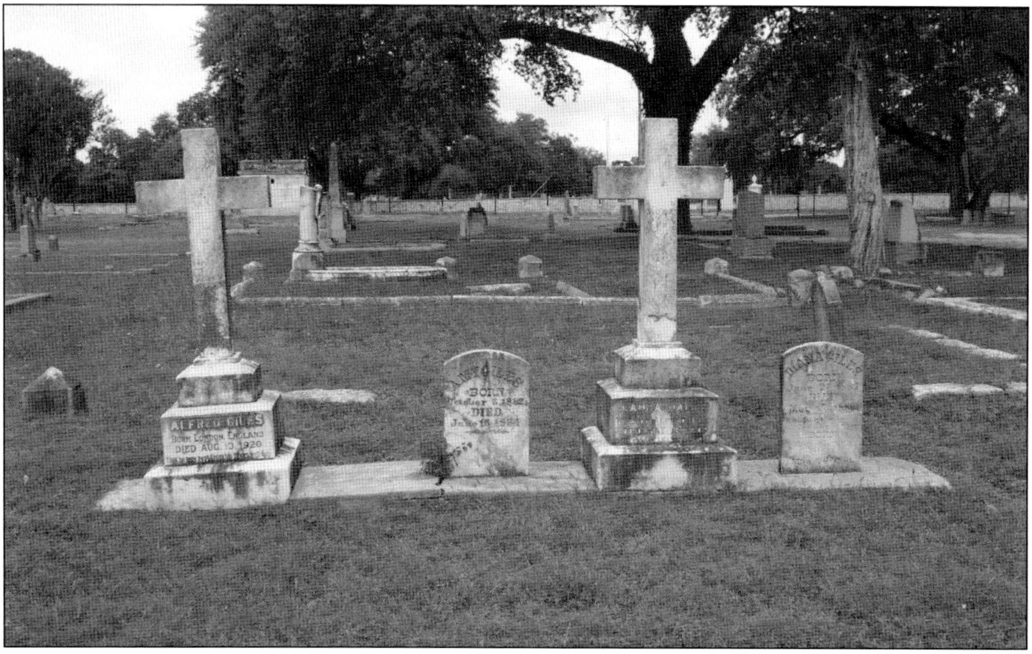

Alfred Giles is perhaps the best-known architect of the 19th and early 20th centuries in the Southwest and Mexico. Examples of his work are the Steves Homestead and the Bexar County Courthouse. He was also well known for raising Poll Angus cattle and Angora goats. Born in London, he came to San Antonio in 1875. In 1881, he married Laura James, daughter of John James.

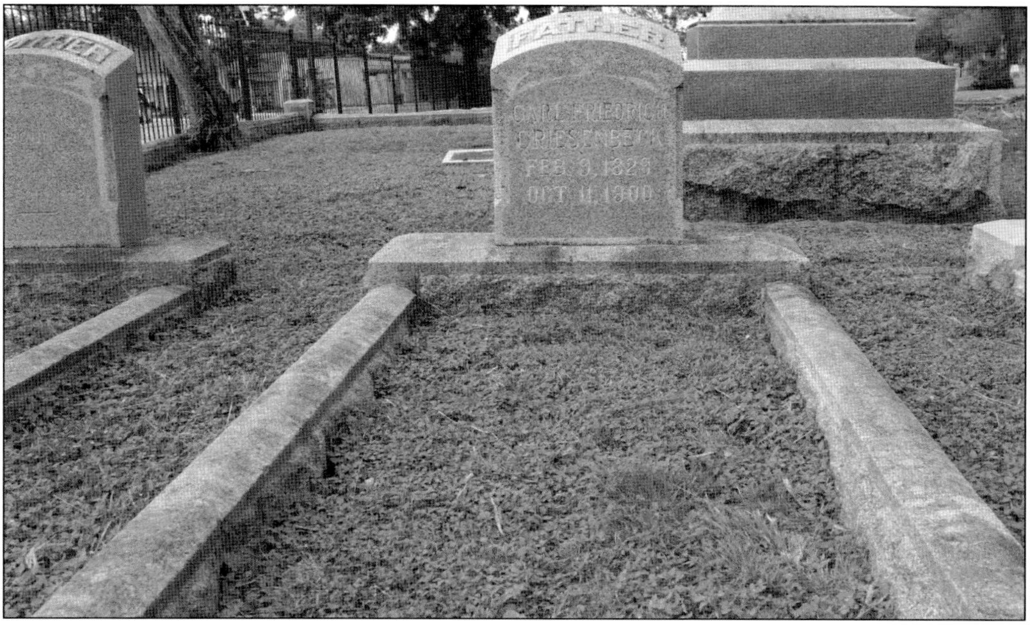

Born in Prussia in 1829, Carl Friedrich Griesenbeck arrived in Galveston in 1849. He worked as a farmer, postal clerk, and store clerk. During the Civil War, he was a commission agent in partnership with Governor Madero of Mexico. He worked as a cashier in John Twohig's bank for 23 years, before returning to the commission business. He was a founder of the German-English school and the Casino Association.

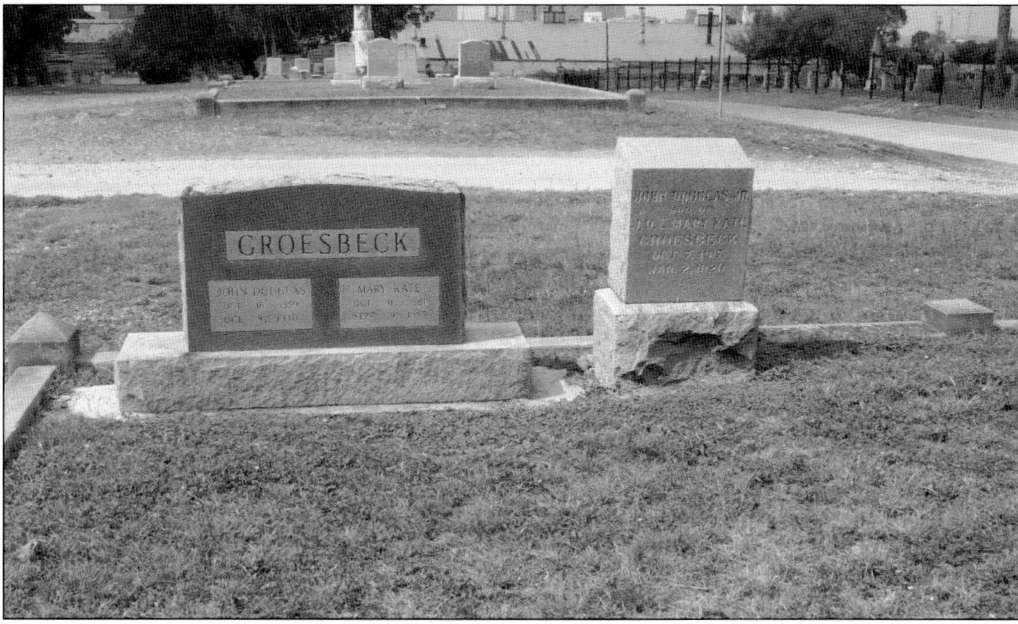

John D. Groesbeck, born in 1815 in New York, began his career as a railroad surveyor. With the Panic of 1837, Groesbeck decided to move to Texas. With Dr. Levi Jones, he surveyed and platted the town of Galveston. When his health began to fail, he moved to San Antonio where he went into business with Nat Lewis and John C. French as a government contractor.

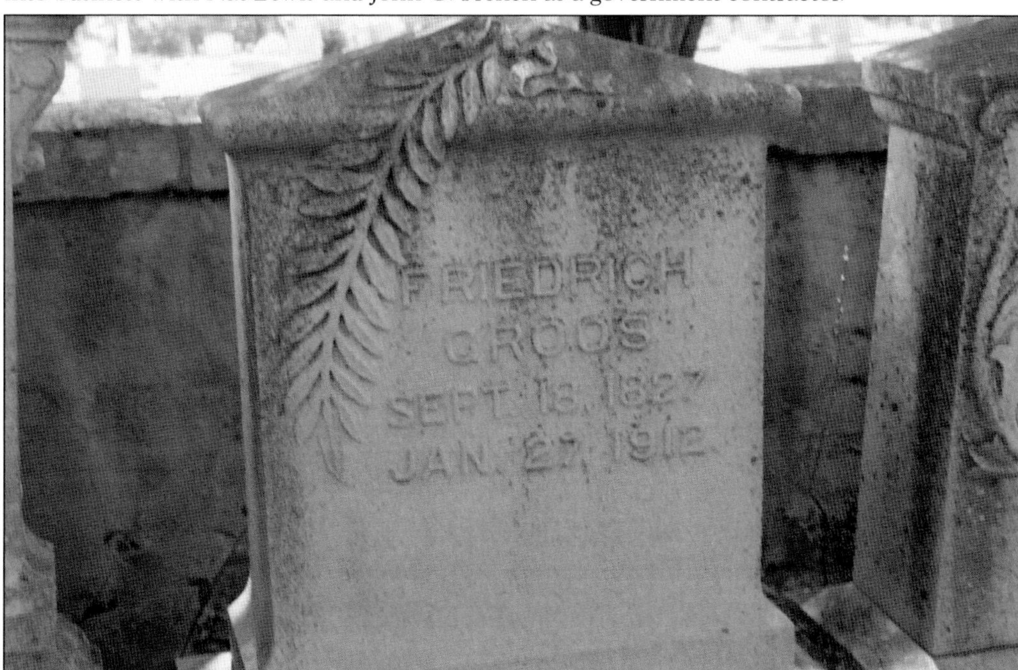

Friedrich Wilhelm Groos, and his brothers Gustav and Karl, arrived at Galveston in 1848. Friedrich became a partner with Bryan Callaghan in a mercantile and freighting business in Eagle Pass. In 1854, he and his brothers organized F. Groos and Co. The merchandising business eventually resulted in a bank. The private bank was nationalized in 1912 as the Groos National Bank.

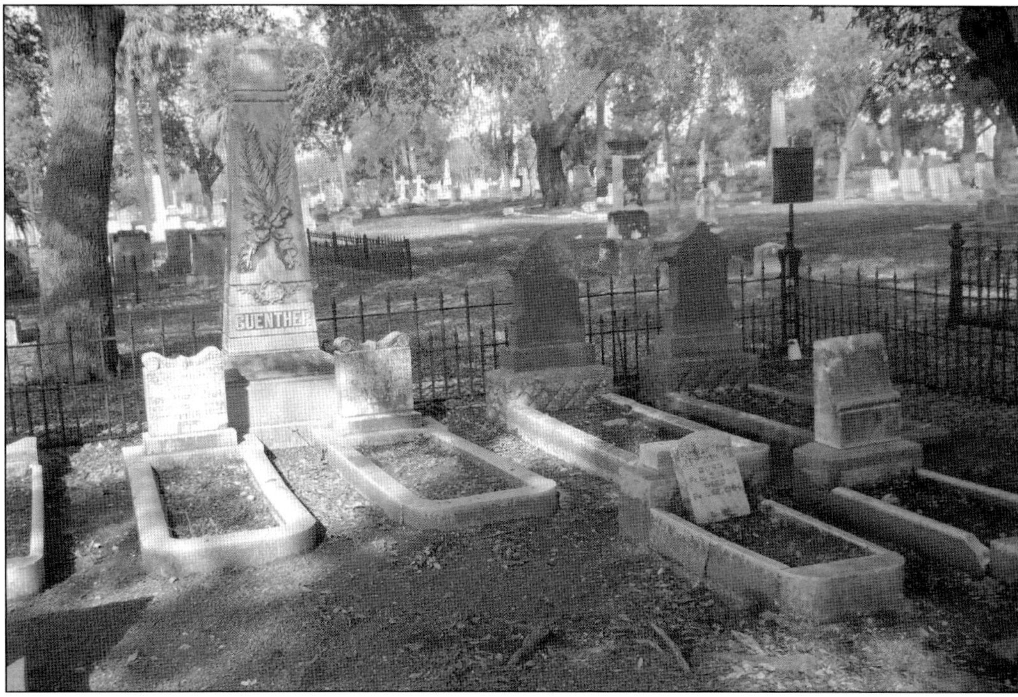

Notice the wheat that adorns the Guenther obelisk. Wheat may represent home, prosperity, or affection. Here, it may well represent all of those. Carl Hilmar Guenther, born in Saxony, Germany, built the first mill in San Antonio in 1859. For almost 10 years he owned a mill in Fredericksburg, where he married Dorothea Pape in 1855. The milling operation is still in business as Pioneer Flour Mills.

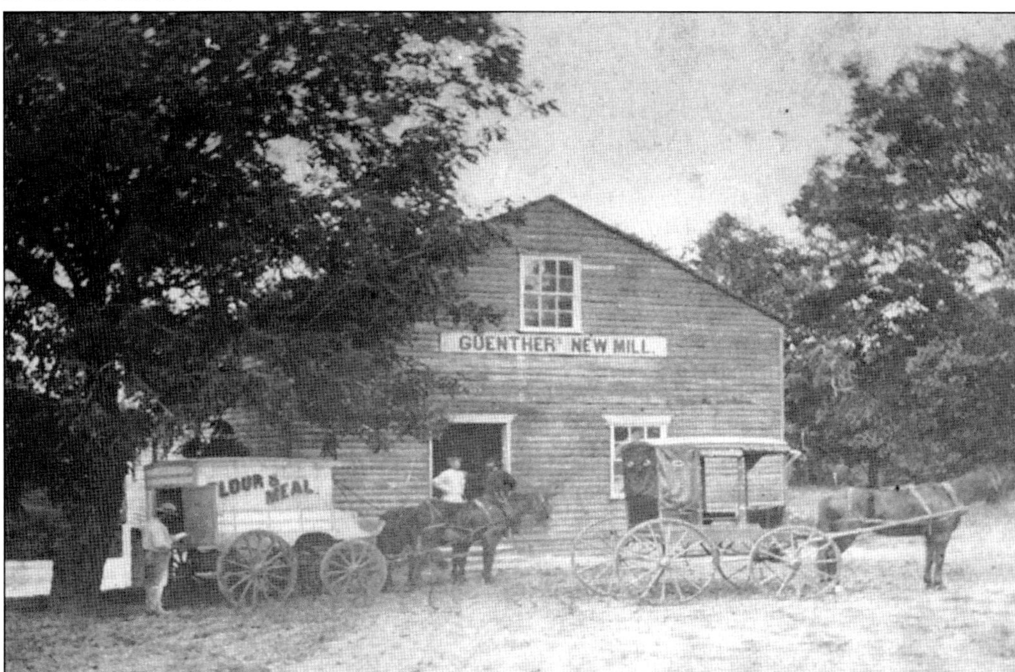

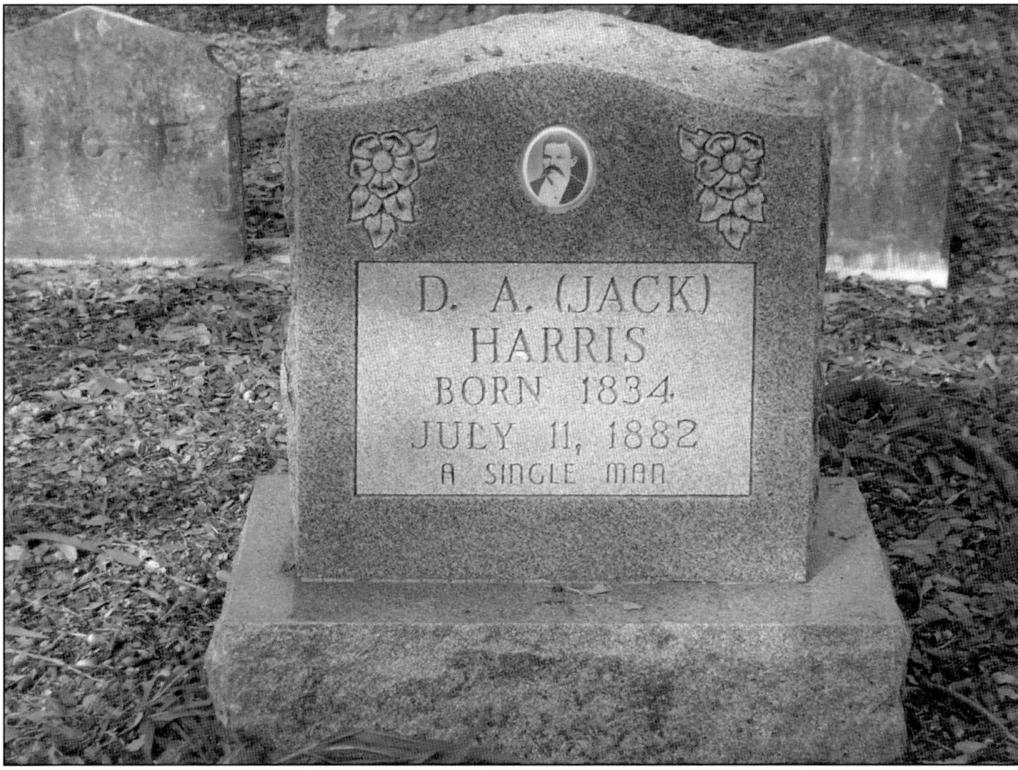

Connecticut-born Jack Harris served on San Antonio's police force and, during the Civil War, was a member of the 2nd Texas Cavalry. In 1872, he opened a saloon at West Commerce and Soledad Streets. On July 11, 1882, Austin city marshal Ben Thompson killed Harris over a gambling debt. His original gravestone was stolen and replaced with this one by the Friends of Jack Harris Committee.

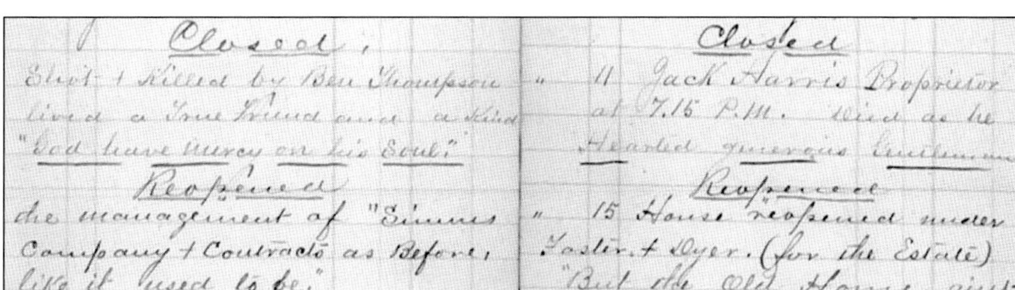

Harris's saloon incorporated a variety theater in 1874, and the name became the Vaudeville Theatre. This extract is from the ledger for the Vaudeville Theatre, kept by Frank Sparrow. Two years after Harris was killed, city marshal Thompson was shot and killed at the Vaudeville. These killings and others made national headlines.

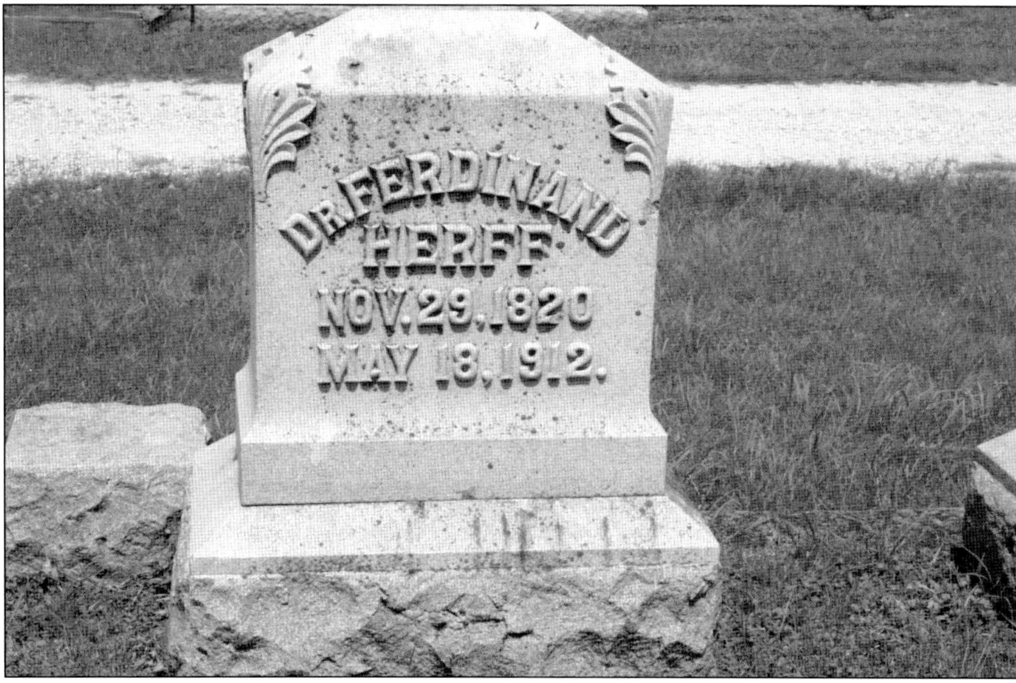

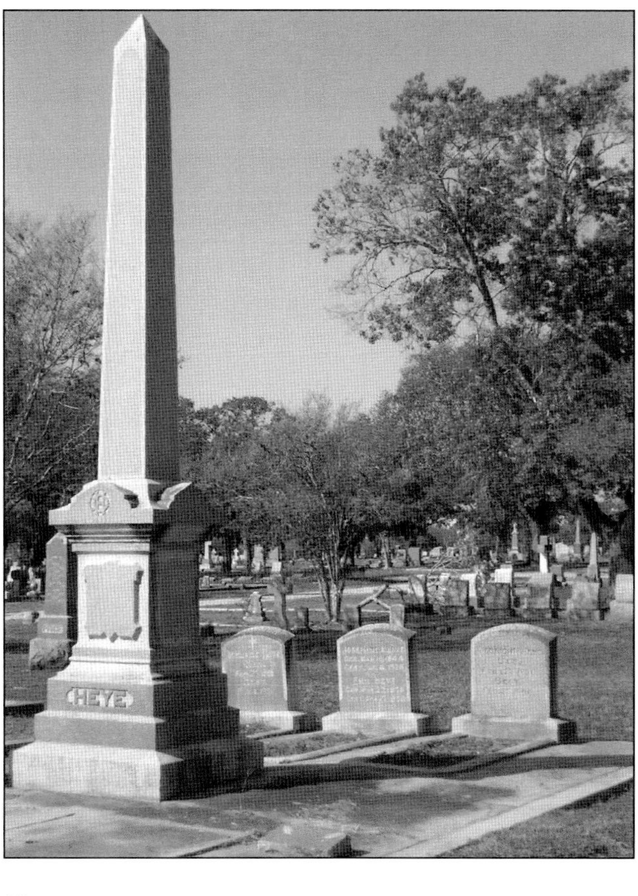

This simple gravestone belies the fact that the grave's inhabitant was a well-known physician, both in Europe and America, in his day. Dr. Ferdinand Charles Herff Sr. came to Texas fleeing his native Germany's 1848 revolution. It is believed that he performed the first hysterectomy in the United States and the first cataract operation in Texas. Once, he performed surgery on an Indian and received an Indian slave girl for his fee.

Born in Holstein, Germany, in April 1837, Diedrich Heye lived in San Antonio for 30 years. He was a member of the Arbeiter Verein and St. John's Lutheran Church. While his family lived at 313 Seventh Street, his business was located on Commerce Street. He dealt in carriage trimming, harnesses, saddles, and other leather products. He died in 1896 and was survived by his wife, Josephine, and seven children.

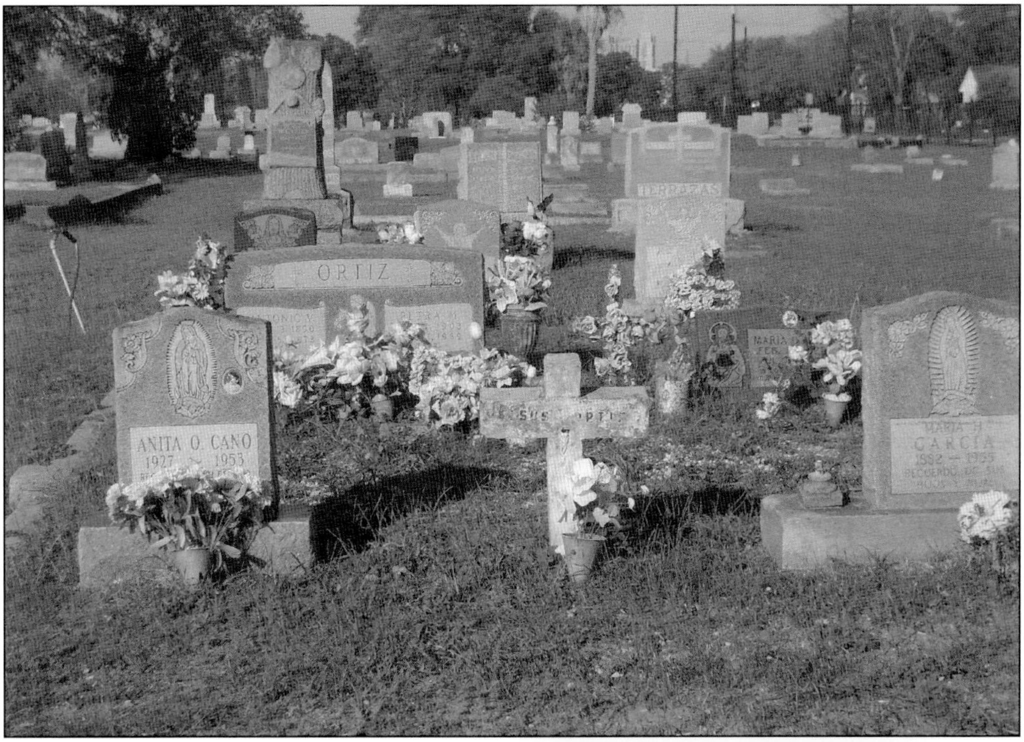

These decorated graves show the love relatives have for those who have passed. A custom brought from Mexico found among many families is Día de los Muertos, held on October 31 and November 1 and 2. During these days, the lives of those who have passed are celebrated by decorating graves, creating altars, and gathering to share memories. The altars will have photographs, favorite foods, and memorabilia.

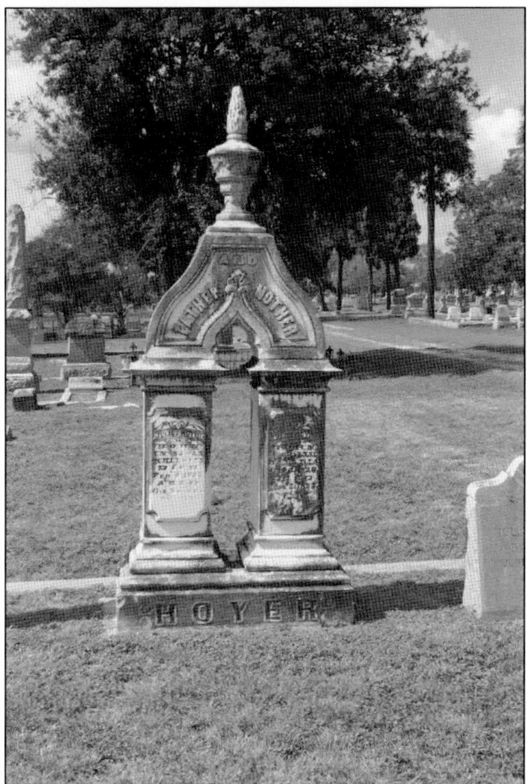

Julius Hoyer, born in Sagan, Schlesien, Germany, in 1820, arrived in Texas in 1840. He joined the Republic of Texas Rangers. As his unit moved toward Mexico, he was left in San Antonio because of illness, and it was here he stayed. He served as justice of the peace and, later, was elected city collector, a post he held for 20 years.

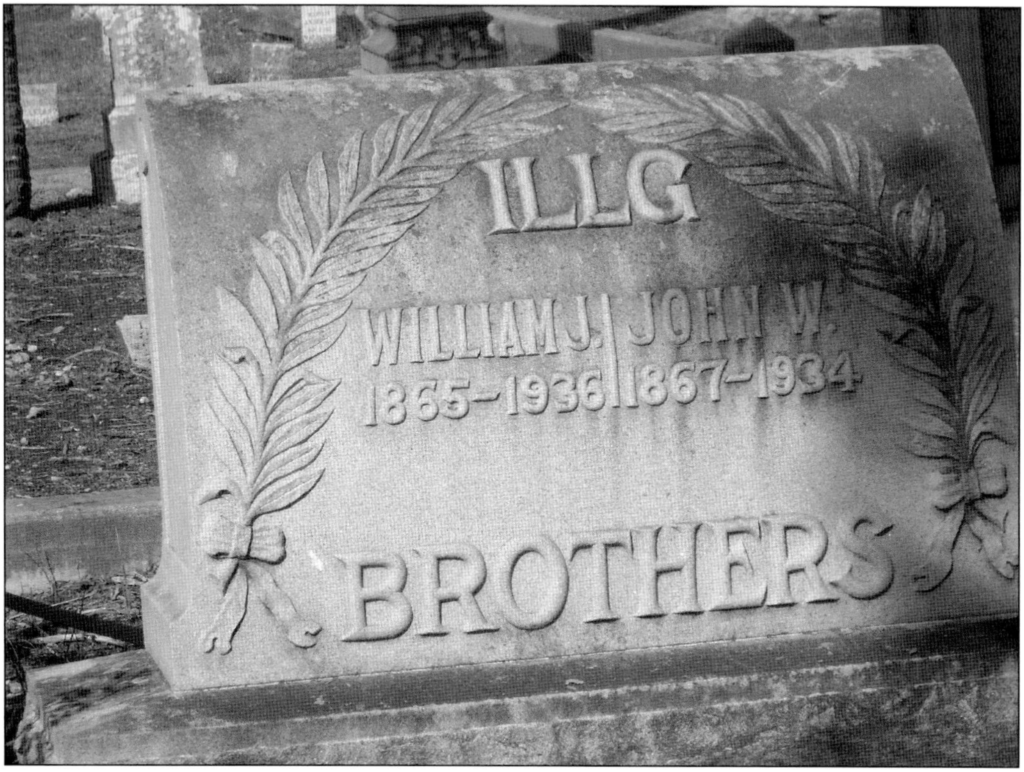

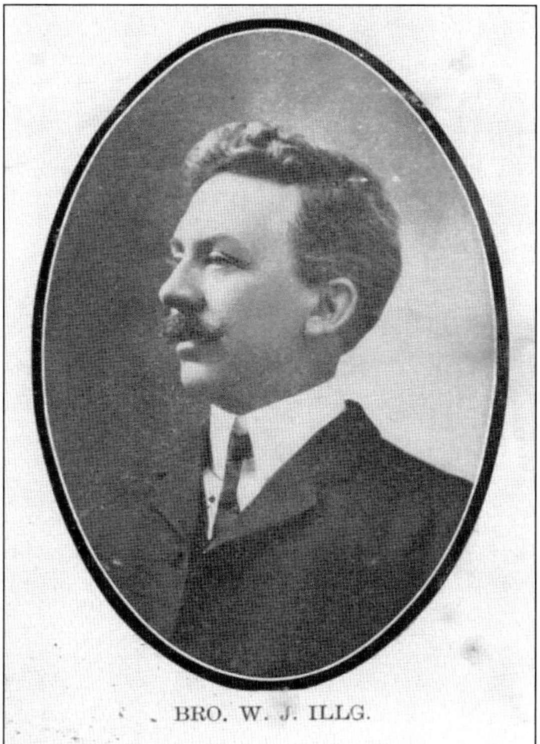
BRO. W. J. ILLG.

The parents of the Illg brothers apparently had difficulty deciding on names for their sons. William John Illg was born in 1865, and his brother John William Illg was born two years later. In 1886, they established Illg Brothers Grocery. John William never married, while William John married and had two daughters. Both brothers were members of St. Mark's Episcopal Church.

This photograph was taken from a publication about the Benevolent and Protective Order of Elks. Conceived by Englishman Charles Algernon Sidney Vivian in 1869, the order was formally organized a year later. It is a fraternal and benevolent organization. Elks seek to assist those in distress whenever possible.

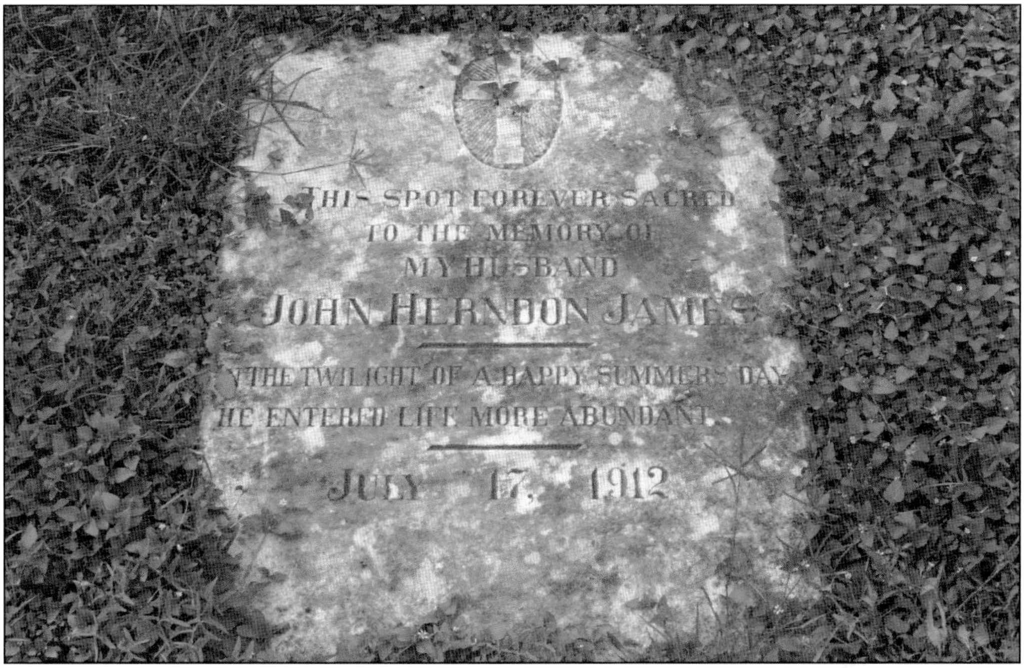

After practicing law for 20 years, Governor Hogg appointed John Herndon James as chief justice of the Fourth Court of Civil Appeals. He was the most universally esteemed man of his profession. Judge James was born in San Antonio in 1852. He studied in Indiana and at Harvard. His father, John James, was an early pioneer in the state, having surveyed more land for townsites than any other surveyor.

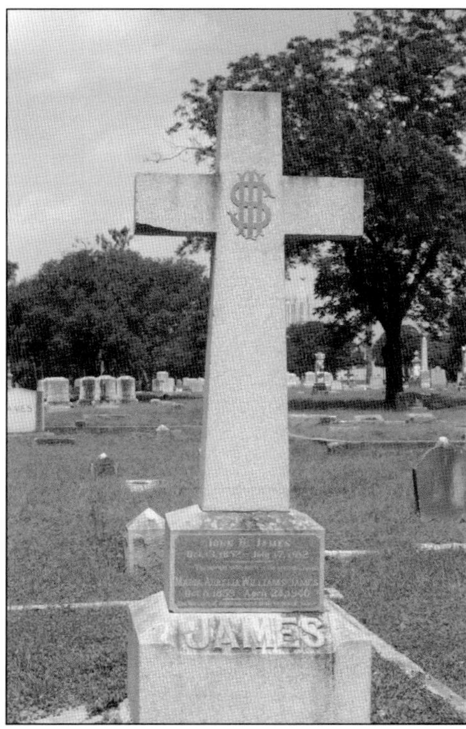

On February 26, 1884, Judge James married Maria Aurelia Williams, whose father had been on Pres. Jefferson Davis's staff. Her mother, Mary Curtis, was a niece of President Tyler. The inscription on the reverse, "This spot forever sacred / to the memory of / my husband," suggests true affection between the couple.

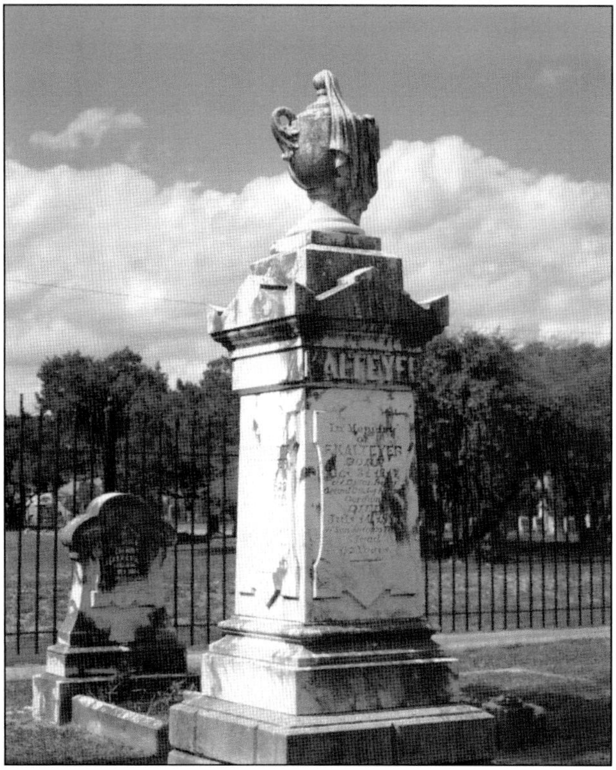

Frederick Kalteyer, a doctor, chemist, and druggist, arrived in Galveston in 1842. He established the first drugstore and made the first soda water there. In 1849, the family moved to San Antonio, where Frederick opened the second drugstore in town on Military Plaza. Known as F. Kalteyer and Son for many years, it eventually became the San Antonio Drug Company. He was also a member of the first fire department.

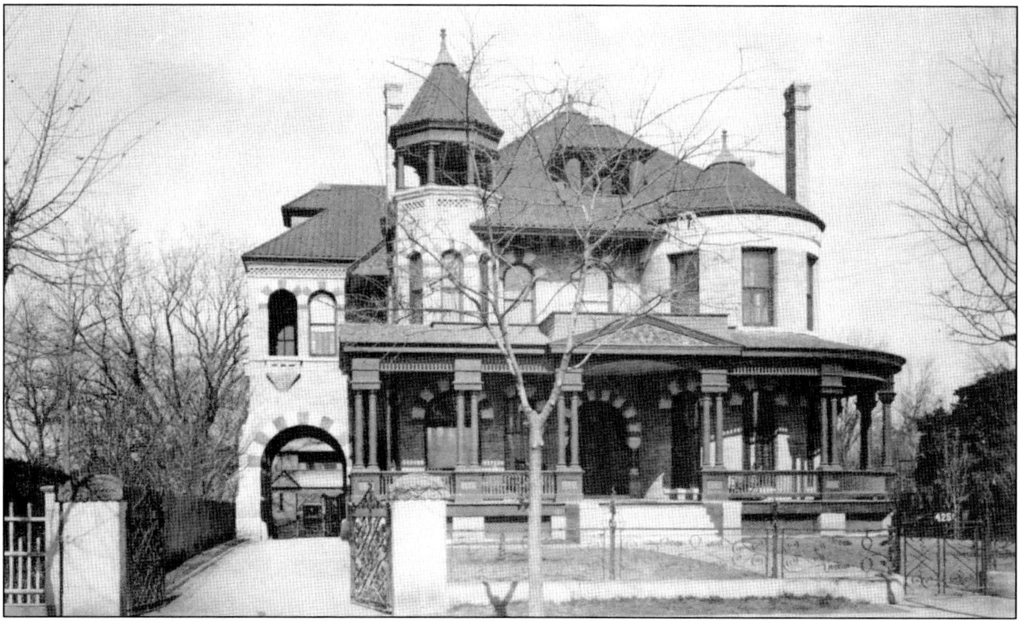

George Henry Kalteyer was born in New Orleans in 1848 to Frederick and Henrietta Kalteyer. He attended St. Mary's College and then traveled to Germany to study chemistry. Upon returning, he worked for his father's drugstore. He later founded the Alamo Cement Company, which became the San Antonio Portland Cement Company. He served as an alderman and was a member of a number of civic organizations.

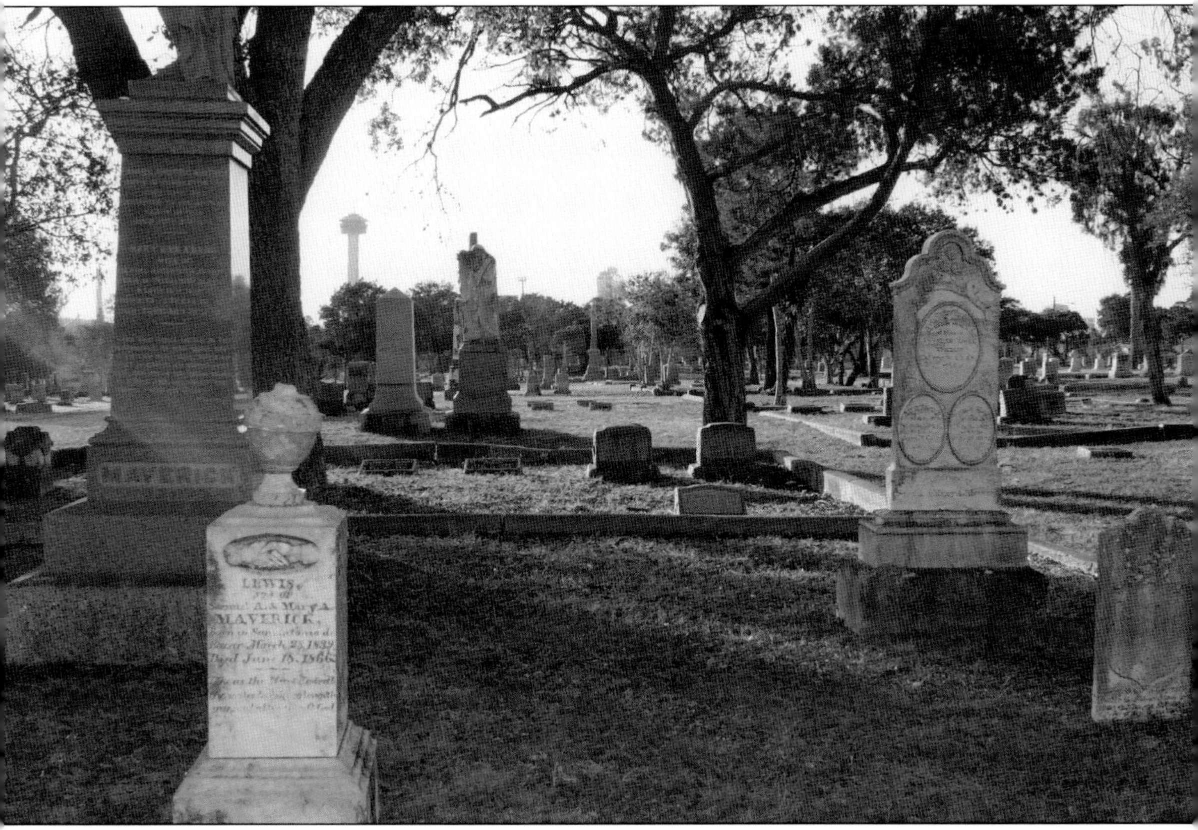

Samuel Augustus Maverick is most often remembered for the word associated with his name "maverick," the term for an unbranded calf. Samuel, born in South Carolina in 1803, graduated from Yale in 1825 and studied law in Virginia, before coming to Texas in 1835. Later that year, he served with Ben Milam in the Siege of Bexar. He then went to Washington-on-the-Brazos as a delegate to the independence convention. Afterward, he practiced law and engaged heavily in land speculation, eventually acquiring over 300,000 acres. He served in the legislature of the Republic of Texas and state legislature (1851–1863). He was the city's mayor in 1839 and for a term during the Civil War. His wife, Mary, was instrumental in establishing St. Mark's Episcopal Church. Her memoirs paint a vivid picture of life in early Texas.

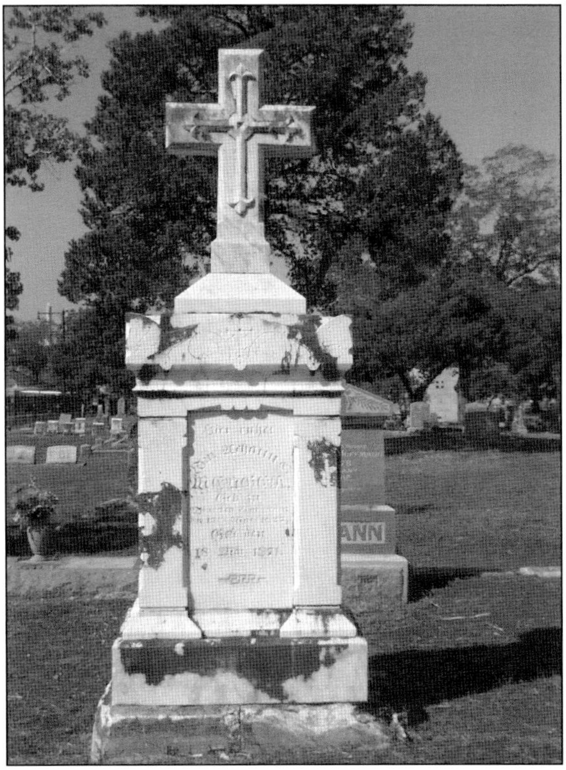

William Menger arrived in San Antonio in 1847, establishing a brewery in 1855 with Charles Degen as brewmaster. Hops and malt were imported from New York. In 1858, he contracted with John H. Kampmann to build the Menger Hotel. Menger, captain of the volunteer fire department, purchased the city's first steam fire engine shipped by rail from New York to Columbus, Texas, and from there by ox carts.

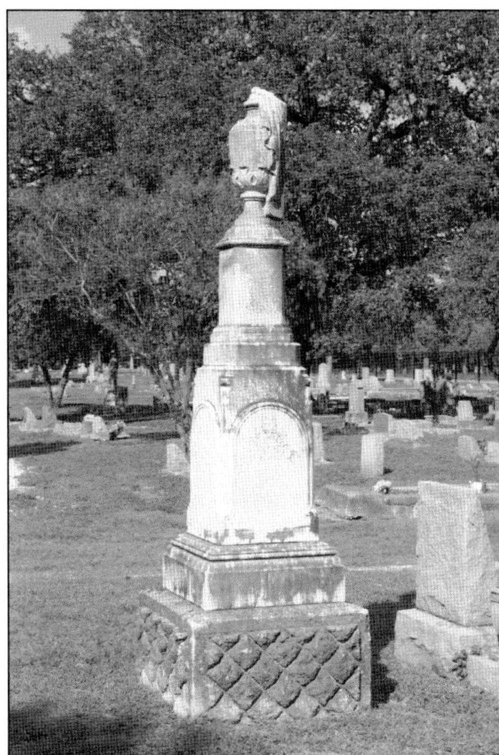

August Nette Sr. opened the city's first drugstore in the 1850s at the corner of Commerce and St. Mary's Streets. Later, he established a meat extract factory. His son August Nette Jr. grew up in San Antonio but studied pharmacy and chemistry in Germany. The son continued his father's drugstore, held a US weather observer position, and was superintendent of the San Antonio Gas Factory.

Franklin Lafayette Paschal was born in Georgia in 1810. He arrived in time for the Texas Revolution, after which he enlisted in the army of the Republic of Texas. Then he became a Texas Ranger under John Hays. After settling in San Antonio in 1839, he held a succession of positions, including assessor, coroner, and sheriff. He then served in the Texas legislature, on city council, and as tax collector.

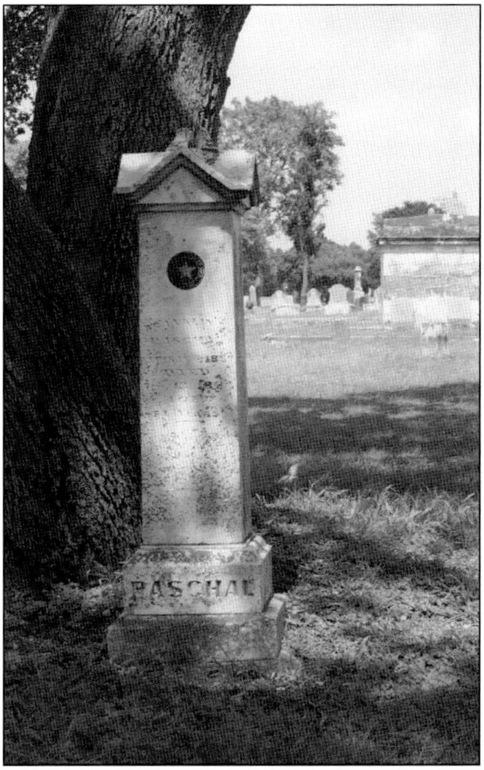

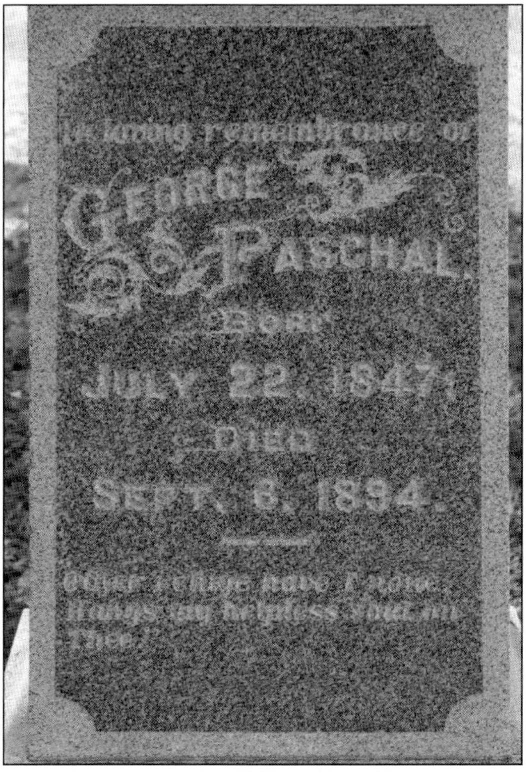

George Paschal was raised in San Antonio and became one of the leading lawyers in the Southwest. He served as district attorney for eight years before being elected mayor. He died in office after 18 months. He had married Emma Elizabeth Basmer, daughter of E.H. Basmer of Germany, a noted scientist, who established an astronomy laboratory near Houston.

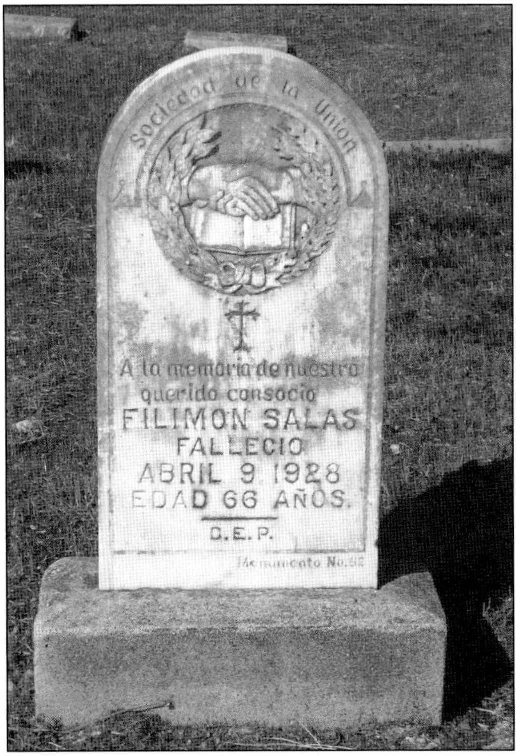

Born in Mexico in 1872, Filimon Salas and his wife, Felicitas, came to the United States in 1902. Filimon worked as a tailor for J.E. Pancoast and Henry Kohler. Burial locations of family members are in both City Cemetery No. 1 and San Fernando No. 2. The Sociedad de la Union was a mutual aid society primarily for Hispanics. It provided financial, educational, burial, and other assistance.

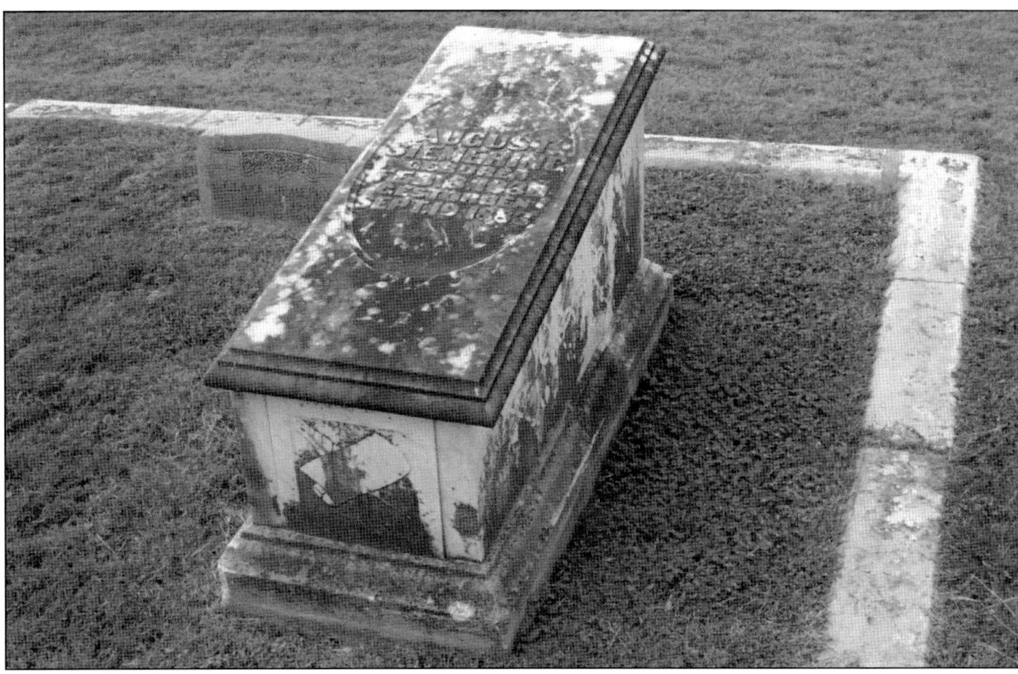

August Siemering, born in Germany in 1828, left the country with the uprising of 1848. In Texas, he taught school until the Civil War. Although a Unionist, he served in the Confederate army. In 1865, he founded the *Freie Presse für Texas*. He also contributed to the *San Antonio Express* and other newspapers. Siemering is buried in a false crypt, which covers an in-ground burial.

Edward Steves Sr. arrived in Texas in 1849 aboard the *Neptune*. He married Johanna Kloepper in 1857 and temporarily settled in Kendall County. In 1866, the family moved to San Antonio and established a lumber business. In 1876, John H. Kampmann built a home for Steves in the King William area believed to have been designed by Alfred Giles. That home is now open to the public by the San Antonio Conservation Society. Son Albert continued the business. He was elected alderman in 1911, and in 1913, when Mayor A.H. Jones died, he succeeded as mayor. Albert also served as a director of the Alamo National Bank and San Antonio Zoological Society, and volunteered with the Turner Hook and Ladder Company, Beethoven Maennerchor, and numerous other organizations.

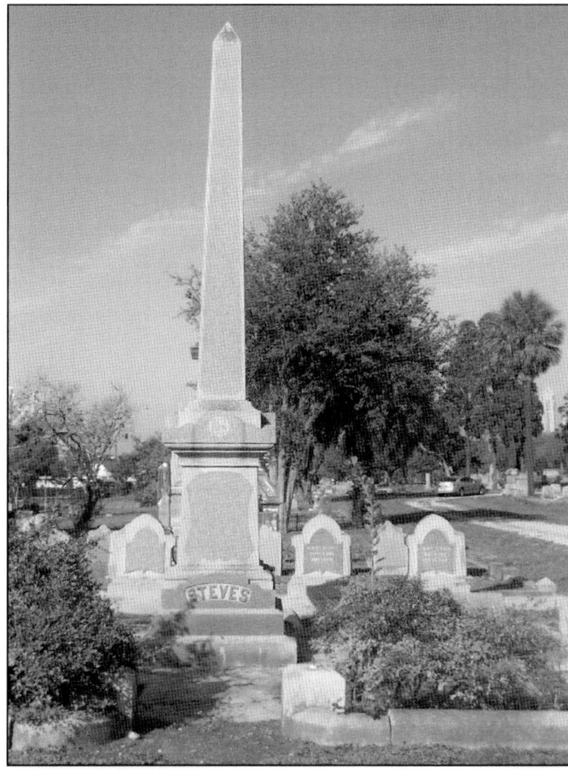

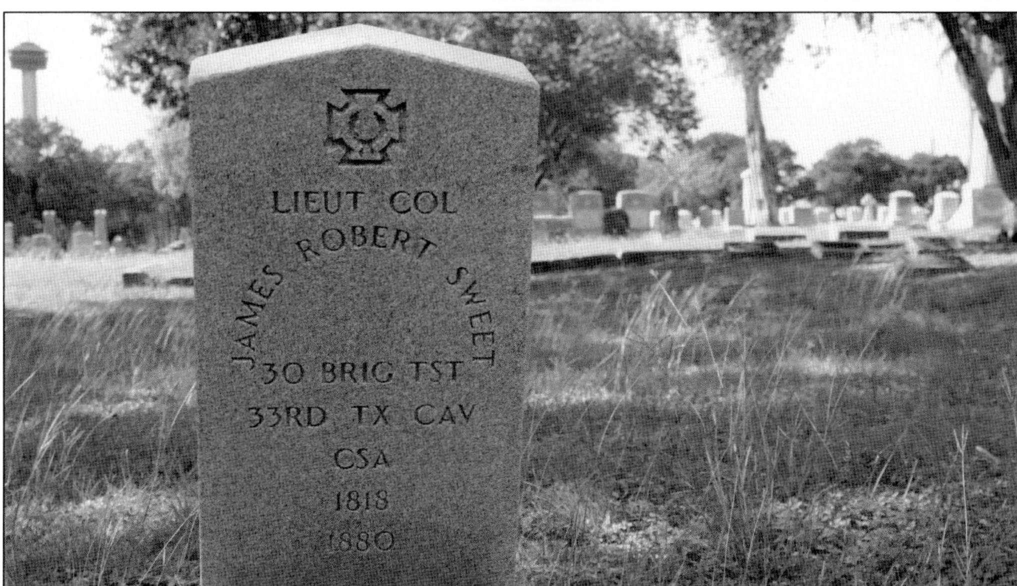

From Nova Scotia, James Sweet eloped with Charlotte James, sister of John James, and came to San Antonio. Sweet sold his home to George Brackenridge, which is now part of the University of the Incarnate Word property. He was elected mayor on two separate occasions. During the Civil War, he served in the 14th Texas Cavalry. After the war, he and others formed the Colony of Cordova in Mexico.

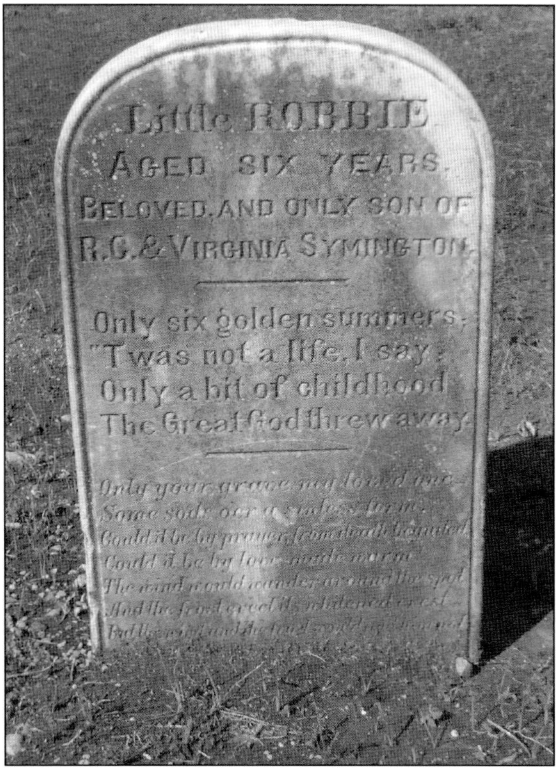

The death of children has always been difficult to fathom. That seems to be true of Robert and Virginia Symington. The words on the gravestone ring with pain—death took their only son. In 1898, Virginia died of paralysis and exhaustion. Between 1910 and 1920, Robert and daughter Edith moved to St. Louis, Missouri, where they remained, Robert passing in 1942. Edith remained single and taught school.

Nicolas Tengg Sr. and his family came to Texas from Germany just after the Civil War and worked in a store owned by Julius Berends, a family friend. When Berends returned to Germany in 1874, Tengg purchased the store. The stationery store and bookstore was a local institution for 100 years, later operated by Nic Tengg, Jr. and Julius Tengg. It closed in 1964.

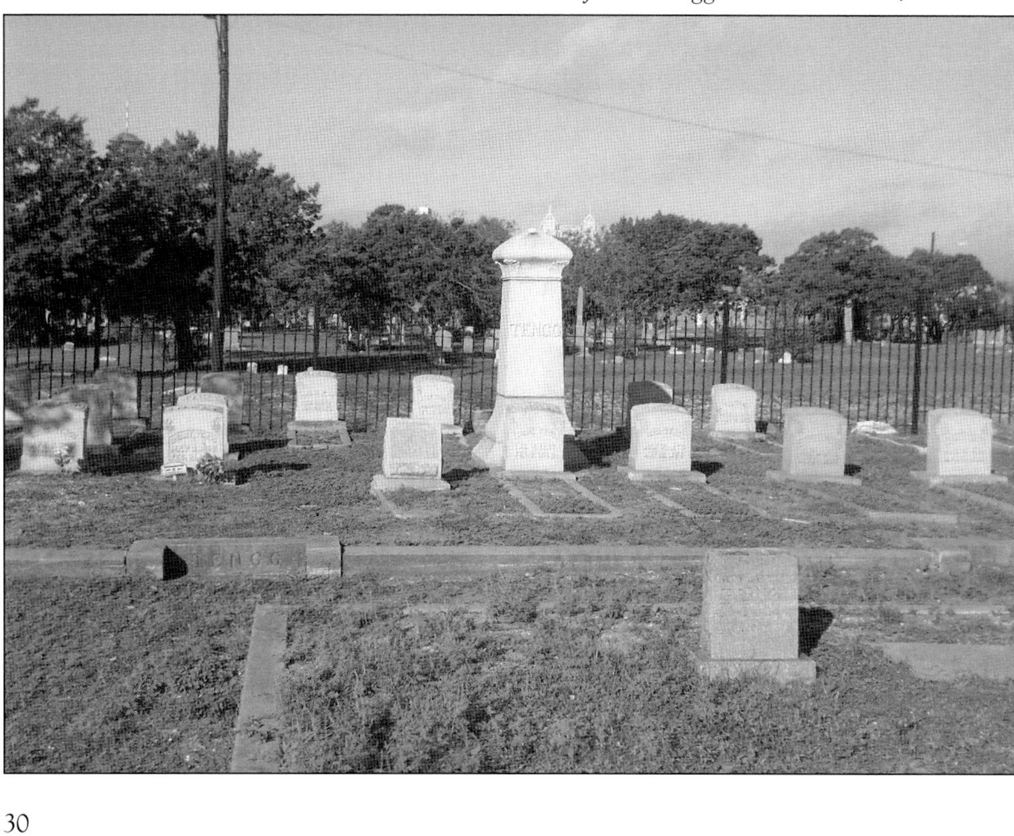

This beautiful monument is to Mary Maverick Terrell, wife of Edwin Terrell and daughter of Samuel and Mary Maverick. Born in Indiana in 1848, Edwin Holland Terrell was a businessman, diplomat, and authority on international law, having attended DePauw University and Harvard Law School before moving to San Antonio in 1877. He served as minister to Belgium from 1889 until 1892, when he returned to San Antonio permanently.

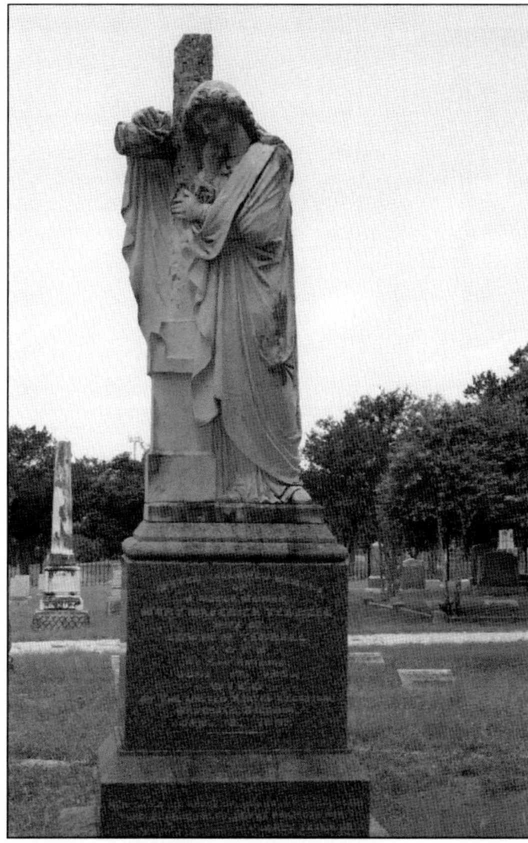

Born in May 1936, Eugene James Toscano died from a combination of measles and pneumonia. He lies next to his grandfather, Richard O. Toscano, who had passed only a month after his birth. Richard's parents were from Spain and his wife, Eugene's, grandmother was from the Canary Islands. Richard's wife rests in San Fernando Cemetery No. 2.

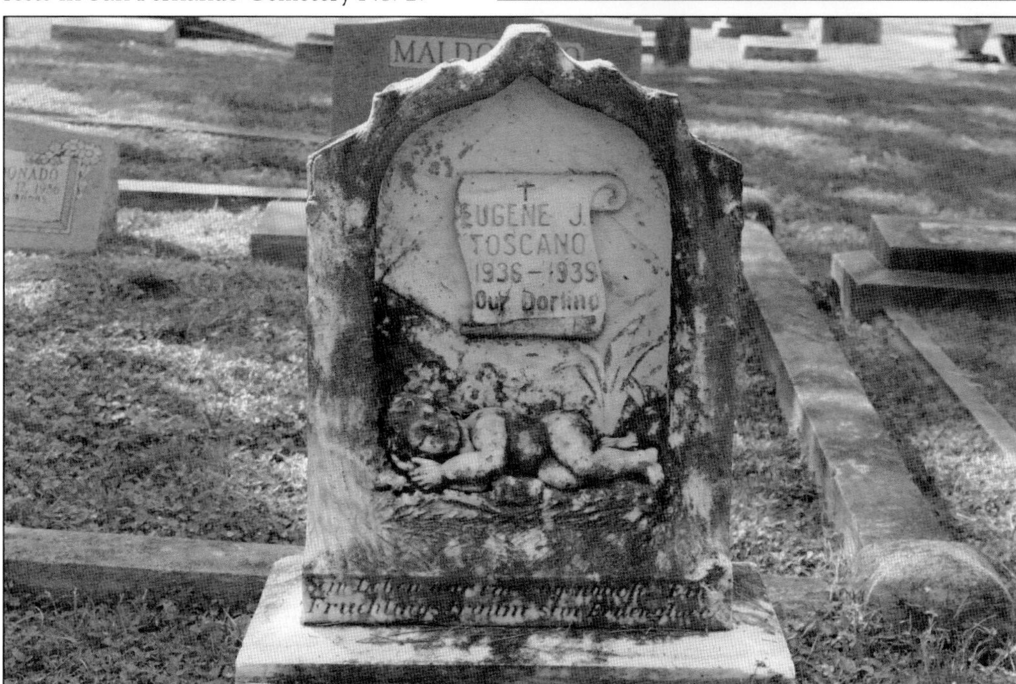

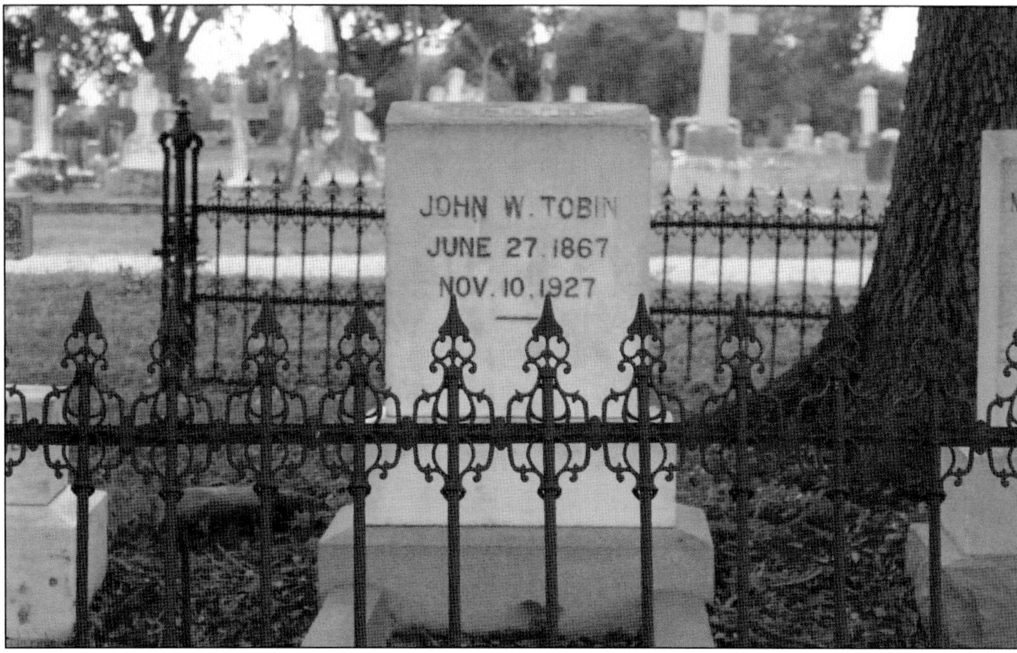

John Wallace Tobin, born in San Antonio in 1867, began his working life with the city engineer's office. He soon left for railroads, becoming a chief engineer for the International & Great Northern Railway. For the rest of his career, he served the city and county, first as an alderman, then fire chief, and later as county treasurer and sheriff. He passed away while serving as mayor.

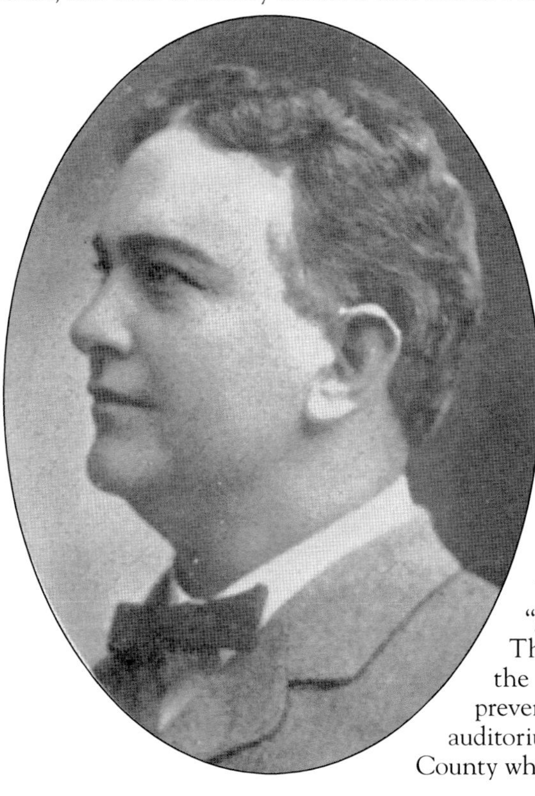

For 20 years, between 1900 and 1923, John Wallace Tobin was known as Bexar County's "gunless sheriff." In 1923, he was elected mayor. The two highlights of his career as mayor were the building of Olmos Dam, as part of efforts to prevent floods like that of 1921, and the municipal auditorium, built as a memorial to those from Bexar County who lost their lives during World War I.

Maria Cuellar worked at Joske's Department Store for 25 years. She began part time in the hosiery department in 1941 while still attending Lanier High School. When she was promoted to an office job, she quit because she preferred working with customers. She and her husband, Gilbert, were married in Our Lady of Guadalupe Catholic Church in 1951.

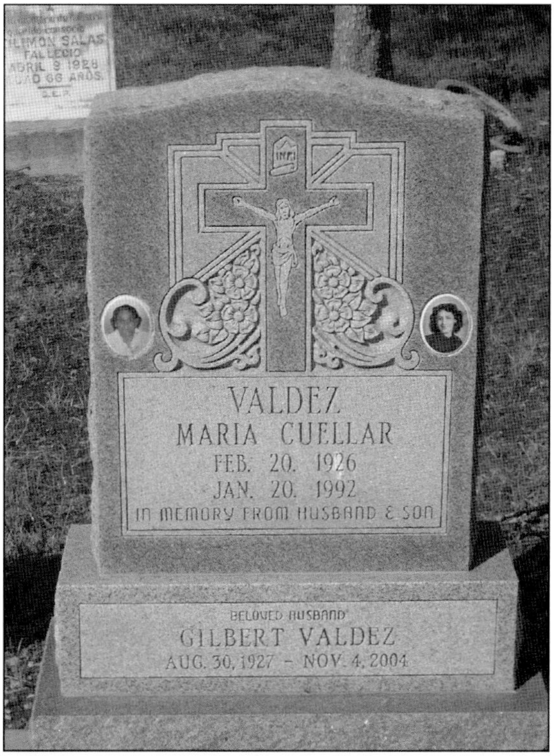

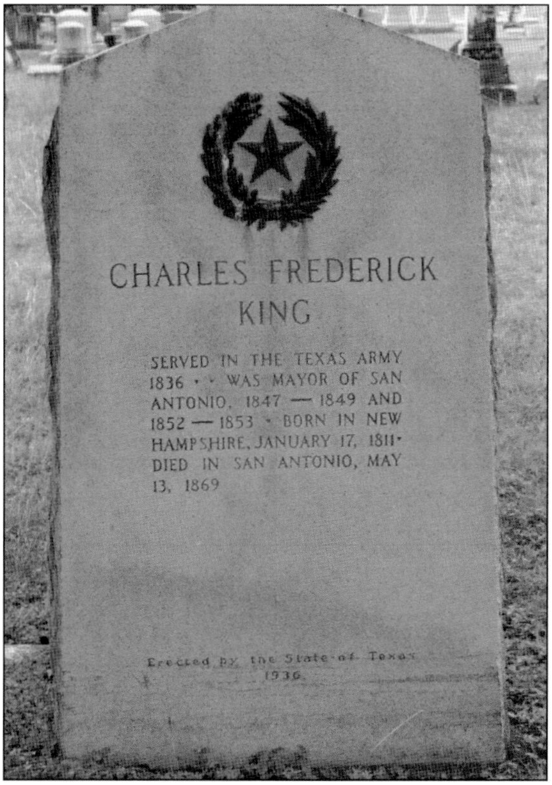

Charles Frederick King, born in New Hampshire in 1812, arrived in Texas in 1835 and fought at the Battle of San Jacinto. He served as a Texas Ranger for many years, chasing Indians and bandits across the frontier, and also served as sheriff of Bastrop and Travis Counties, mayor of San Antonio for two nonconsecutive terms, and collector of customs. He once wrote, "I believe no one dies a natural death in Texas."

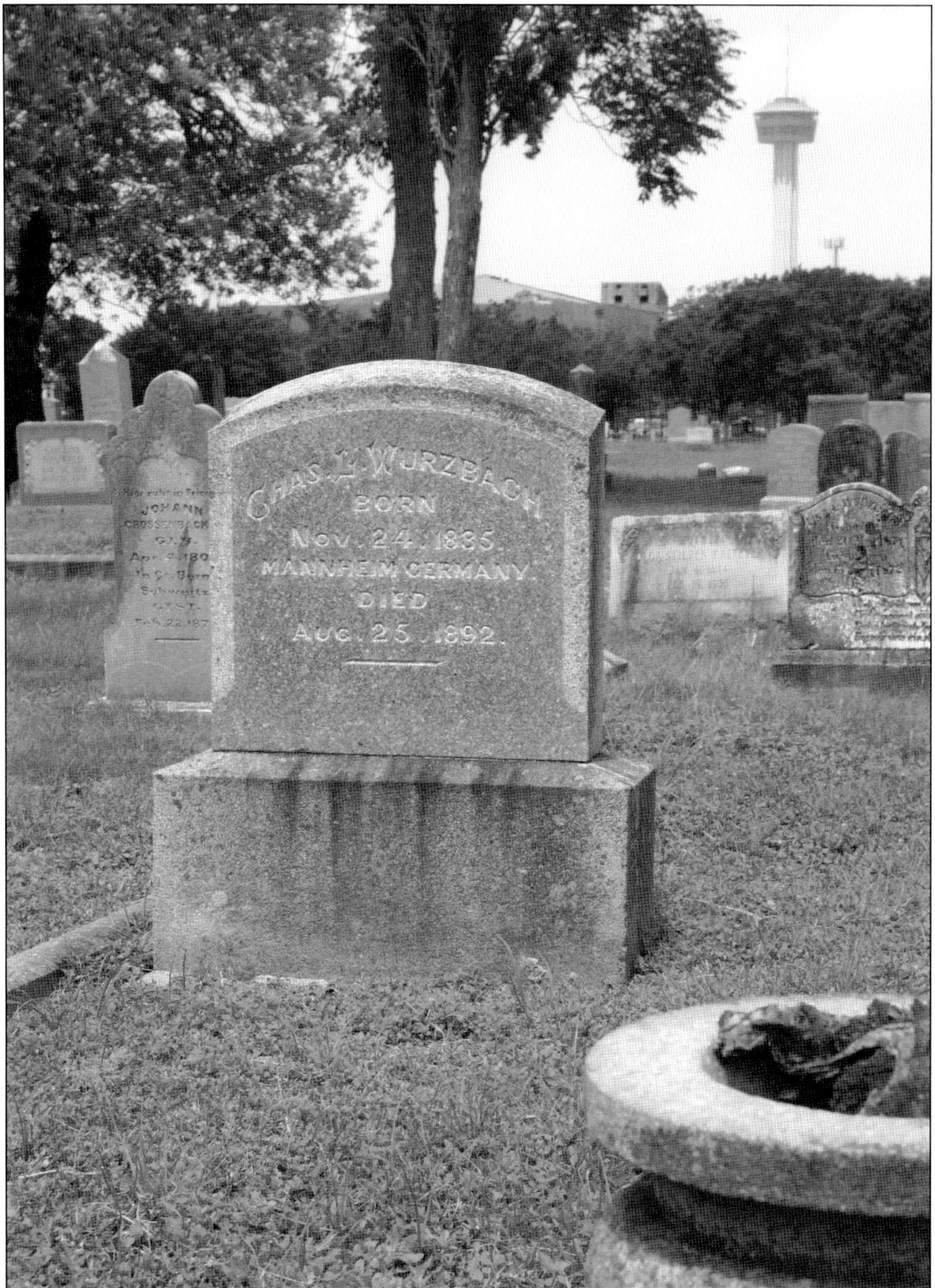

Although coming to the United States as an immigrant, Charles Wurzbach spent his life serving this country. During the Civil War, he worked his way up from trumpeter to adjutant general. After that war, he was elected city attorney, where he was the first to codify city ordinances. From 1884 to 1890, he was county judge. He served in the 16th, 17th, 18th, and 22nd Texas legislatures.

Two

City Cemeteries Nos. 2–6

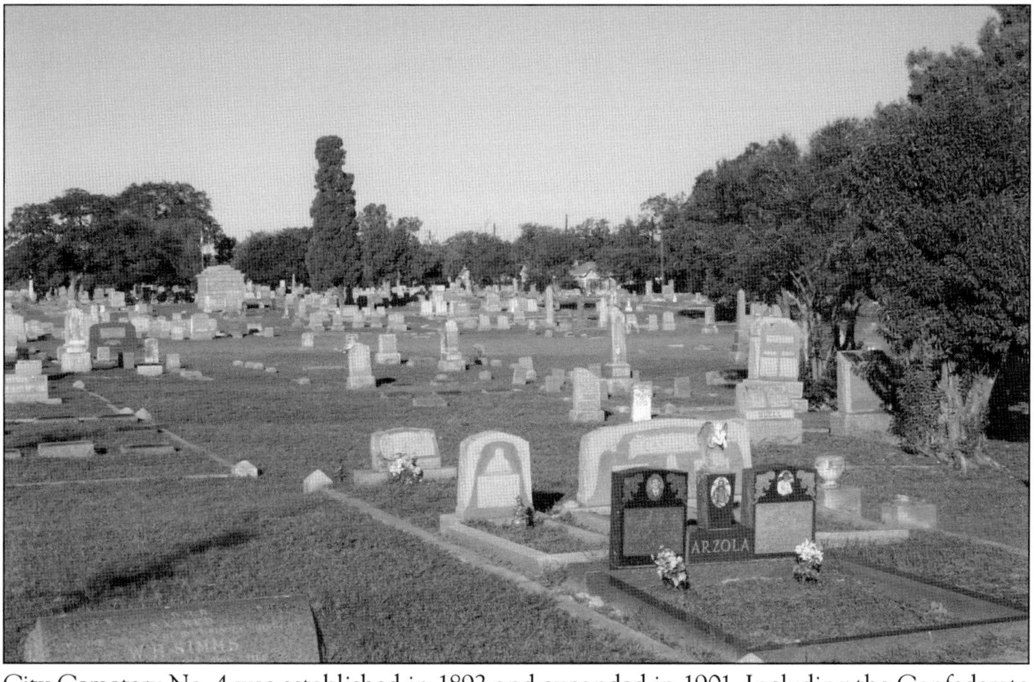

City Cemetery No. 4 was established in 1892 and expanded in 1901. Including the Confederate Cemetery, which is within its bounds, this cemetery contains 10.5 acres. Also within it are special lots for the Order of Railway Conductors, San Antonio Typographical Union No. 172, San Antonio Fire Department, and the Natchez Trace Tribe No. 4, Improved Order of Red Men.

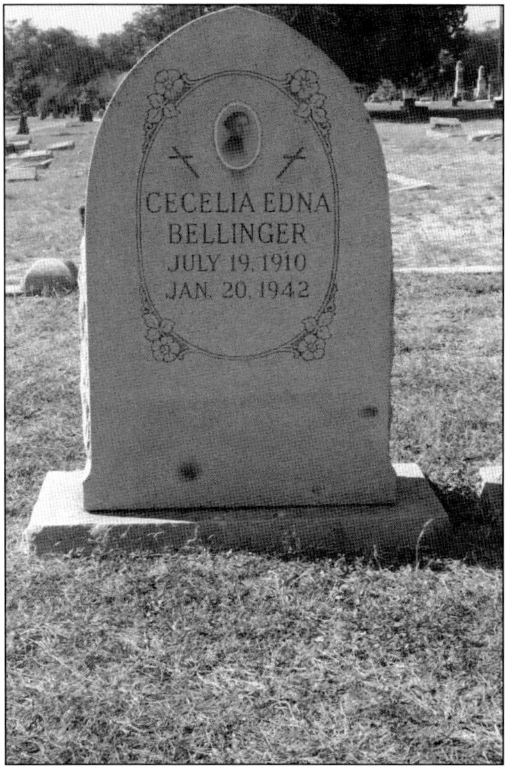

The young woman in the picture on this gravestone was Cecelia Edna Bellinger, daughter of Charles and Celestine Bellinger. Cecelia was only 31 at the time of her death. At age five, she was stricken with paralysis, and although she was able to attend St. Peter Claver Academy, she often suffered from various illnesses. Her father was the undisputed king of local African American politics in the early 1900s. [3]

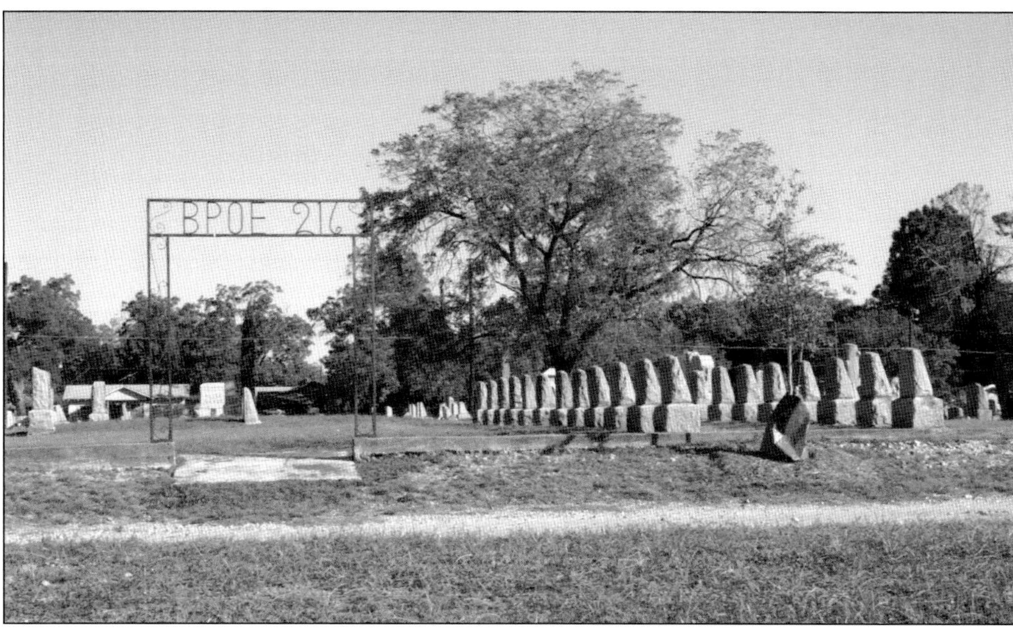

Within City Cemetery No. 6 is this section for the Benevolent and Protective Order of Elks, San Antonio Lodge No. 216. The local lodge was organized on November 14, 1891. Originally, there were about 40 individuals. By about 1904, there were 393 members who met on the second floor, over the Bon Ton restaurant, at 127 West Commerce Street. The Elks continue their charitable works. [6]

Dr. James H. Bindley moved to San Antonio shortly after receiving his medical degree from Cincinnati College of Medicine. He was an eye, ear, nose, and throat specialist. In the early 1900s, he was working with serum therapy and scarlet fever. Like many of his generation, he also was involved with charitable causes. In his spare time, he enjoyed outdoor sports and automobiling. [6]

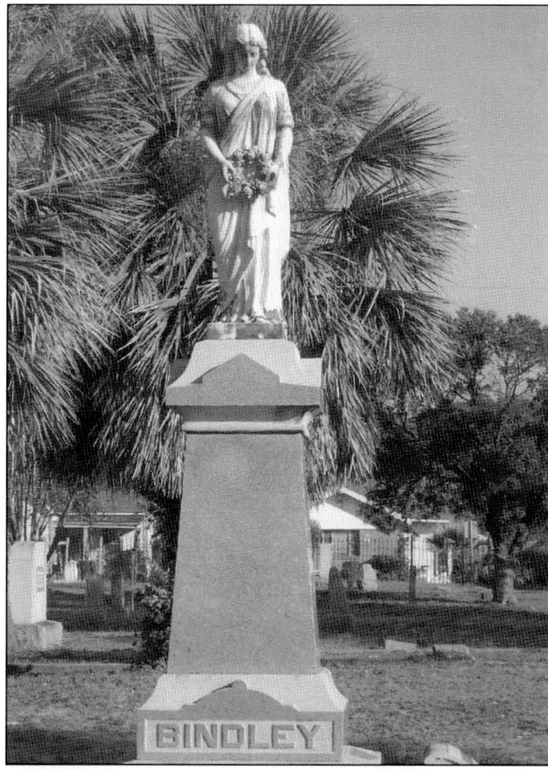

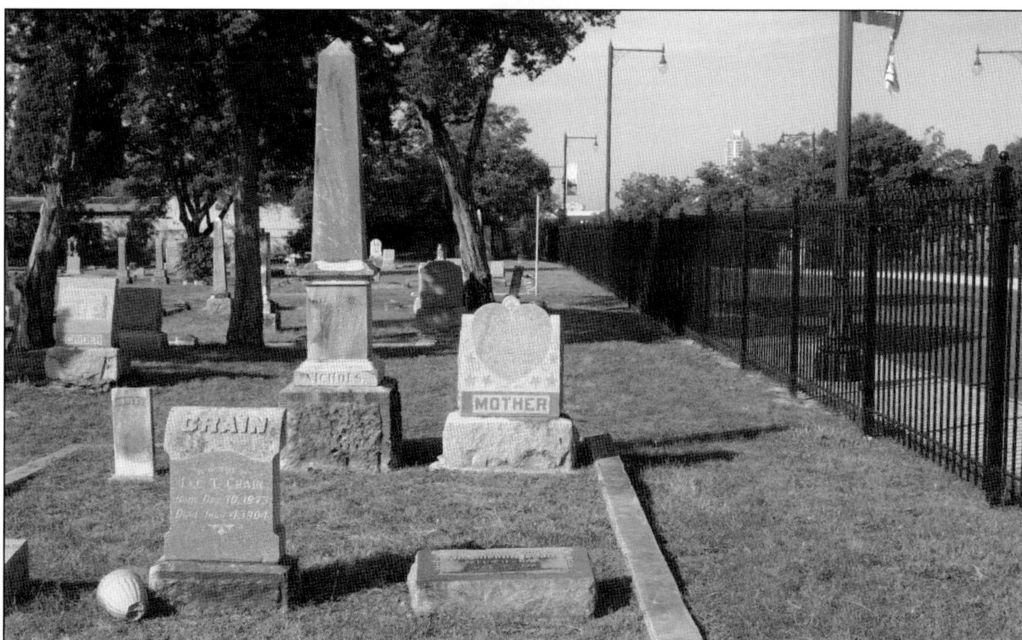

The small, flat stone on the right in front is that of Ada Nichols Crain, longtime principal of Highland Park Elementary School; she was originally from Canada. Next to her is her husband, Lee, who was a clerk for the San Antonio & Aransas Pass Railroad when he died in 1904. Ada's parents, Alex and Ellen, are at the rear. [2]

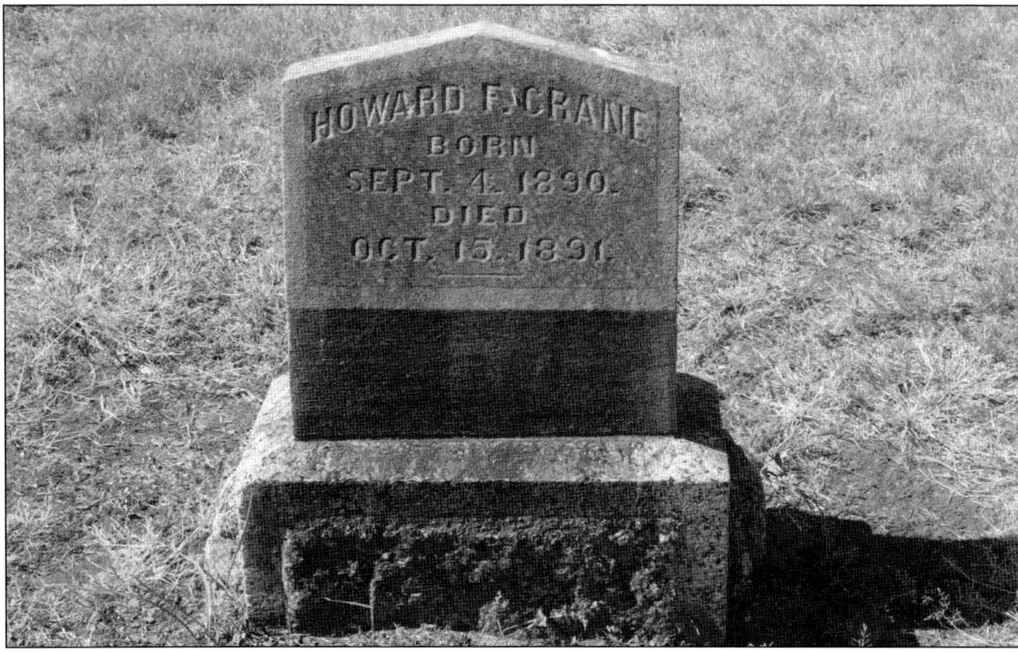

Howard French Crane was only one year, one month, and eleven days old when he passed on October 15, 1891. His parents, Charles E., a special agent for the Washington Life Insurance Company, and Jeannie F., lived in the West End, now the area of Woodlawn Lake and St. Mary's University. The cause of death was tuberculosis and meningitis, according to Dr. L.L. Lacey. [3]

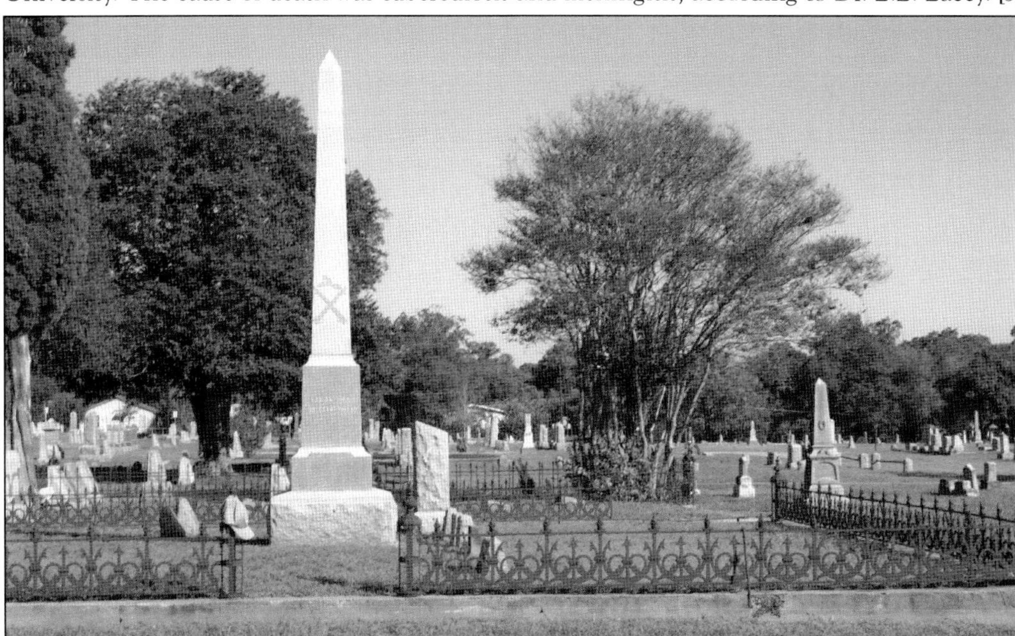

In 1903, the City of San Antonio donated a plot of land in City Cemetery No. 4 as a resting place for firemen. It is surrounded by a stone wall with a metal fence on top. Among the first buried there was John Grover, who fell from a ladder while fighting a fire. Fred Strauss was killed when the engine he was driving overturned. [4]

Albrecht Carl Dittmar was born in Darmstadt, Germany, and came to the United States during the 1848–1849 revolution. The family settled in Seguin, later in New Braunfels, and finally in San Antonio. Albrecht was a linguist, attorney, scientist, and artist. He also owned several farms. In 1867, he temporarily returned to Germany to marry Emmy Von Rehfues, whose father was the founder of the University of Bonn's natural history museum. [2]

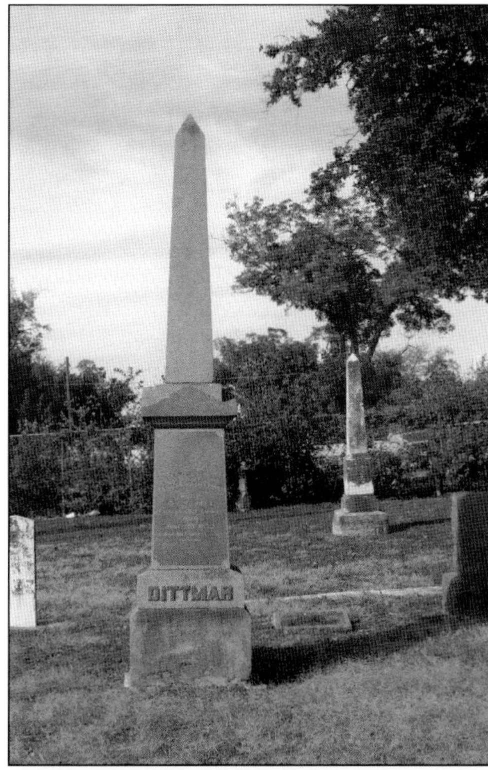

This stone for Albert Dittmar of the 33rd Cavalry Regiment, is for the same man as Albrecht Dittmar. The Confederate unit was formed from part of Duff's Regiment, and men were recruited in San Antonio, Port Lavaca, and Kaufman County. It spent its service time along the Lower Rio Grande. Although serving in the Confederacy, Dittmar opposed secession and slavery. [2]

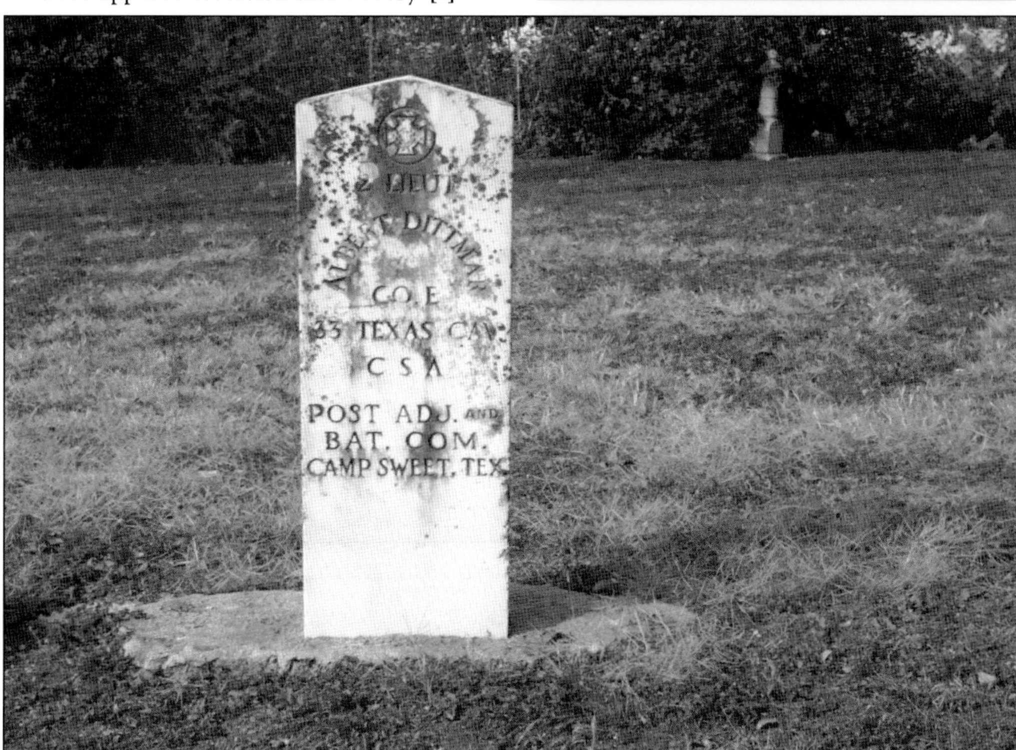

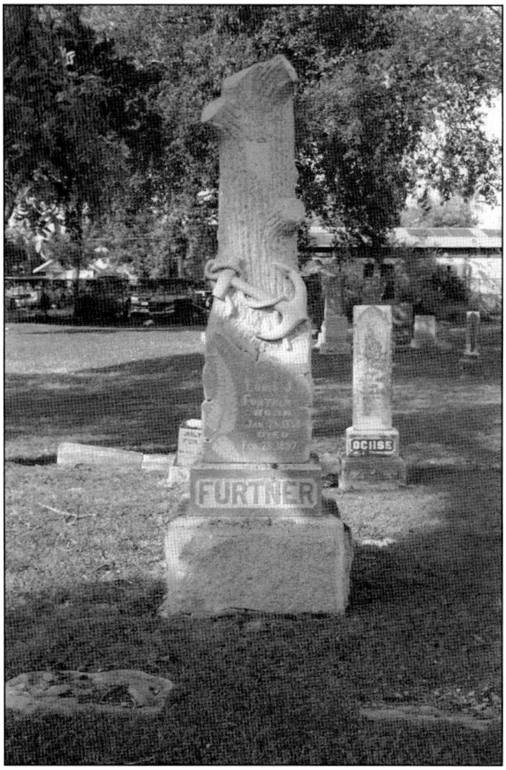

Louis J. Furtner first appears in San Antonio's 1883–1884 city directory as a proprietor of the Hotel Maverick Bar with Thomas Campbell. In 1895–1896, he had the Opera House Bar and was married to Julia Norris. The tree with branches cut off is a common symbol of the Woodmen of the World. The anchor often symbolizes hope and steadfastness. [2]

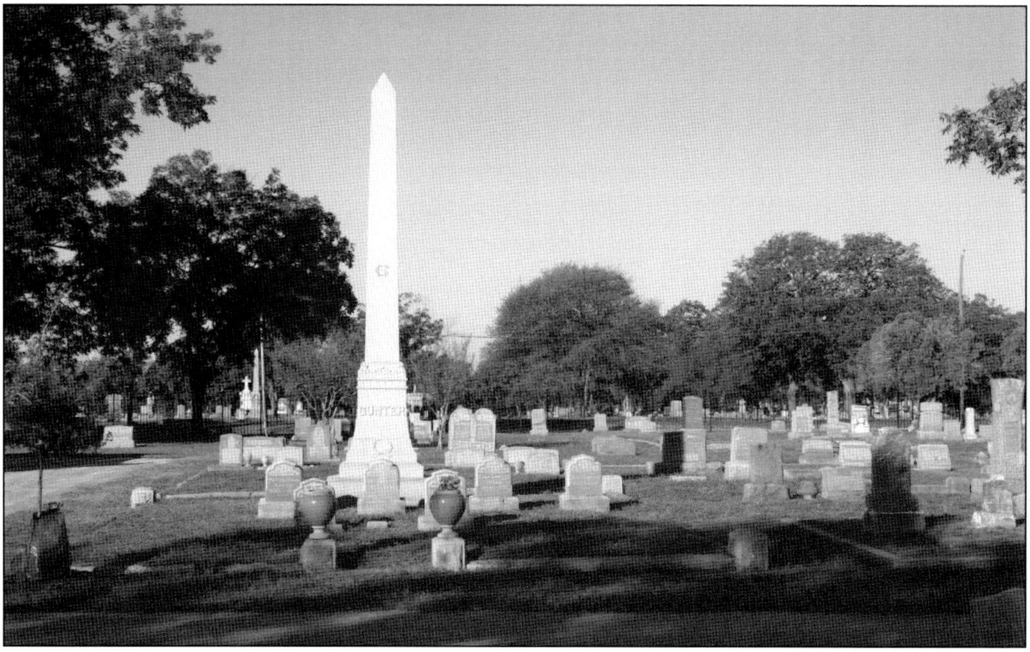

The Gunter Hotel was the city's largest hotel when it opened in 1909, two years after Jot Gunter, who helped acquire the property, had passed. Born in 1845 in North Carolina, Gunter was a farm boy. At the age of 16, he served under Dick Dowling at Sabine Pass during the Civil War. Later, he practiced law and became one of the state's leading cattlemen. [6]

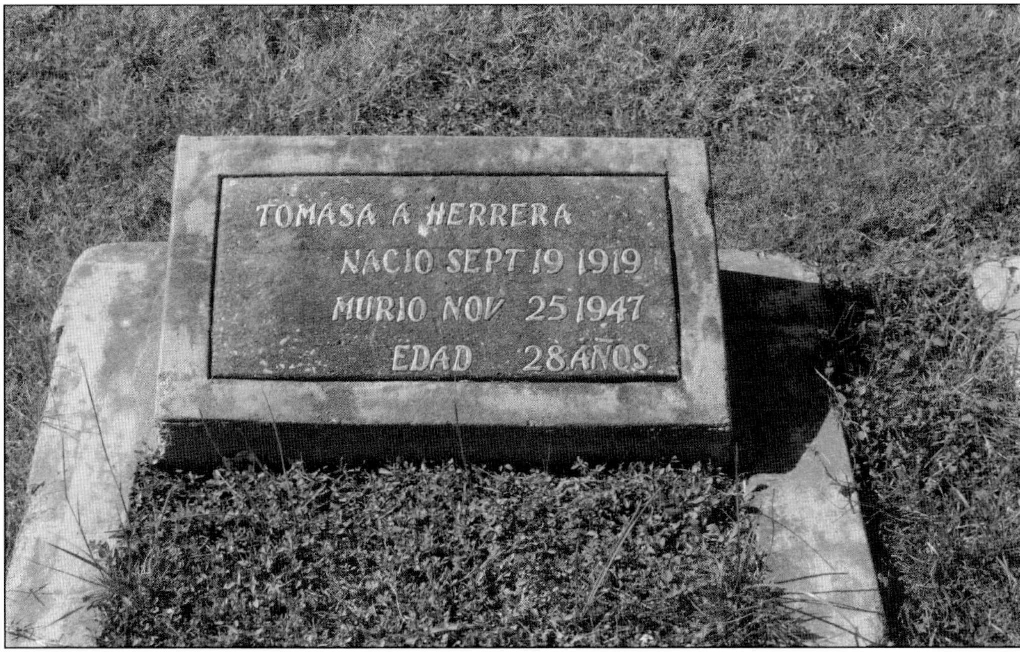

Tomasa Herrera was born in Austin, the child of Mexican immigrants Tomas Herrera and Agrapina Avila. Tomasa had moved to San Antonio five years before her death by tuberculosis in 1947 and worked for Frederick's. She had found a home with Severo and Gabriela Rangel. Note the simple cement marker and thin metal lettering, with a font often used for house numbers. [3]

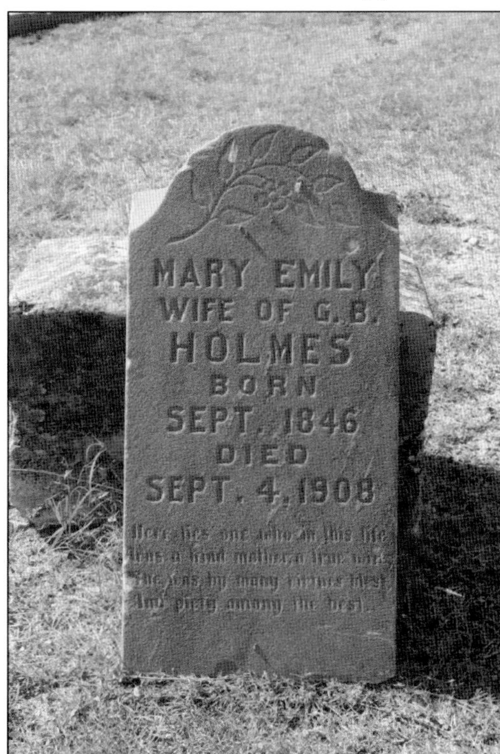

Like so many gravestones, Mary Emily Holmes's is broken but still legible. It poses one problem. While the stone gives the name of Mary Emily Holmes, the newspaper account of her death refers to her as May Holmes. She and her husband, George B. Holmes, and their eight children had arrived in San Antonio from Arkansas just two months before her death. [3]

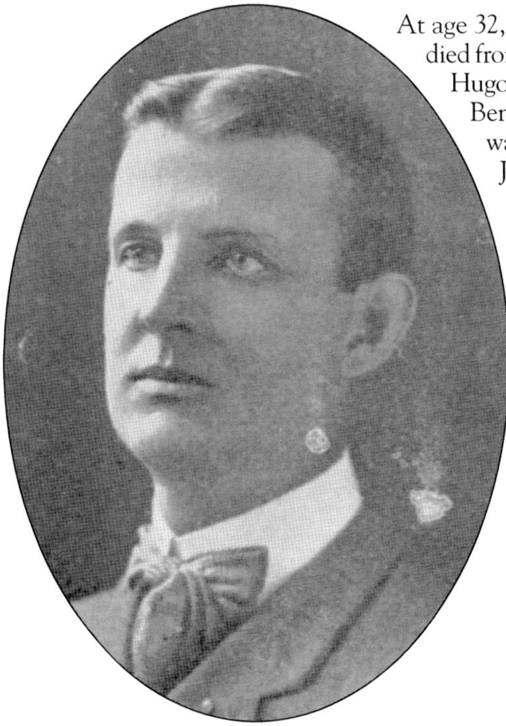

At age 32, Victor Hugo, president of Hugo and Schmeltzer, died from a stroke. Victor had succeeded his father, Charles Hugo, as president of the company 10 years before. The Benevolent and Protective Order of Elks, of which he was a member, handled the funeral, and Rev. Arthur Jones, pastor of the First Presbyterian Church, presided over the service. [2]

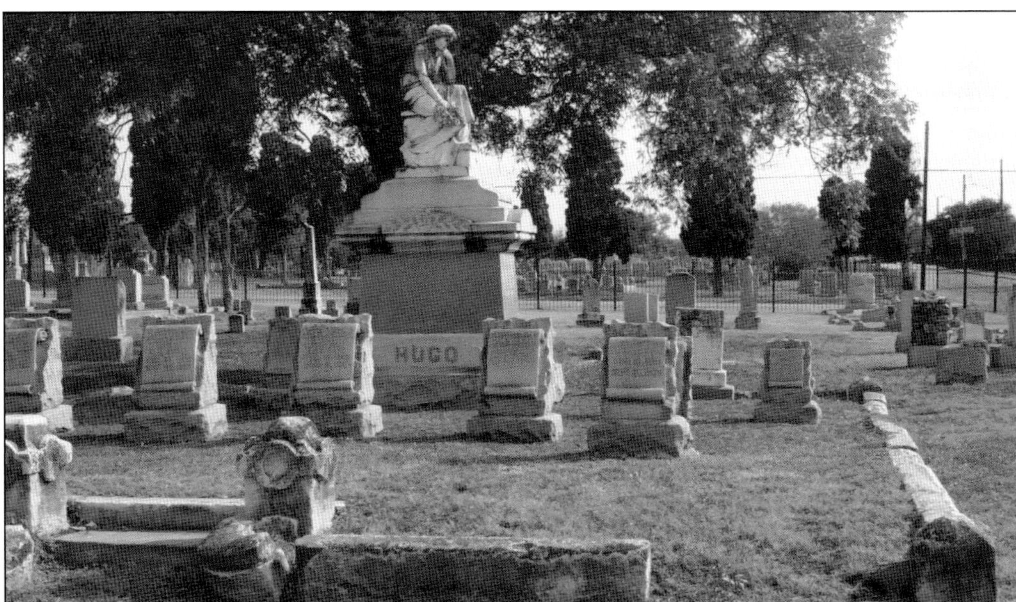

In 1877, Frenchman Augustine Honore Grenet bought the northern portion of the Alamo property from the Catholic Church and built a two-story museum and grocery store complex with two-story wooden arcades, three octagonal turrets, crenellated cornices, and false wooden cannon. Occupying 23,100 square feet, it supplied groceries, dry goods, hardware, and much more. In 1884, the property was sold to Hugo & Schmeltzer. It closed in 1912 and soon was razed. Shown here is the Hugo lot in City Cemetery 2. [2]

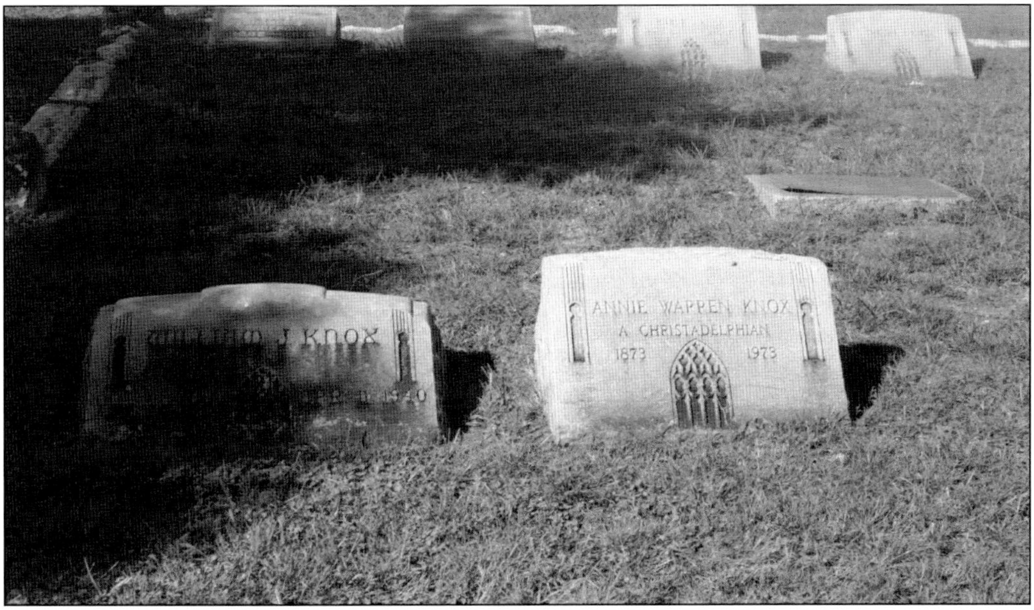

William J. Knox, born in 1866 in Brenham, Texas, was one of the first boys to graduate from San Antonio High School (1885). He was a longtime teacher, principal, and, at his death, assistant superintendent in what is now the San Antonio Independent School District. His wife, Annie, was a native of England. [4]

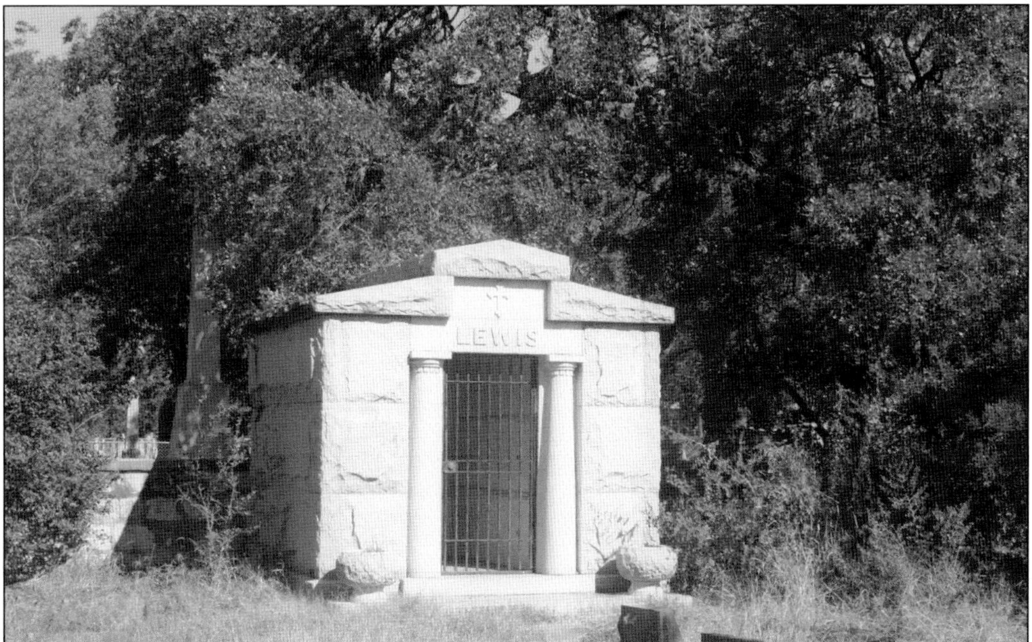

This photograph shows the Lewis family's mausoleum and its monument. Nathaniel Lewis arrived in Texas from Massachusetts in 1830. During the siege of the Alamo, Lewis supposedly smuggled supplies to the defenders before going on scout duty. He was a partner in the mercantile firm of Lewis and Groesbeck and established the city's first gristmill between 1845 and 1846. He was a cattle king, legislator, alderman, and freighter. [5]

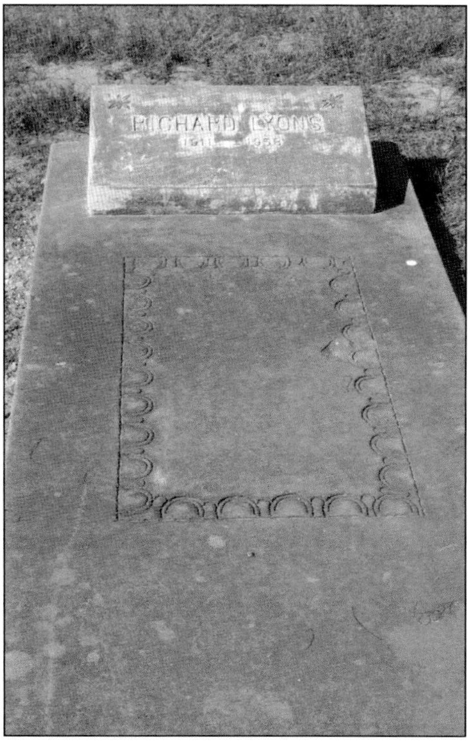

Richard Lyons's grave is a concrete slab with a hand-worked design. The top with his name and dates has two simple flowers etched in. Lyons was an African American who lived at 811 South Mesquite Street. He was born in Oakwood, Texas. At the time of his death, he was a merchandise manager for the Household Furniture Company. [4]

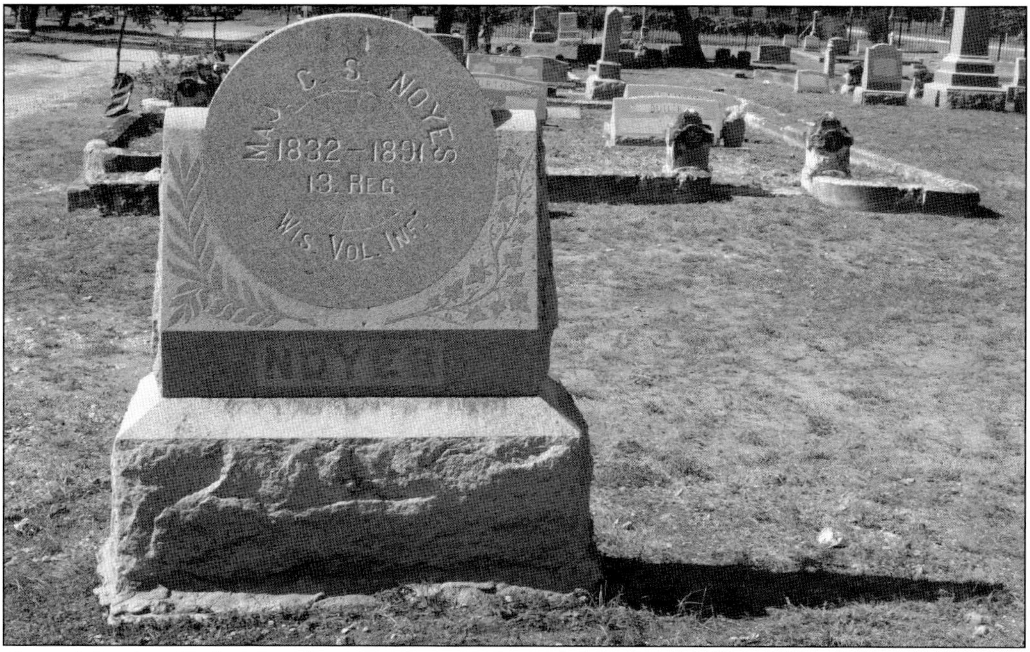

One of the first leather merchants in San Antonio was Maj. Charles S. Noyes, a Union soldier stationed here at the end of the Civil War who decided to remain. Here, he hunted wild cattle and laid out the stage road to Brownsville before partnering with Charles J. Langholz to manufacture saddles, harnesses, and similar items. His sister Jeanette taught at the German-English school and the first high school. [3]

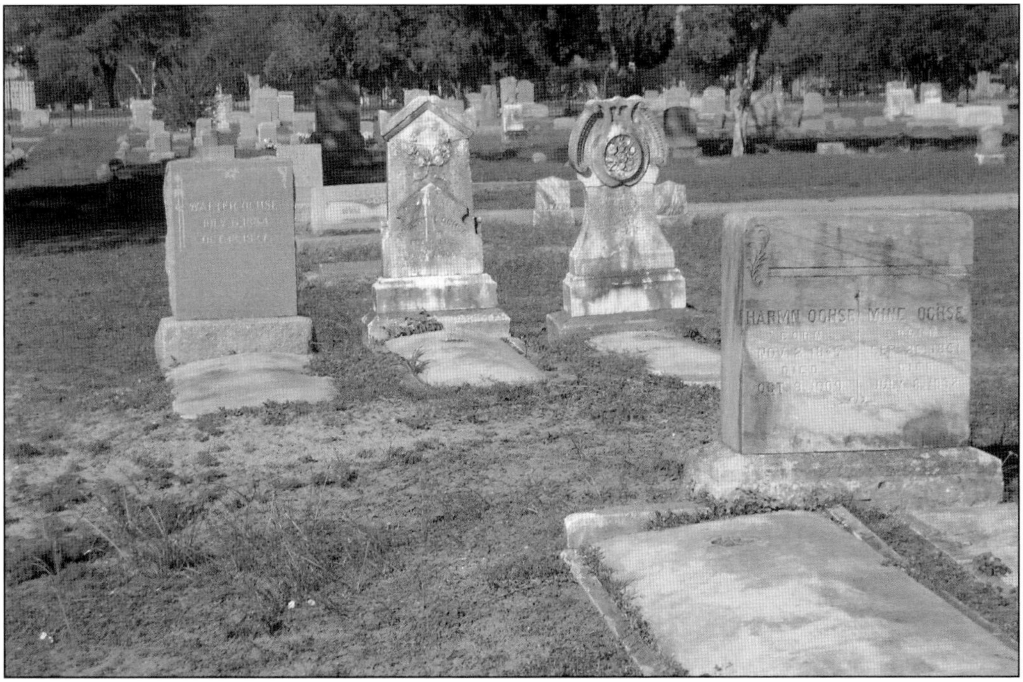

The Ochse lot is an example of a family lot where everyone has their own style, showing some changes over time. Robert H. Ochse (center rear) was killed at age 24 when a railroad car he was working on came loose and ran over him. [6]

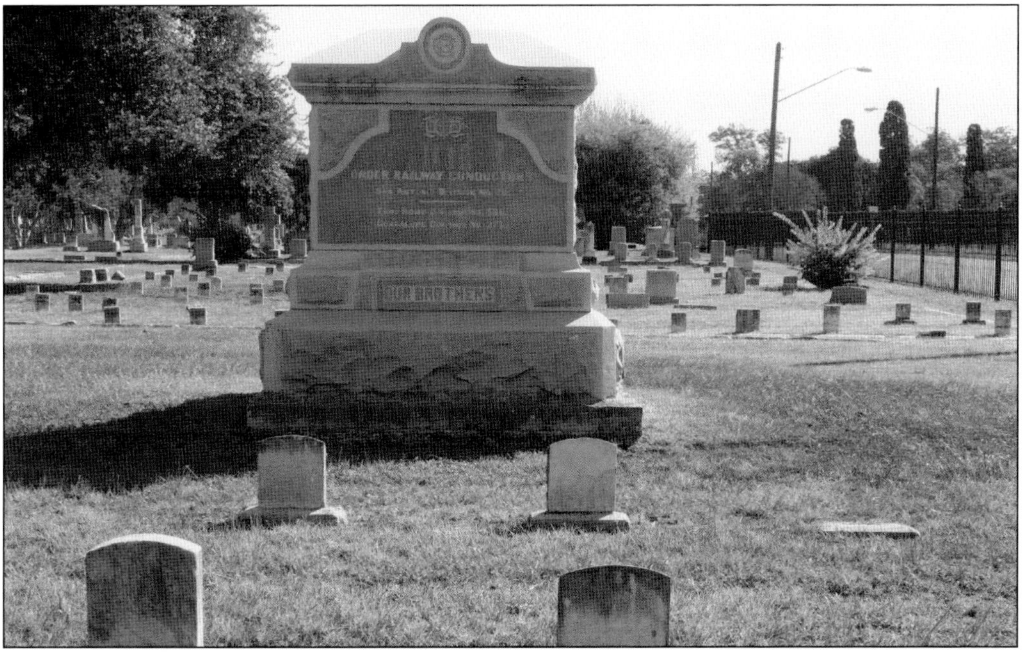

The first conductors' union was formed in 1868 in Illinois as a benefit and temperance society. In 1869, the name was changed to Order of Railway Conductors of America. In 1887, membership was expanded to brakemen, flagmen, and other yard trades. In January 1892, the union struck against the San Antonio & Aransas Pass Railroad, the first of its kind in the United States. It failed. [4]

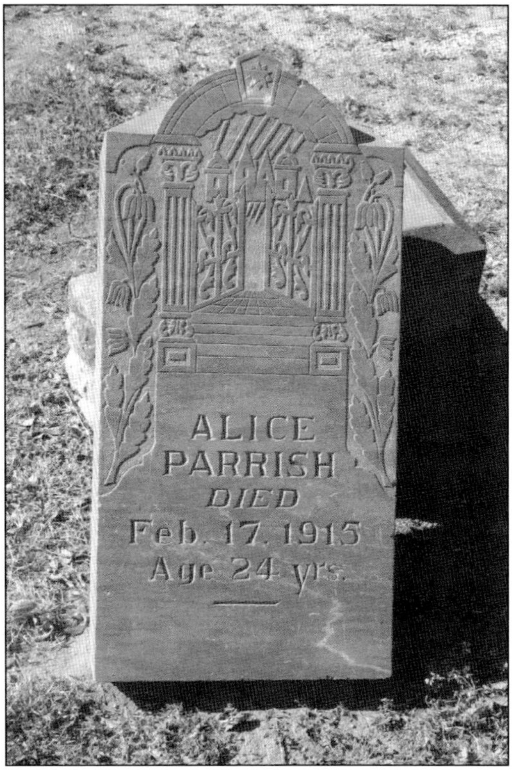

On Tuesday evening, February 16, 1915, Alice Parrish and a gentleman became embroiled in an argument in Gallagher's alley. Soon four shots were heard, the police arrived, and she was taken to the city hospital. The next day, Alice died, and the police captured the gunman, who admitted his crime. [3]

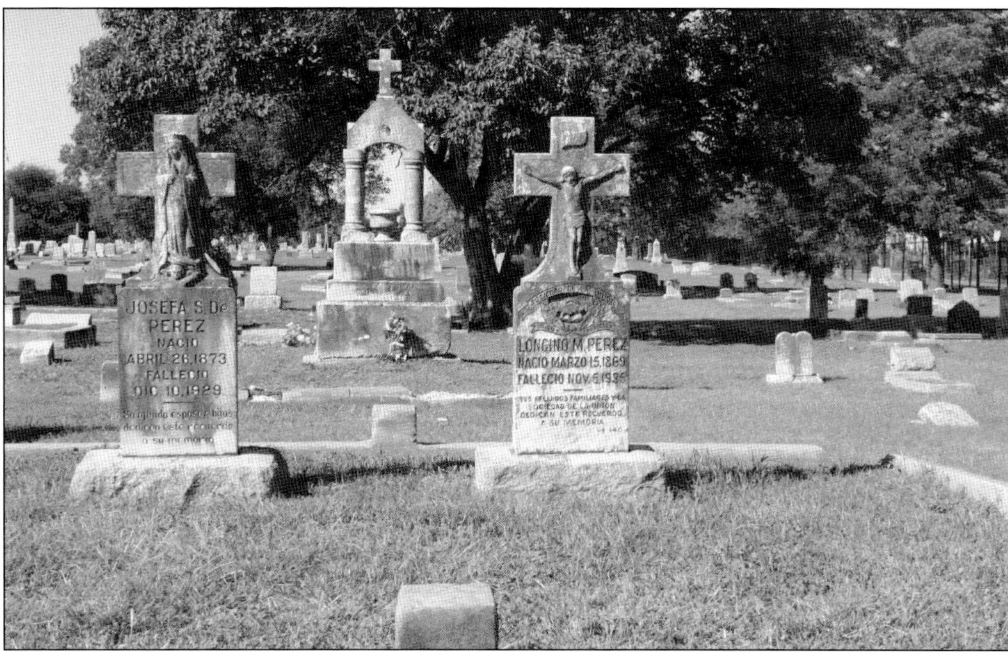

Longino Perez worked as a porter for the Pullman Company during the 1920s. During the Great Depression, he managed as a janitor. He was also a member of the Sociedad de la Union. Notice that Josefa's gravestone features a carving of Mary, while Longino's gravestone shows Jesus on the cross. Behind them in the center is Mrs. Bahia Hyak, born in 1888 and died in 1918. [4]

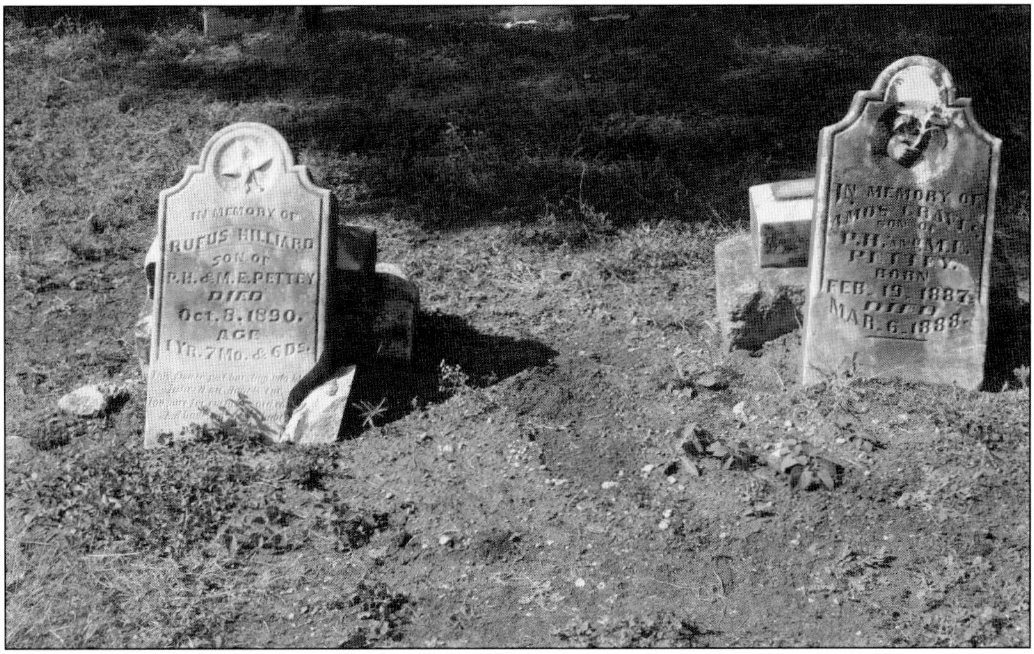

Rufus Hilliard and Amos Graves Pettey are the sons of Philemon and Martha Pettey. Philemon worked as both a hackman and boardinghouse proprietor of the Dalton House and Traveler's House. During the Civil War, he served in Bates Regiment of the Confederate army. After Philemon's death in 1899, Martha had a grocery store until her death in 1918. [3]

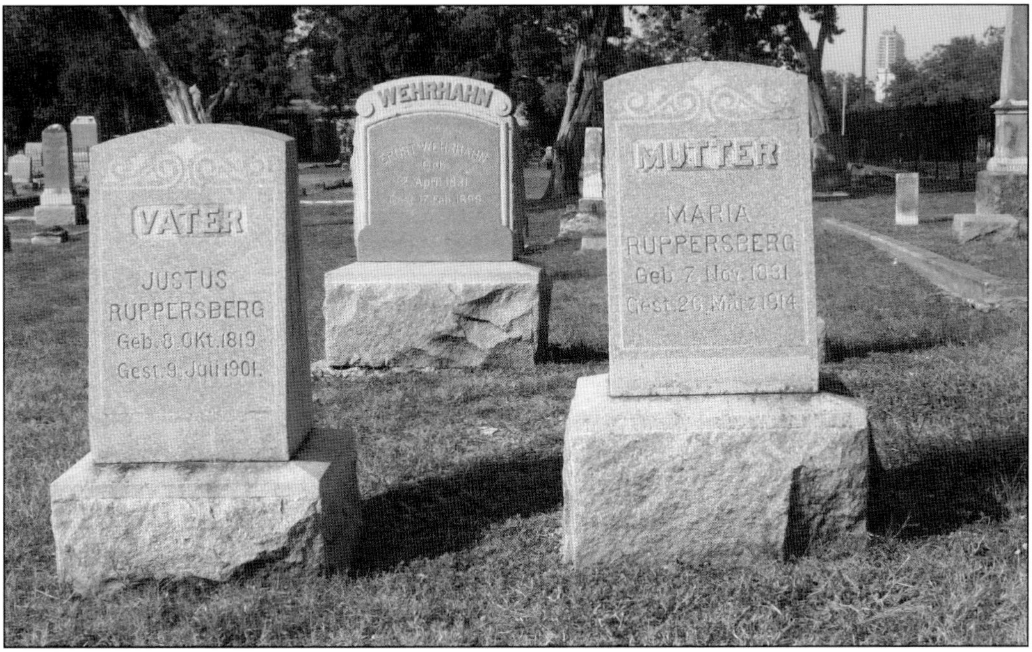

Justus Ruppersberg, born in Prussia, probably arrived in America about 1867, as his son William, born in 1853, lists that year as his arrival date. On the 1880 federal census, Justus is listed as a gardener. By 1889, he was a watchman at the arsenal, according to the city directory. William worked in a grocery store and in a saloon; his last occupation was as a broom manufacturer. [2]

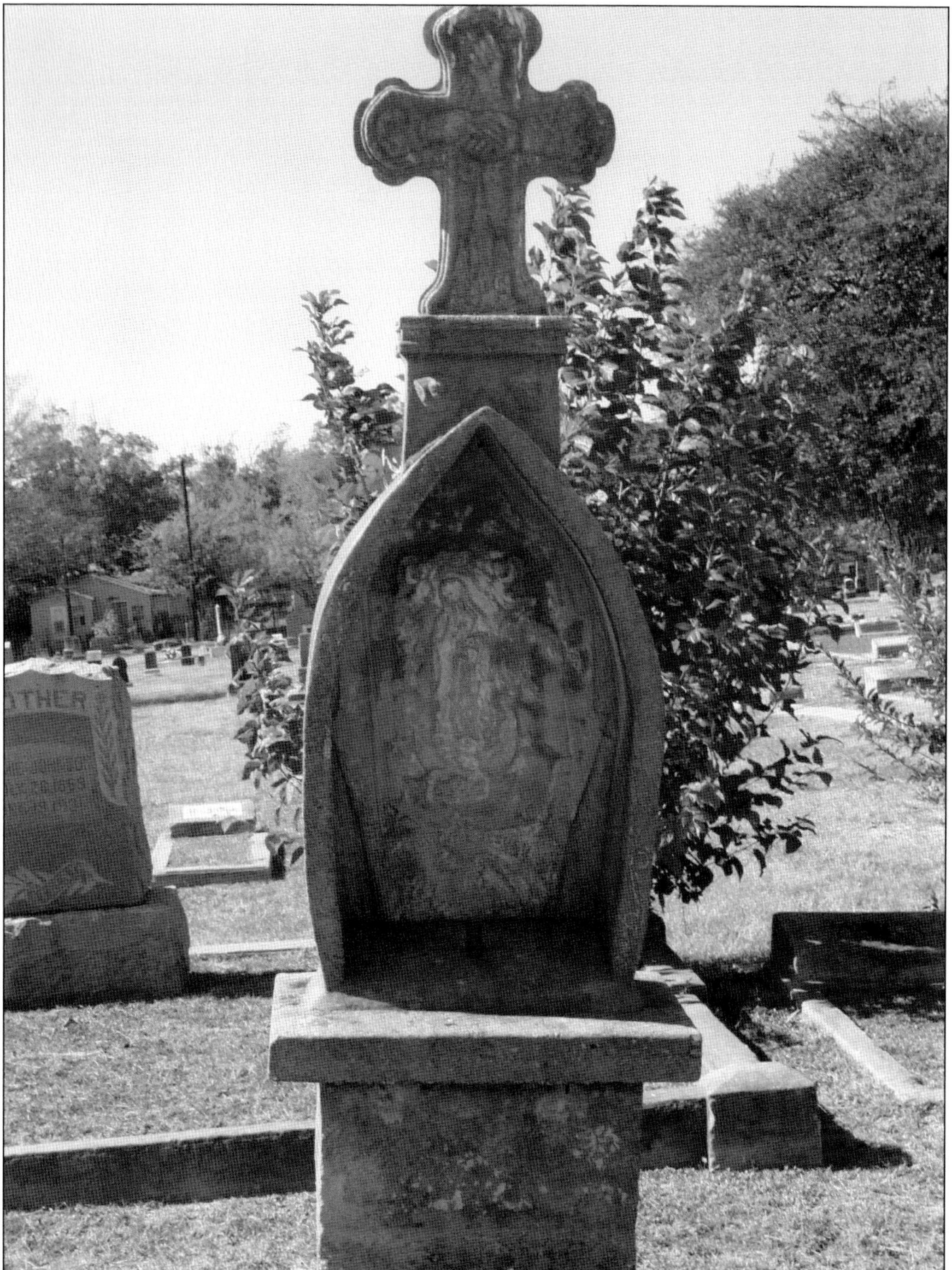

This *nicho* is the most elaborate in the Eastside cemetery complex. On the flat surface is a place for a candle and the usual information about the deceased. Valentina Rivera was born in Mexico on February 14, 1850, and died in San Antonio in July 1901. On the back of the top is Our Lady of Guadalupe held high. Around her are the words of the Hail Mary. Much smaller and simpler nichos can be found in City Cemetery No. 3 and throughout South Texas. [3]

This simple gravestone, just a short distance from the Nat Lewis mausoleum, reflects that Joseph Ryan was the presiding justice of Section B of the Supreme Court Commission of Appeals. Ryan was raised in San Antonio, attended St. Mary's College, and practiced law in the city for over 40 years. He was elected city attorney in 1905 and served until 1913. His younger son died in World War I. [5]

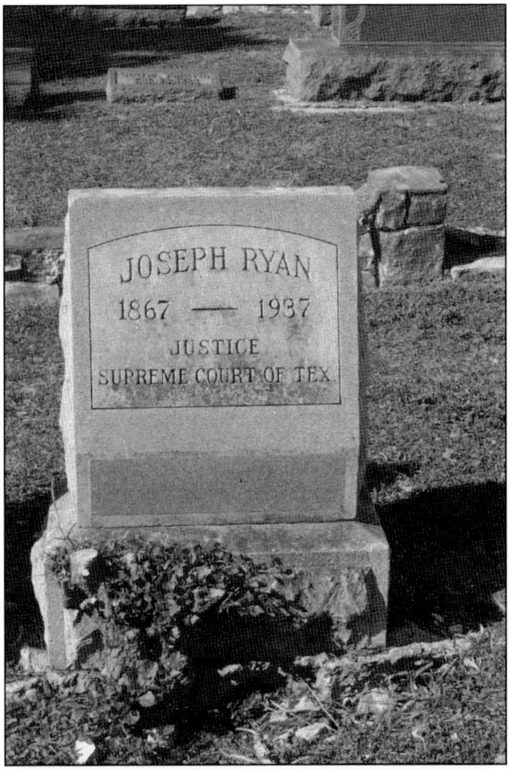

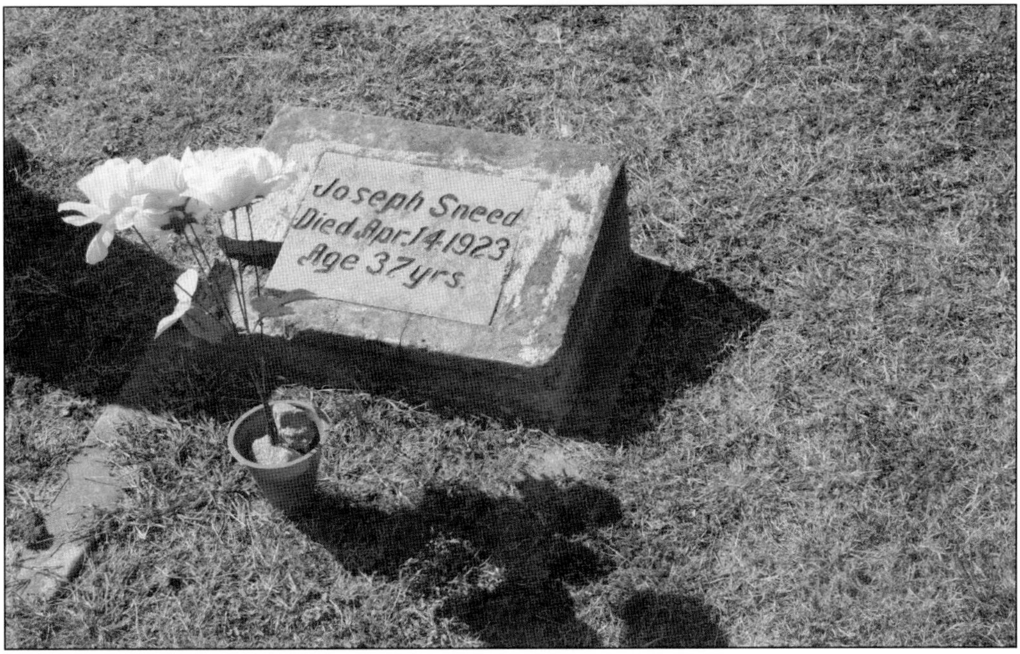

The small flowerpot suggests that someone may remember Joseph Sneed. Joseph was born in 1887 in the small community of St. Hedwig east of San Antonio. At the time of his death, he was a warehouseman for G.A. Stower's furniture store. His wife, Roxana, worked as a washerwoman. The cause of his death is listed as pneumonia and influenza. [3]

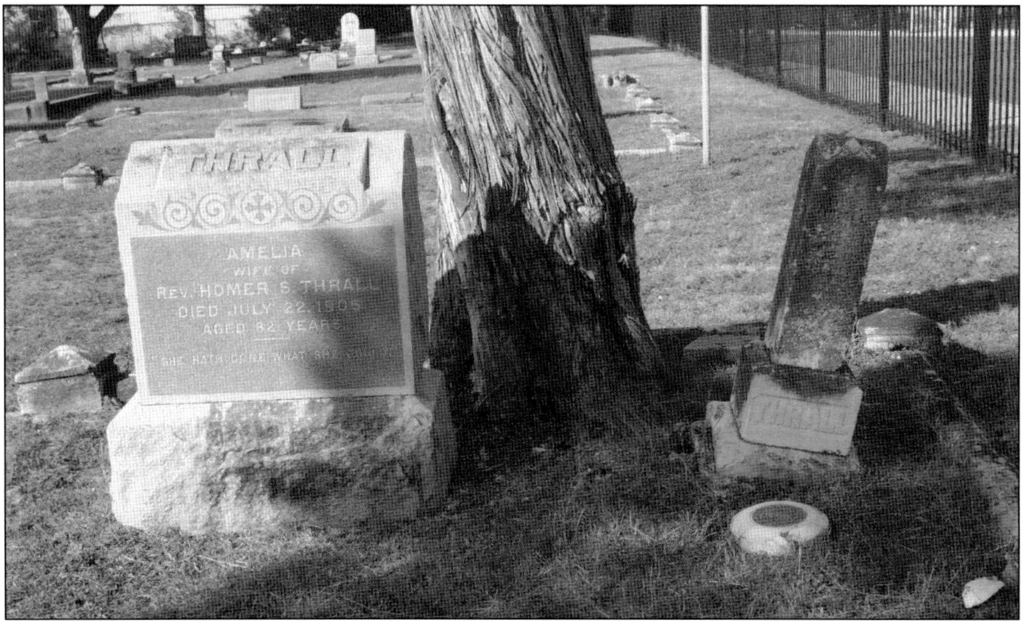

Who would have believed when Homer Spellman Thrall was born in 1819 in Underhill, Vermont, that he would eventually spend over 50 years as a Methodist minister in Texas? As a circuit preacher he made the rounds of churches, homes, and camp meetings, preaching and teaching to all who chose to listen. On the frontier, he would preach with Texas Rangers at hand to protect against Indian raids. The gravestone next to his is that of his second wife, Amelia Trueborn West. [2]

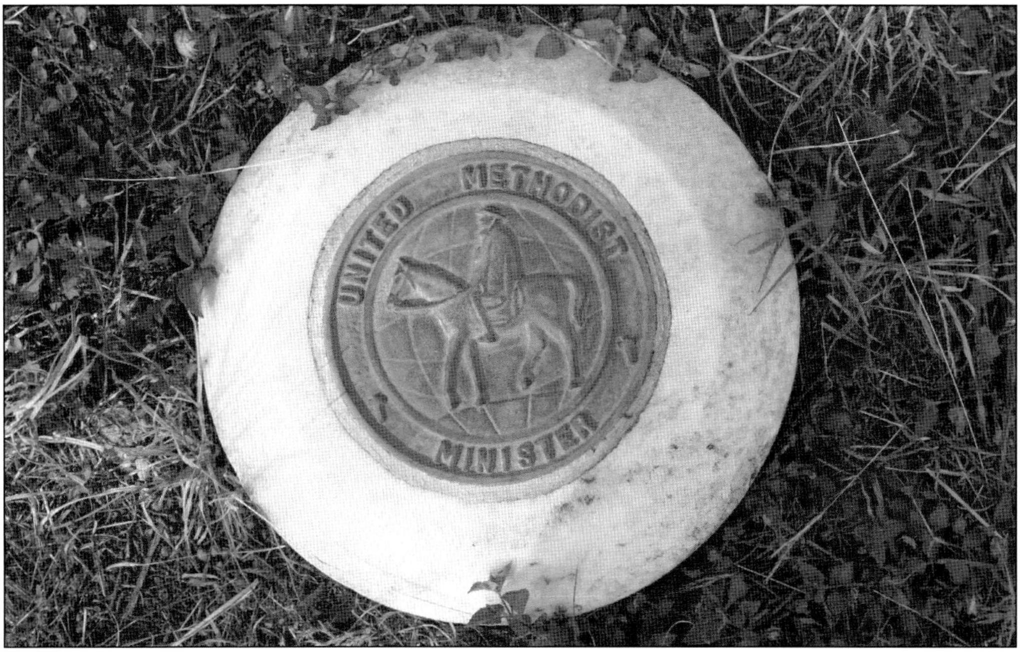

From 1842 until his retirement in November 1891, Thrall served churches in Rutersville, Galveston, Austin, Victoria, Seguin, Del Rio, San Antonio, and others. During the slavery controversy, he remained with the Methodist Episcopal Church South. He helped build Austin's first Methodist church, founded a church newspaper, taught at Rutersville College, and wrote five books. [2]

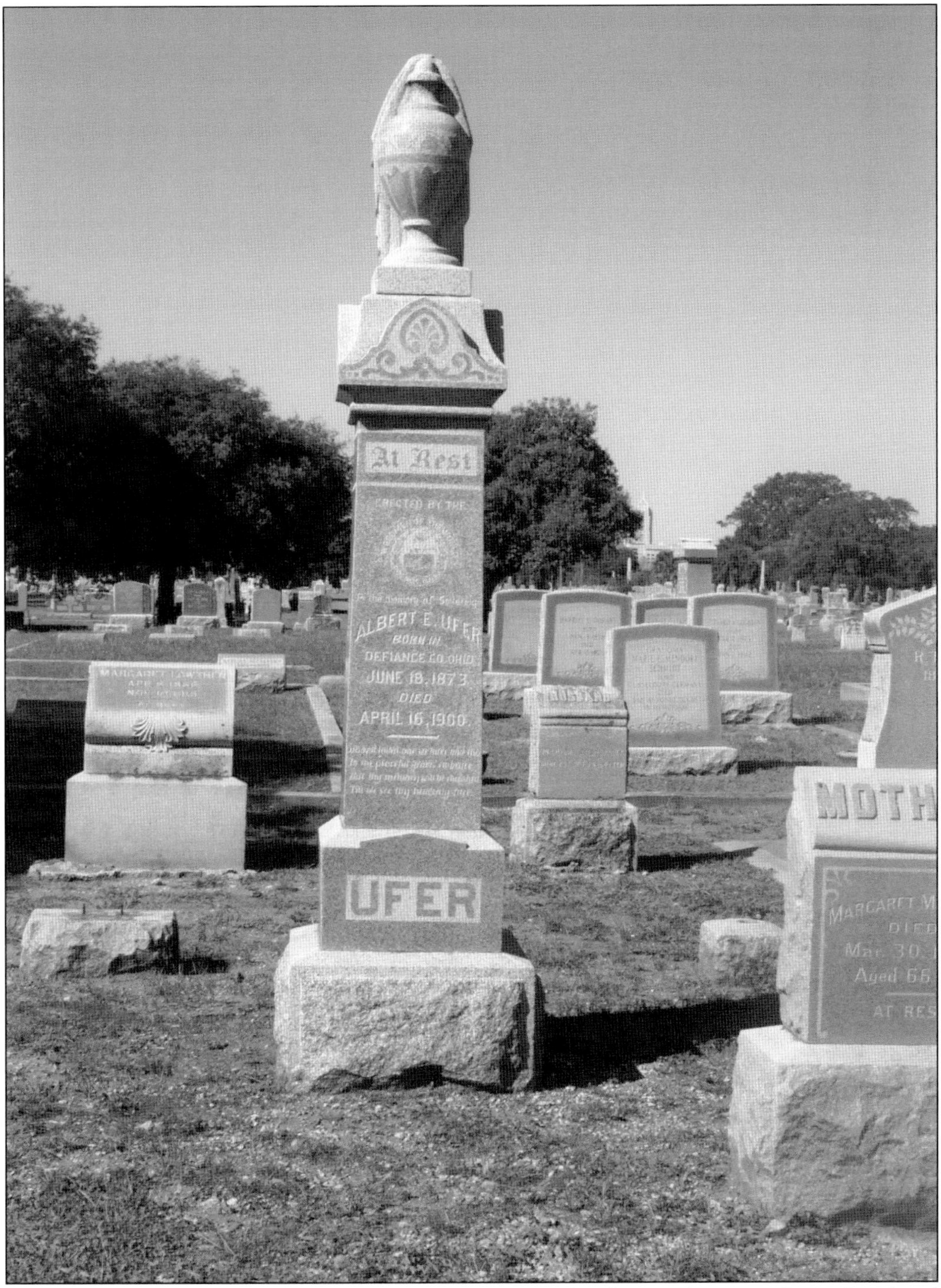

Albert Ufer, known to his friends as Bert, was a fireman for the Southern Pacific Railroad and a member of the Brotherhood of Locomotive Firemen. Originally from Ohio, he married in San Antonio to Anna McIlwane, who had been born in England. Albert Ufer was injured while on a run near Sabinal in January 1900 when the boiler burst, spraying steam into his face. Sadly, he was killed in a tragic accident just a few months later at age 28. [4]

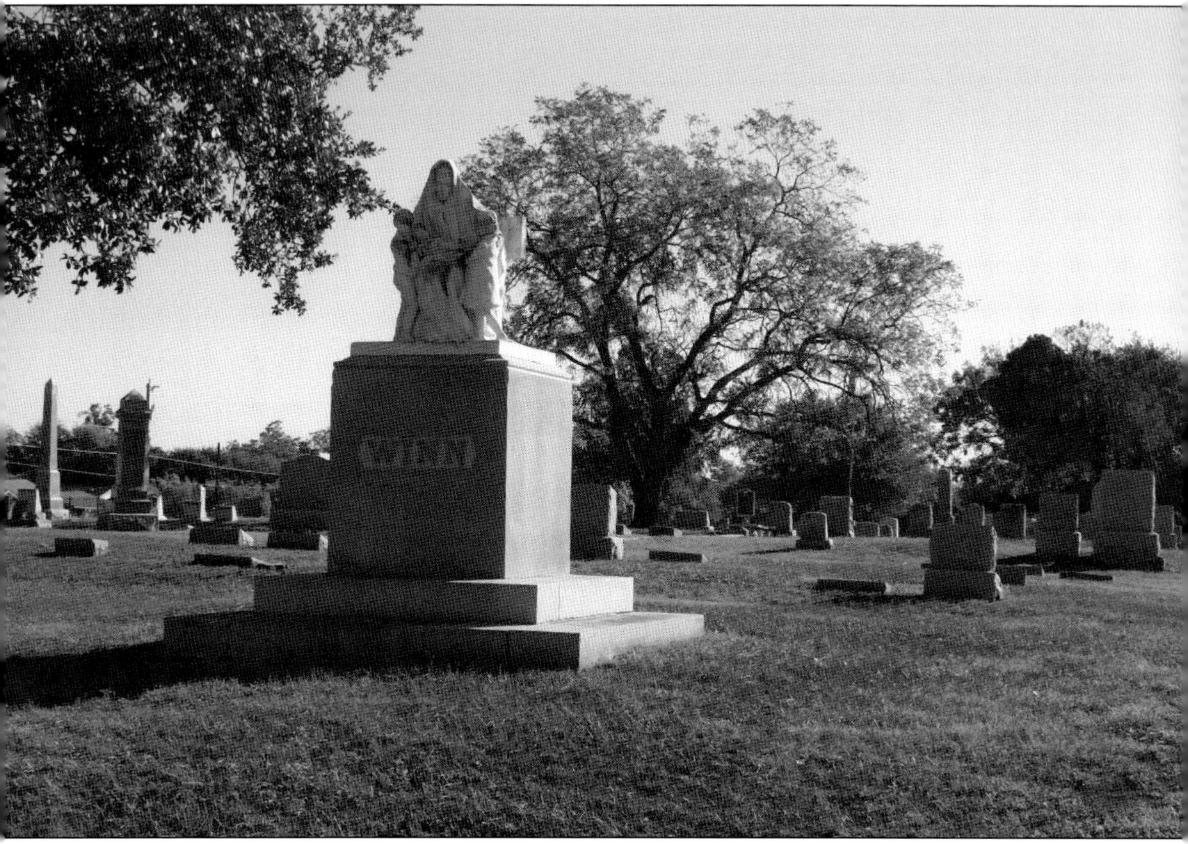

Not only is the marble sculpture by Pompeo Coppini of interest, but so is the story behind it. When still a child, Mattie Winn's family moved from Iowa to Louisiana. Mattie studied nursing and settled in a hospital in New Orleans. Meanwhile, Tom Winn caught typhoid and was sent to the same hospital to recover. Mattie nursed Tom back to health, romance blossomed, and they married. Shortly thereafter Mattie was diagnosed with tuberculosis, and the family moved to San Antonio for her health. In November 1905, Mattie passed. Tom Winn hired Coppini to do the sculpture. Mattie's sister posed as Mattie, and Mattie's daughter and son posed as themselves. The piece was finished in 1908, and the family returned to Louisiana. [6]

Three

Religious

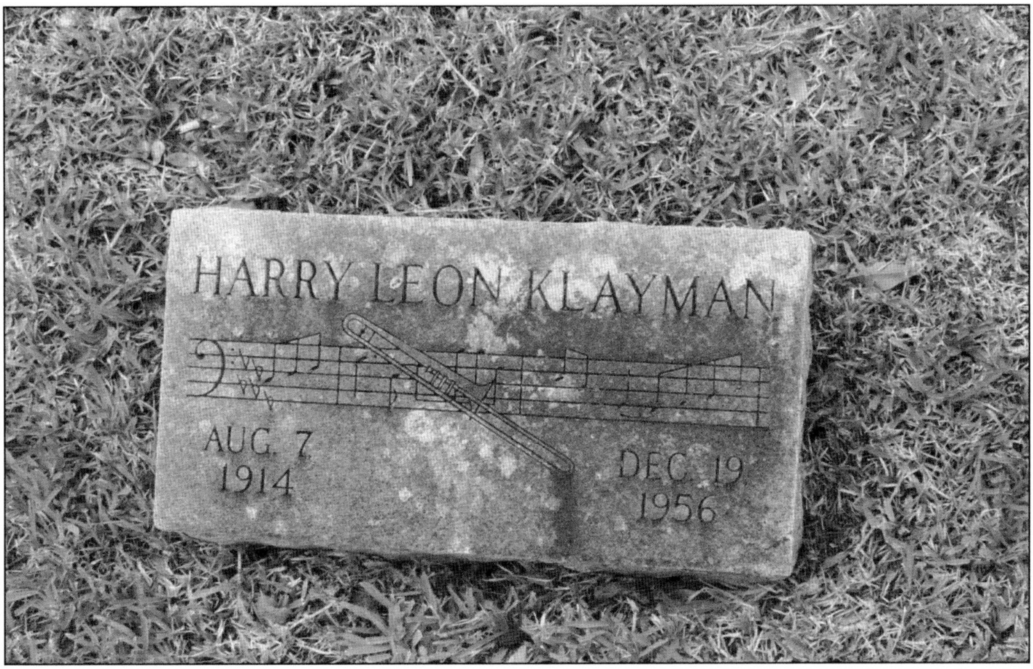

Harry Leon Klayman was born in Boston, Massachusetts, in 1914. In Massachusetts, he was a theater musician. The last 14 years of his life were spent in San Antonio, where he played trombone with the San Antonio Symphony. He also served as librarian and a board member. He taught music at Trinity and St. Mary's Universities. The stone with its trombone and musical notes beautifully portrays his life. [9]

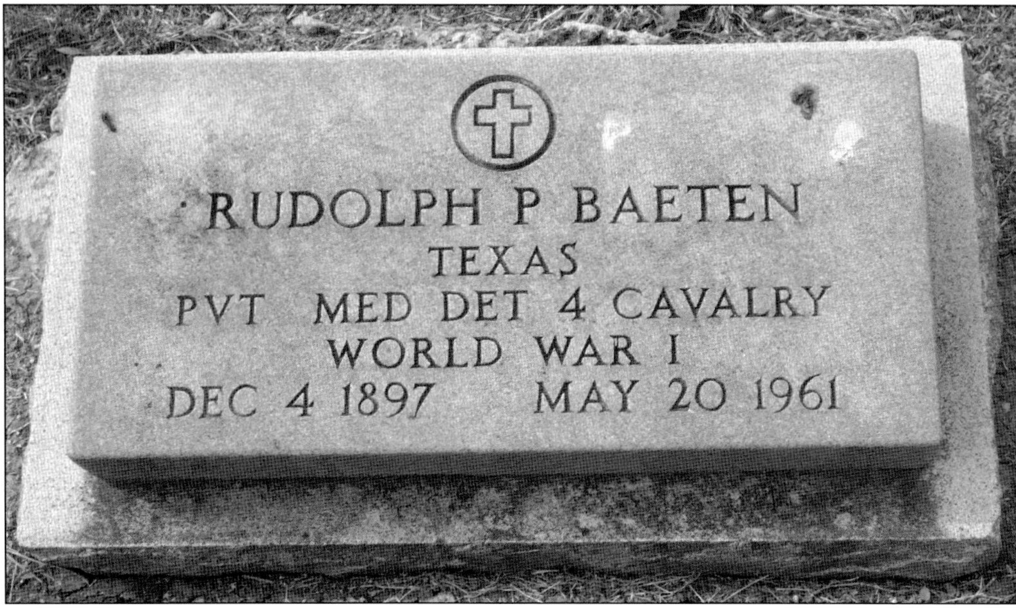

Rudolph P. Baeten was a private in the Army. He was attached to the US Medical Department, Regiment of Cavalry, during World War I. He was discharged from the Army on March 12, 1919. His wife, Claire Ripps Baeten, survived him. [15]

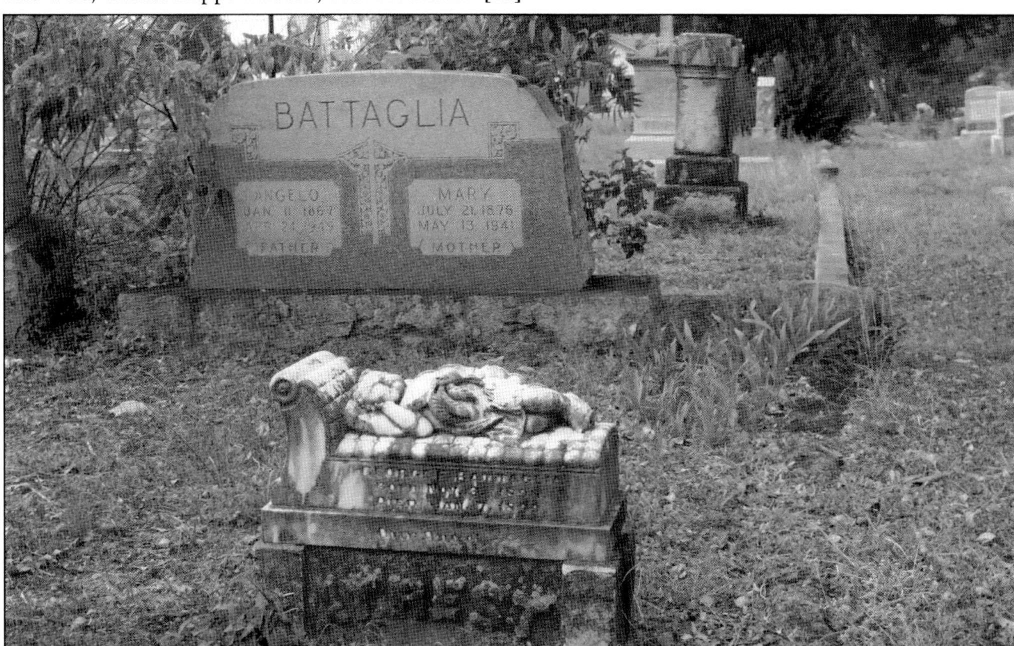

Mary Battaglia, born in 1874 in New Orleans, was the daughter of Italian immigrants. Her husband, Angelo, was born in Italy in 1867. She and Angelo had a daughter and son who survived and a baby, named George, who sadly passed away at two months old. His grave marker shows an infant sleeping. Mary was a member of St. Patrick's Altar Society. Angelo owned the Southern Macaroni Company. When he passed away, he was the last surviving charter member of the Christopher Columbus Society. [13]

Augustine Toutant-Beauregard, a native of Louisiana, came to Texas in 1852 for his health and bought a large ranch in Wilson County. There, he became a prominent cattleman. His brother was Gen. P.G.T. Beauregard, the noted Confederate general. Augustine married Adele De Rigggio of Louisiana and died at the Phillips' boardinghouse on South Alamo Street. [13]

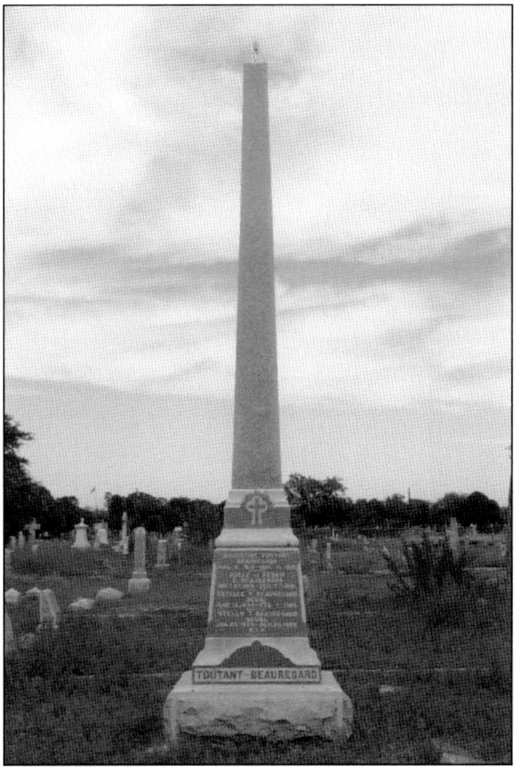

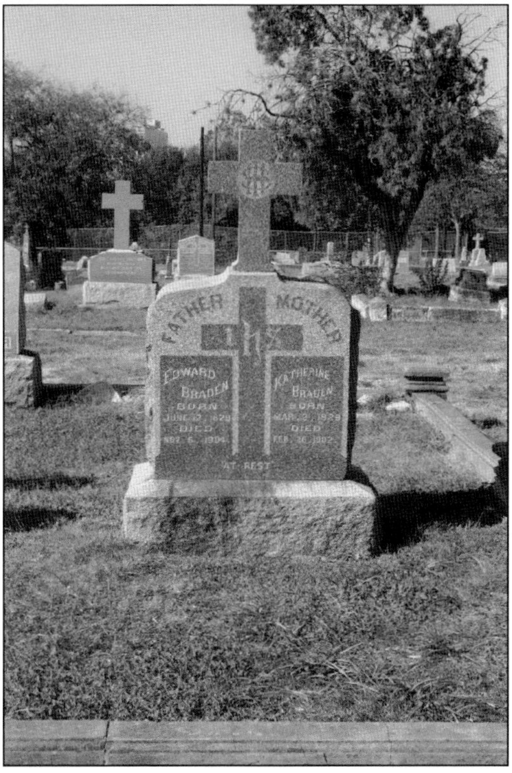

Edward Braden Sr. is best known as a large-building contractor, having been responsible for many of the original buildings at Fort Sam Houston, including the tower. He was also in charge of construction of the current San Antonio City Hall. Born in Germany, he came to Texas in 1846. After serving in the Confederacy during the Civil War, he opened the Texas House, later called the Braden Hotel. [15]

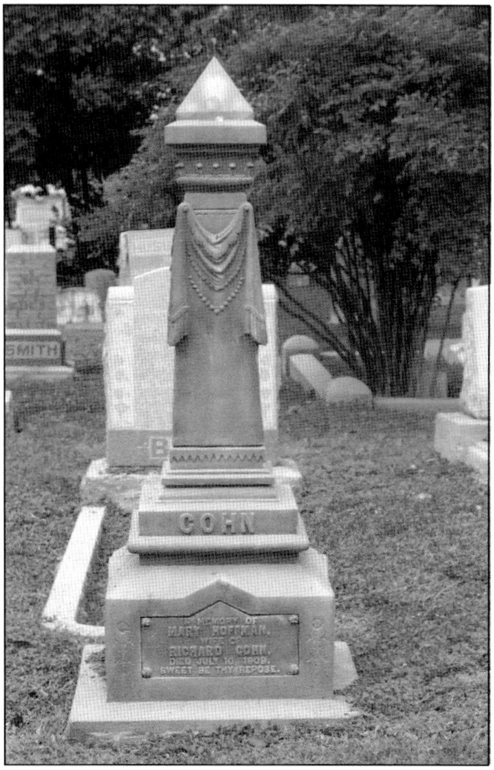

Richard and Mary Cohn were owners of the San Pedro Drugstore located at 910 ½ West Commerce Street. Richard started as an apothecary clerk at a store in Galveston, Texas, around 1880. Although German born, he became a US citizen on September 25, 1906. [9]

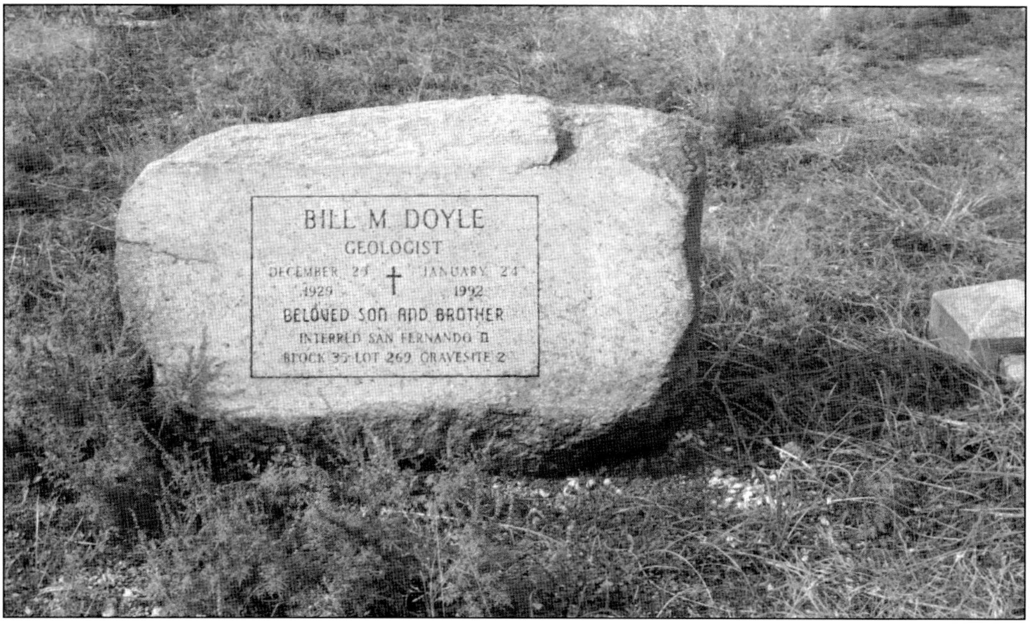

This large rock is an appropriate marker for a petroleum geologist. Bill Doyle attended St. Gerard High School and the University of Texas at Austin. He was a member of the American Association of Petroleum Geologists and the South Texas Geological Association. It is interesting that the funeral was held at St. Pius X Catholic Church, his burial was at San Fernando Cemetery No. 2, and this marker was placed in St. Mary's Cemetery. [13]

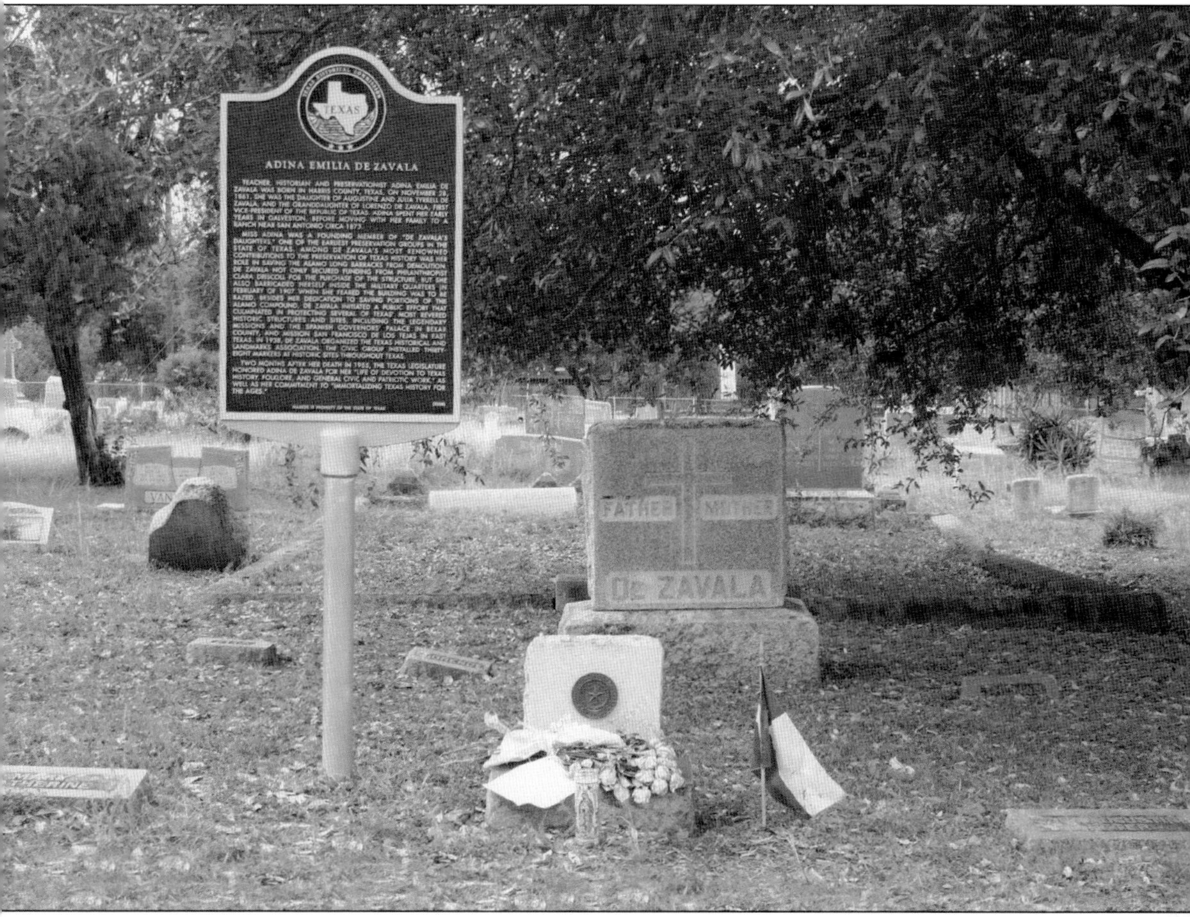

Adina Emilia de Zavala, born in 1861, was a granddaughter of Lorenzo de Zavala, the first vice president of the Republic of Texas. She was instrumental in saving the long barracks of the Alamo from destruction by getting Clara Driscoll to purchase the property. She was also instrumental in the preservation of the Spanish Governor's Palace. Adina was a charter member of the Texas Historical Association and a member of several other organizations. [13]

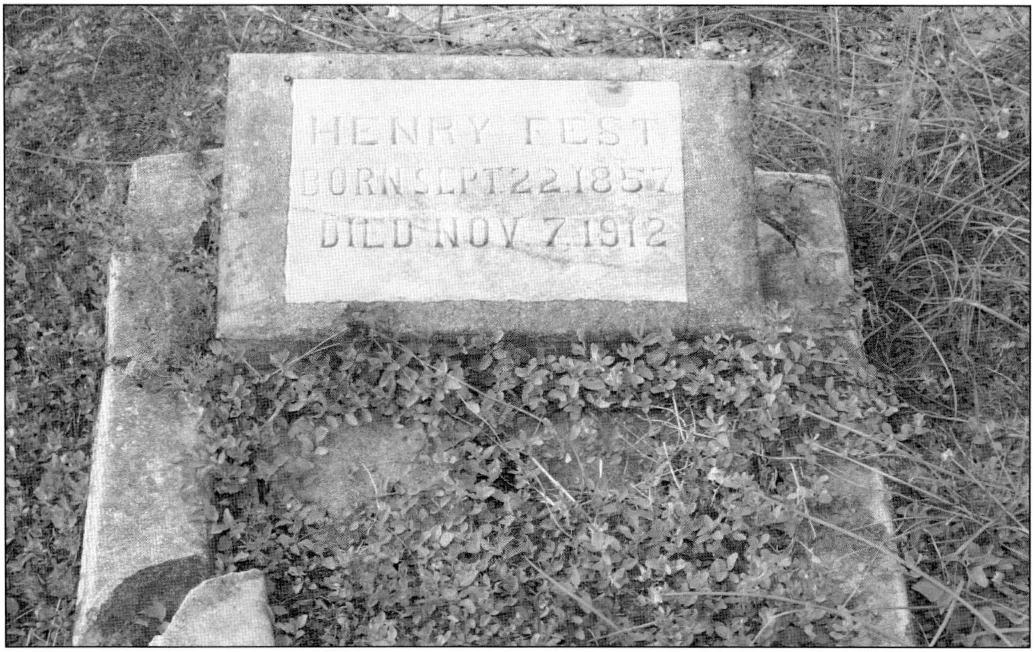

Henry Fest was the son of Simon Fest of an early pioneer family from Alsace. After two trips up the cattle trails to Kansas, Henry opened a butcher shop. Later, he opened a mercantile store and, finally, the Fest Department Store. He was a member of the Trail Driver's Association and St. Henry's Catholic Church. [13]

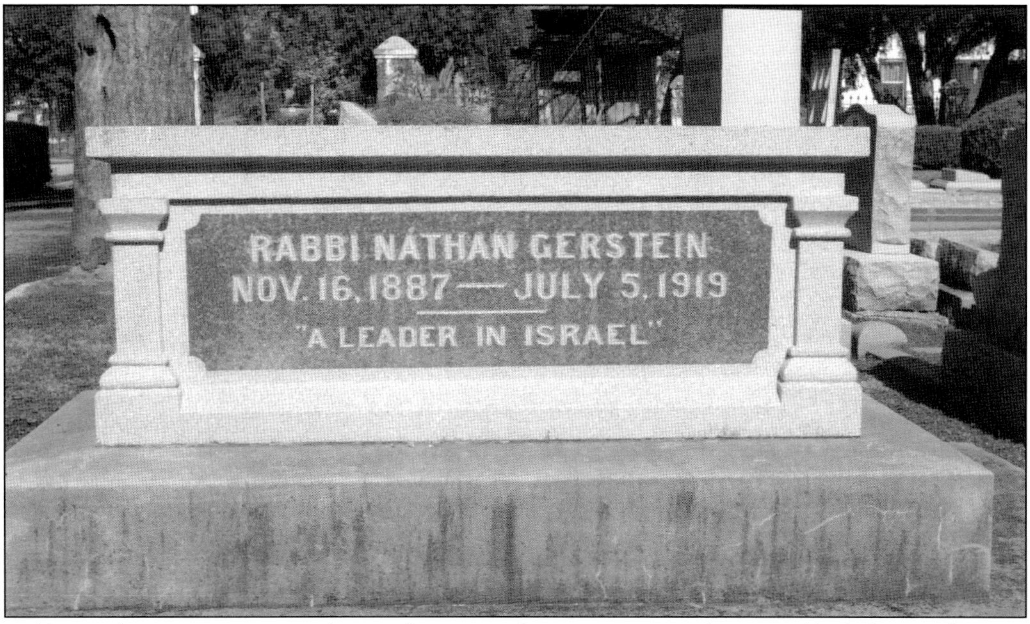

Rabbi Nathan Gerstein passed away from spinal meningitis. He became ill while traveling on his way to New York to get approval to build a new synagogue on Main Avenue in San Antonio. Rabbi Gerstein was actively involved with several organizations such as Alzafar Shrine, Knights of Pythias, Elks, Hermann Sons, Charlton Temple, and several more. He was also greatly concerned about the welfare of soldiers. [10]

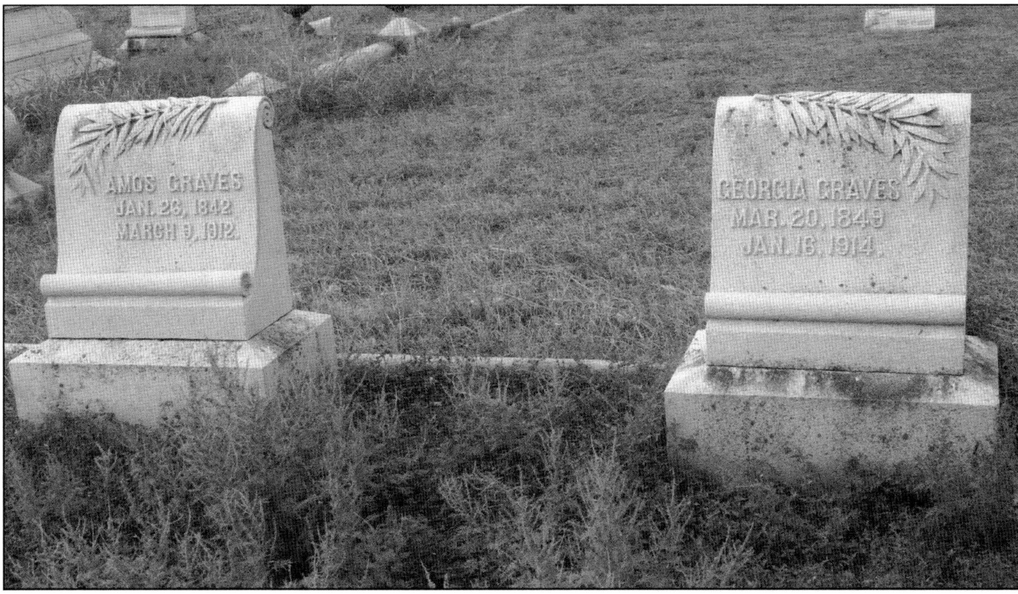

Dr. Amos Maverick Graves Sr. was born in Mississippi in 1842. During the Civil War, he rode with Confederate general Nathan Bedford Forrest. After the war, he went on to medical school, graduating in 1868. In 1876 he moved to Texas, ranching in Frio County. Two years later, he moved to San Antonio. From 1888 to 1902, he was medical director of Galveston, Harrisburg, & San Antonio Railroad. He built and promoted San Antonio Union Stockyards and packinghouses known as Union Meat Company. He married Georgia Riley Smith of Missouri in 1869. He was considered the foremost physician and surgeon in the city during his time here. [13]

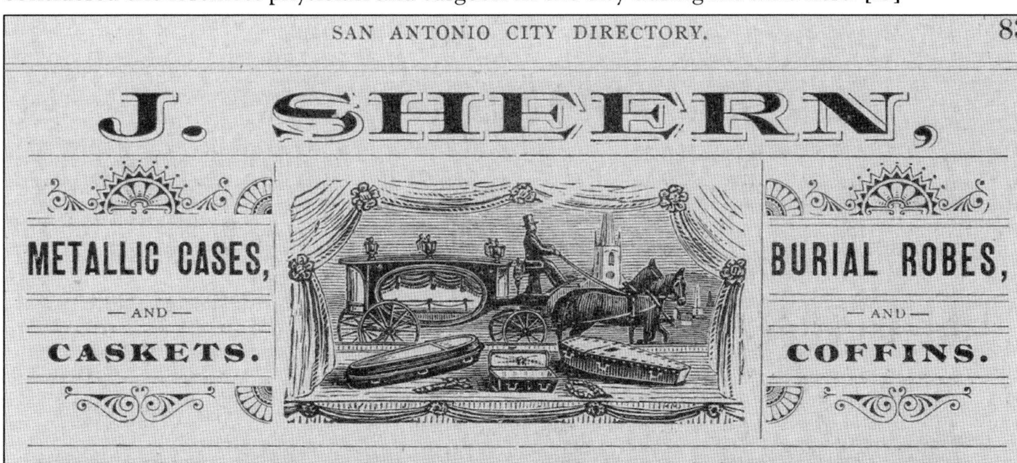

This advertisement for J. Sheern appeared in the 1883–1884 *San Antonio City Directory*. Prior to 1900, several undertaking establishments operated in San Antonio. Most did not last very long. Joseph Sheern's business was an exception. He appears in the first city directory in 1877 and remained independent until 1891.

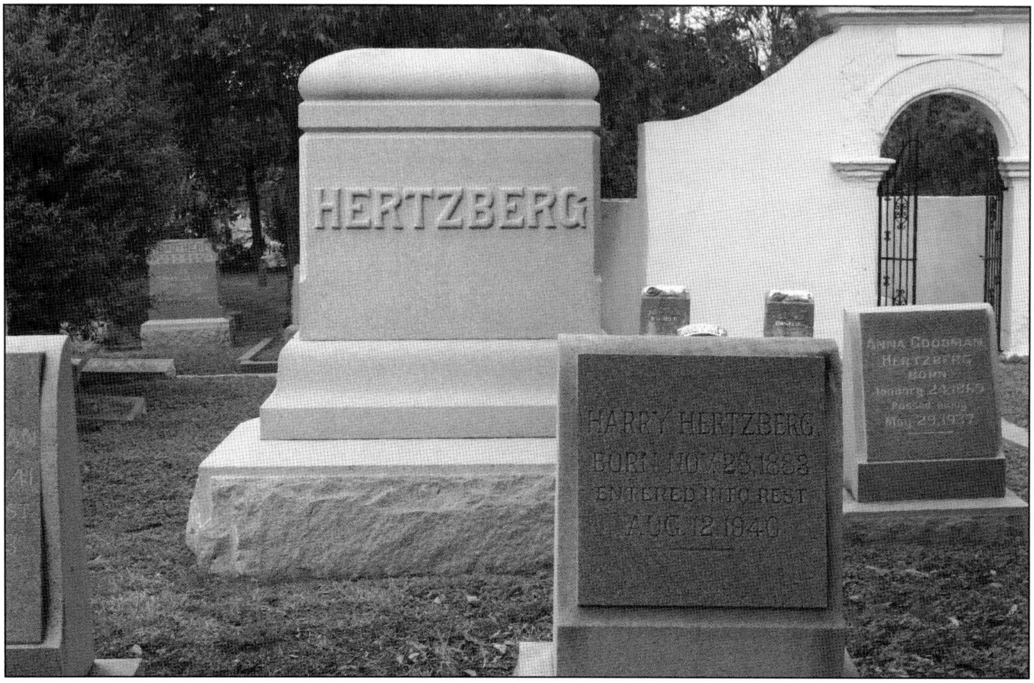

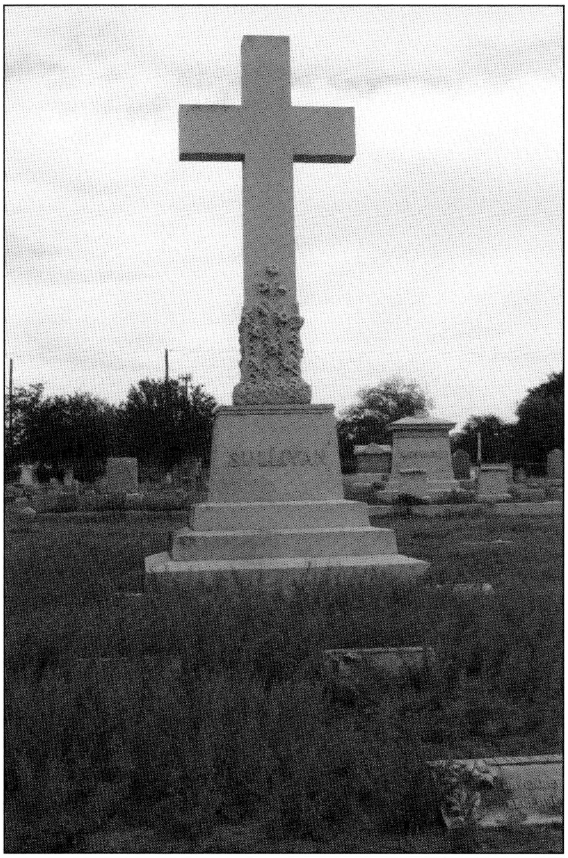

Harry Hertzberg, son of Eli and Anna Hertzberg, was born and raised in San Antonio. He was admitted to the bar in 1904 and served in the Texas Senate during the 1919–1922 terms. He is most known for his civic work as a member of the public library board, zoological society, and Witte Museum board. He was a charter member and national president of the Circus Fans of America Association. [9]

Irishman Daniel Sullivan was born on December 24, 1845. In Texas, at the beginning of the Civil War, he enlisted in the Confederate 1st Texas Cavalry. He served at Brownsville, Mansfield, and Yellow Bayou, Louisiana, and at Sabine Pass. After the war, he went into merchandising wholesale and retail groceries with banking interests in Indianola. In 1884, he moved his banking to San Antonio and discontinued the mercantile business. [13]

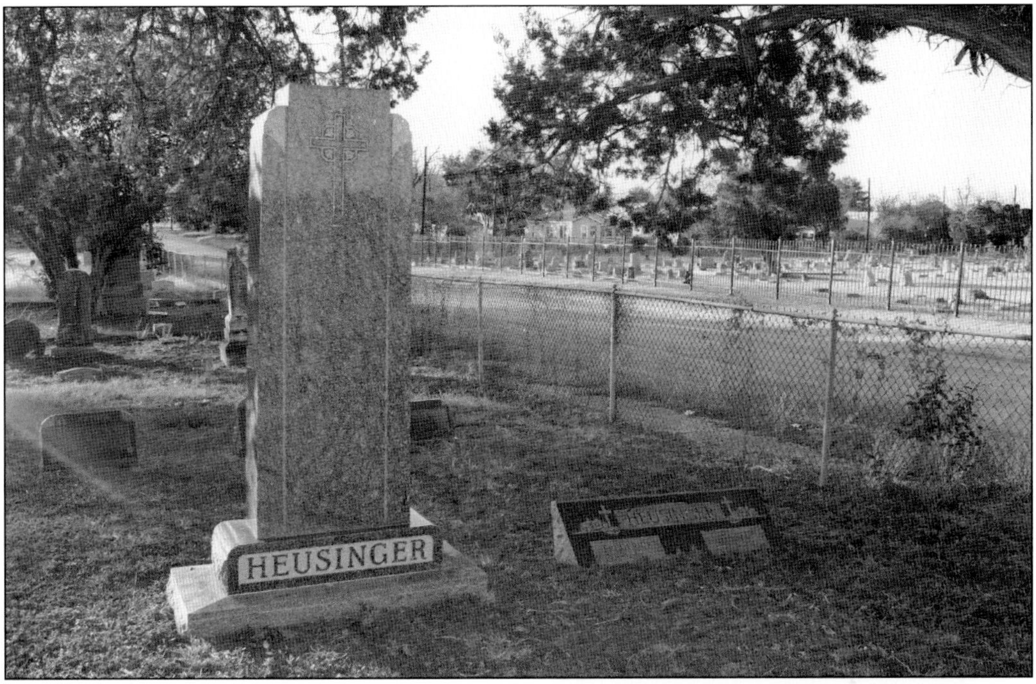

Edward W. Heusinger was born in San Antonio on June 9, 1874, the son of Adolph and Anna. Adolph and his brother Julius arrived in San Antonio in 1850, when it had a population of about 4,000. Adolph went into the mercantile business with Honore Grenet where the Crocket Hotel is presently located.

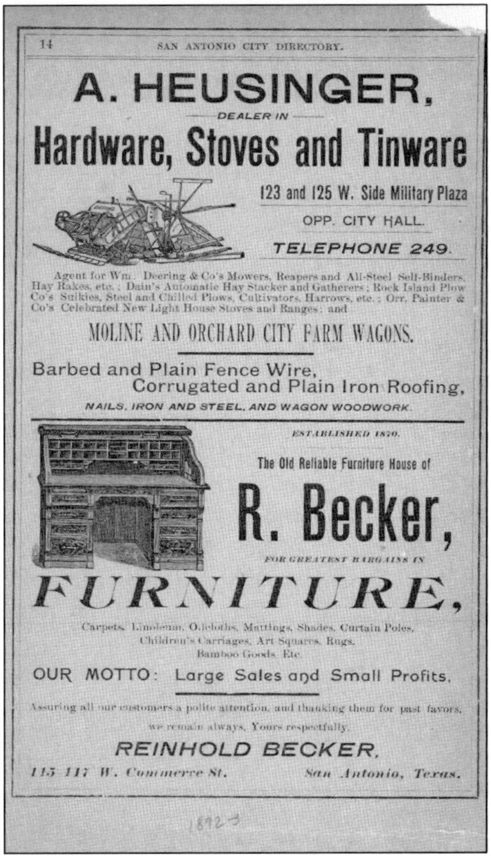
14 SAN ANTONIO CITY DIRECTORY.

A. HEUSINGER,

DEALER IN

Hardware, Stoves and Tinware

123 and 125 W. Side Military Plaza

OPP. CITY HALL.

TELEPHONE 249.

Agent for Wm. Deering & Co's Mowers, Reapers and All-Steel Self-Binders, Hay Rakes, etc.; Dain's Automatic Hay Stacker and Gatherers; Rock Island Plow Co's Sulkies, Steel and Chilled Plows, Cultivators, Harrows, etc.; Orr, Painter & Co's Celebrated New Light House Stoves and Ranges; and

MOLINE AND ORCHARD CITY FARM WAGONS.

Barbed and Plain Fence Wire, Corrugated and Plain Iron Roofing,

NAILS, IRON AND STEEL, AND WAGON WOODWORK.

ESTABLISHED 1870.

The Old Reliable Furniture House of

R. Becker,

FOR GREATEST BARGAINS IN

FURNITURE,

Carpets, Linoleum, Oilcloths, Mattings, Shades, Curtain Poles, Children's Carriages, Art Squares, Rugs, Bamboo Goods, Etc.

OUR MOTTO: Large Sales and Small Profits.

Assuring all our customers a polite attention, and thanking them for past favors, we remain always, Yours respectfully,

REINHOLD BECKER,

115-117 W. Commerce St. San Antonio, Texas.

1892-3

In 1873, Adolph Heusinger opened a hardware store on Commerce Street. Edward W. Heusinger was educated at the German-English school in San Antonio. He became associated with his father's business and was secretary of A.E. Staacke Automobile Company. He was one of the founders of the San Antonio Scientific Society. He was a member of the Royal Geographical Society and a specialist in the origin of races in the Pacific region. He published a book on the mission establishment among the Indians of Texas. Edward Heusinger married Teodolinda Bruni, a descendant of Francisco de Arocha, a Canary Island settler. [13]

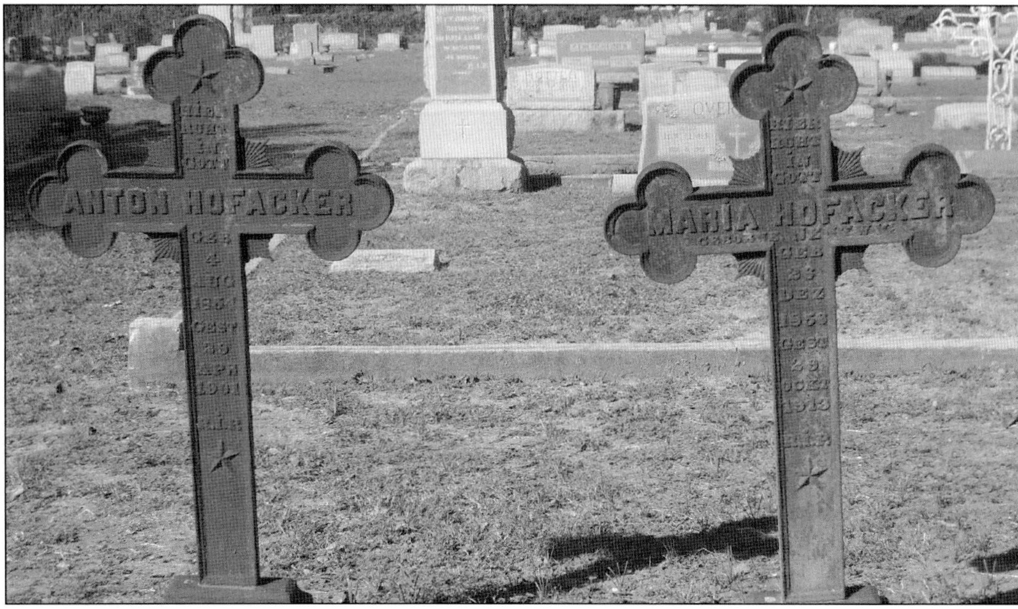

Anton and Maria (Nentwig) Hofacker were both born of German parents. Their banns were announced at St. Joseph's Lutheran Church on April 12, 1891. Their graves are marked with typical German markers. Alamo Iron Works in San Antonio made these metal crosses. The star or pentacle (*Drudenfuss* in German) at the top and bottom of each cross were believed to ward off the devil in German folklore. [13]

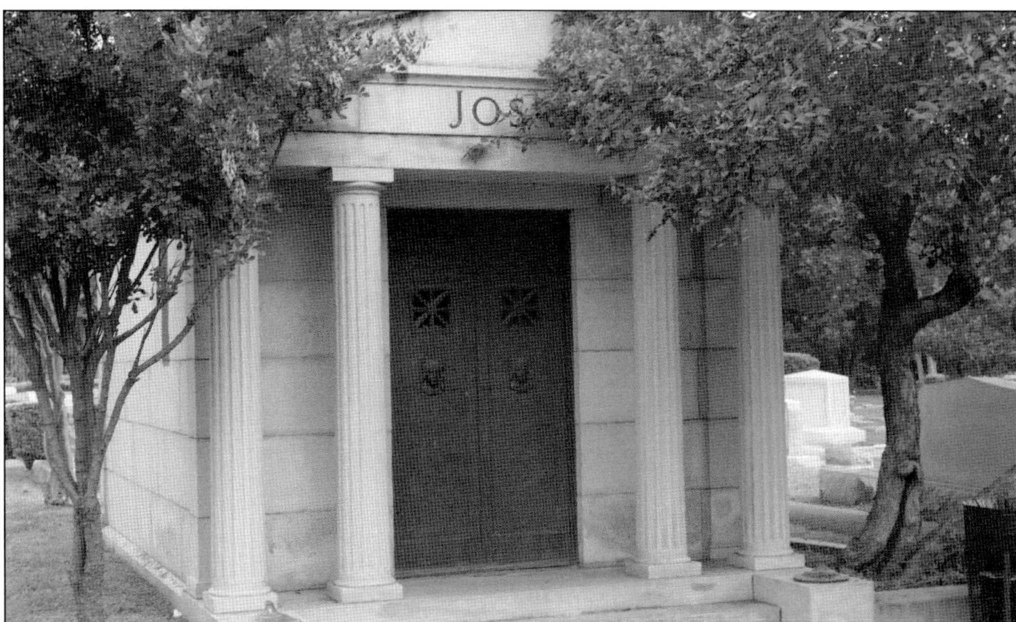

In 1900, Alexander Joske became sole owner of the business his father had begun in 1873, and by the time he died in 1925, it was the largest department store south of St. Louis and between the Mississippi River and the Rockies. He had a searchlight mounted on the store's roof, which guided James Doolittle in landing at Kelly Field in 1922. Alexander also wrote opinion pieces in the local newspapers. [9]

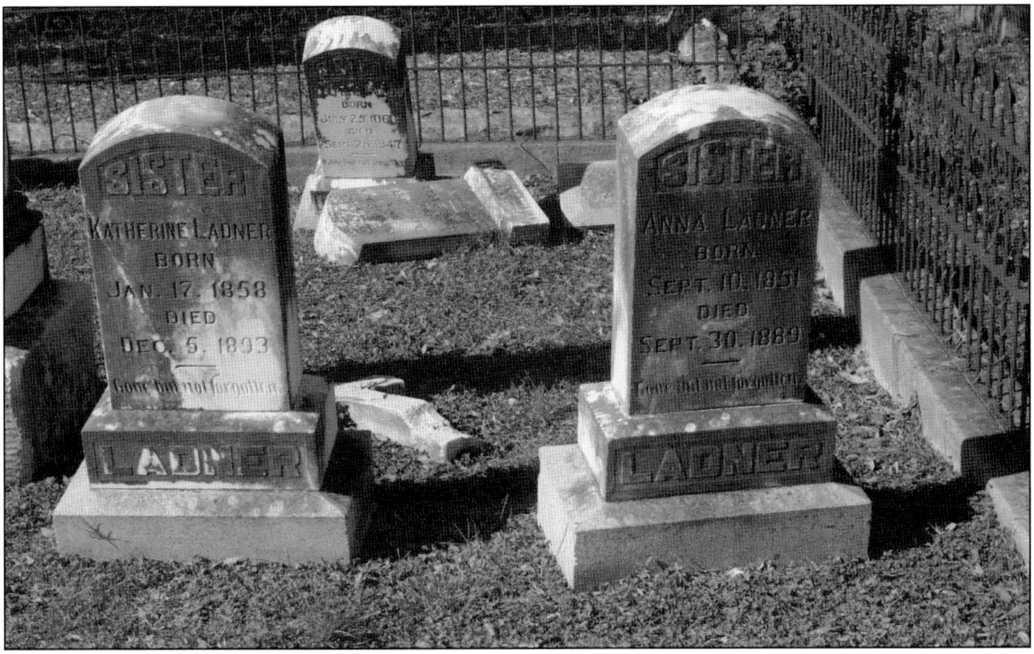

Anna Ladner is buried with her sisters Katherine Ladner, Josephine Ladner, and Louisa Heinen. Anna died at the age of 38 after a short illness. Their parents were Nicholas and Catherine Ladner, who were born in Europe. The girls were born in Texas. They lived on the family farm. [15]

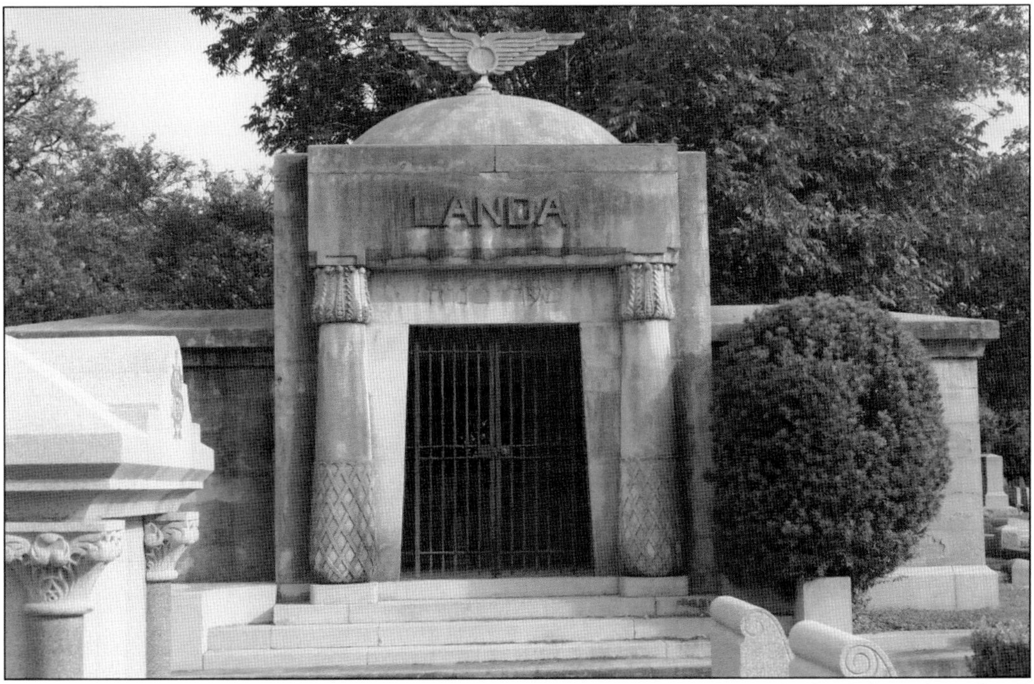

Harry Landa's father believed in hard work, which is why Harry was working for his father after school. When he became a teen, he moved to Austin and invested in a feed store with his time and money. Later, he sold his businesses and moved to San Antonio. After recovering from a serious wound, he moved back to New Braunfels and developed the natural resources of Landa Estates. [9]

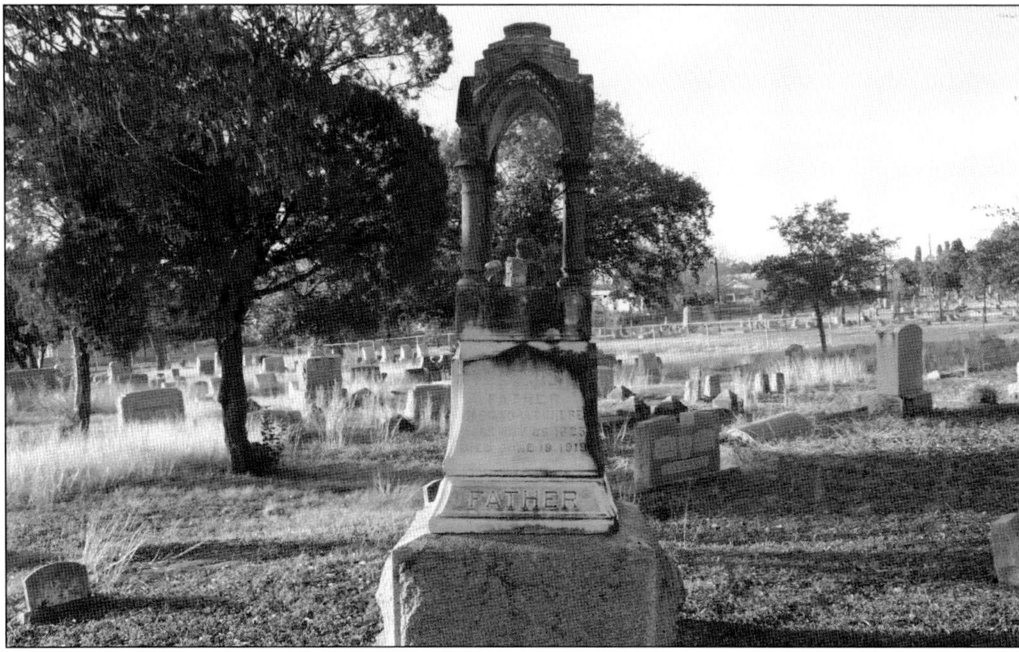

In 1894, Gaetano Lucchese and his family emigrated from Italy. He had been born in 1825 in Sicily. His wife, Josephine Colliti, was from Vicari, Italy. Gaetano was a veteran of the Garibaldi Revolution and served in the National Guard when Garibaldi went to Sicily. He was a shoemaker and father of Sam Lucchese of Lucchese Book & Shoe Factory. [13]

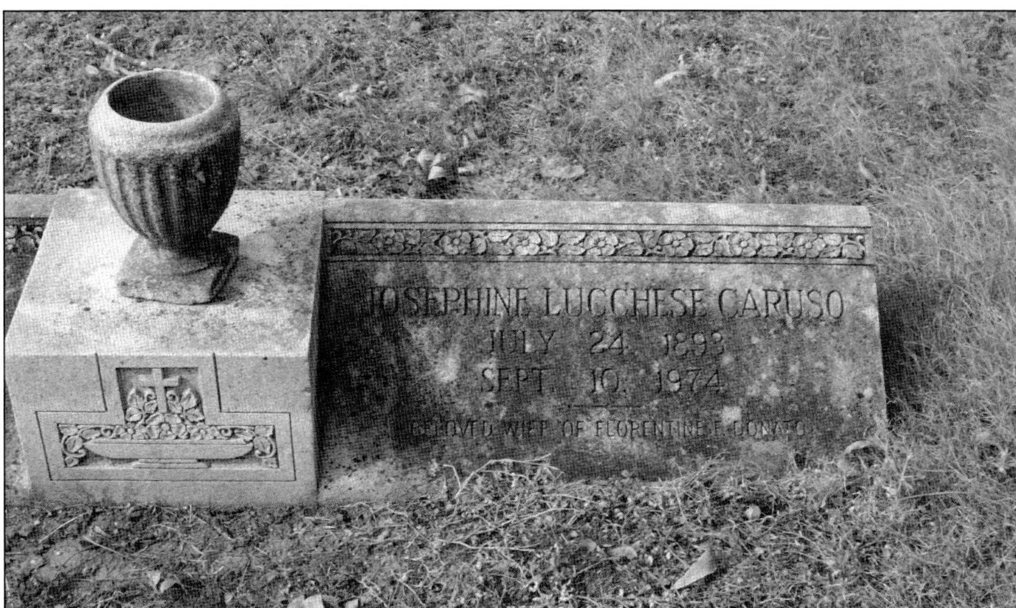

This small marker of Josephine Lucchese belies the fact that she was one of the world's premier opera stars of the 1920s and 1930s. A daughter of Sam Lucchese, she grew up here, eventually studying music in New York. Her debut was at the Aeolian Hall, New York, in 1922. From 1929 to 1936, she performed throughout Europe and America. From 1956 to 1971, she taught music at the University of Texas. [13]

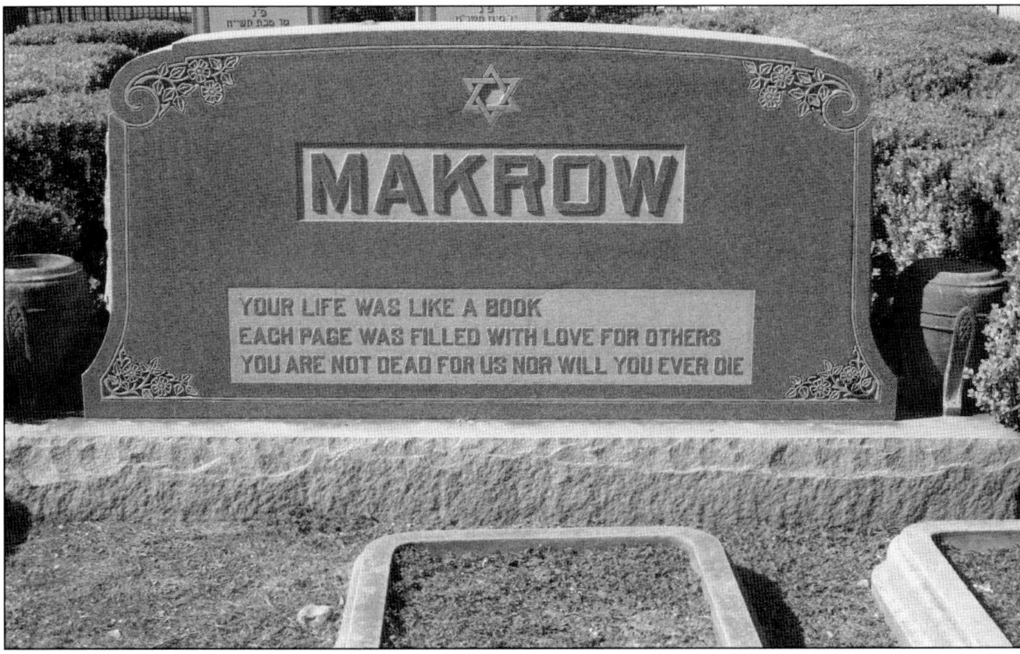

Gregory and Anne Makrow lived in Alice, Jim Wells County. There, he owned a dry goods store. He was born in Russia in 1883 but lived in Alice for 40 years before his death in 1964. He was a member of B'nai Israel Synagogue of Corpus Christi and the Scottish Rite. The inscription on the gravestone says much about the man. [10]

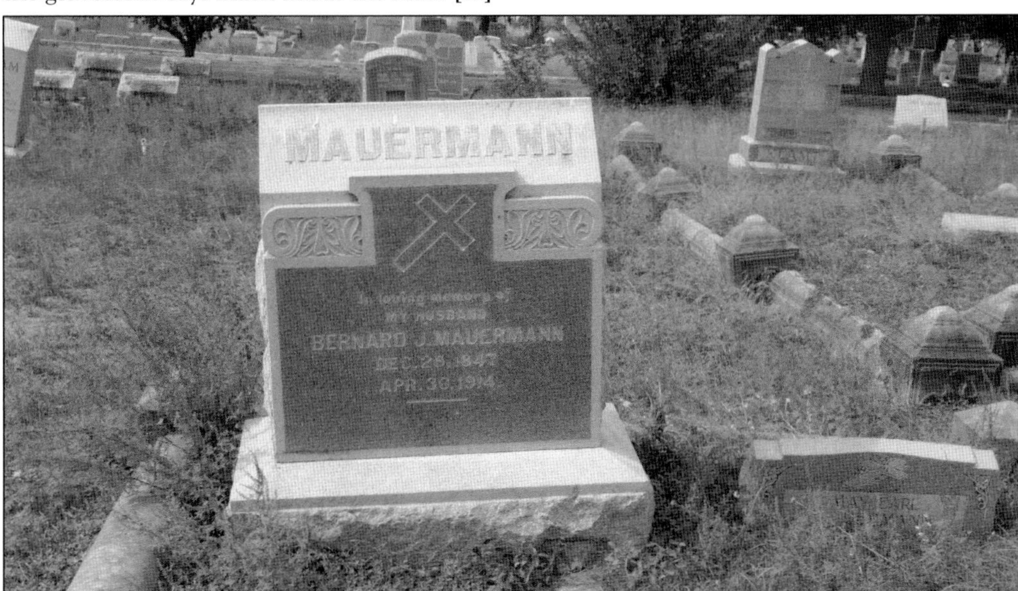

Bernard J. Mauermann, of Austria, came to San Antonio in 1853 with his parents. During the Civil War, he joined one of the Union cavalry regiments organized in Texas. He was a power in local politics during the Bryan Callaghan era, serving for a time as an alderman. He was a member of the volunteer fire department at one time, the TurnVerein, Beethoven Maennerchor, and other organizations. [13]

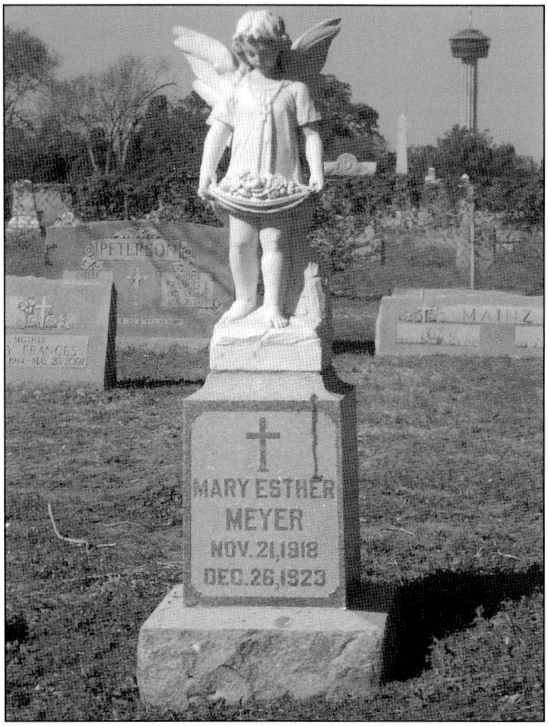

Mary Esther Meyer had just turned five when she passed in 1923. Her parents, Charles W. and Kunngunda Dielman, were from Texas. Charles was an insurance agent with F.A. Burtschell who worked out of the Moore Building, selling insurance of all kinds. The sad young angel atop her grave must reflect the sadness her parents felt. [14]

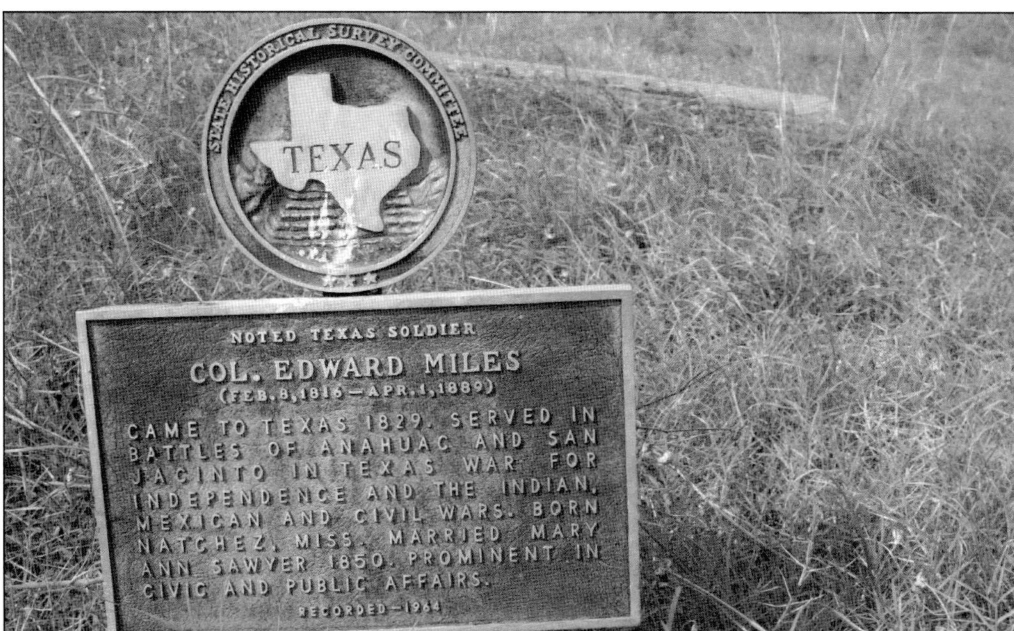

Edward Hamilton Miles served in three wars. He fought during the Texas Revolution and was a veteran of the Battle of San Jacinto. When the Mexican War began in 1846, he enlisted in the US Army and fought at Buena Vista, Monterrey, and Chapultapec. During the Civil War, he served the Confederacy in Texas and Oklahoma. His life ended in 1889 when he was run over by a buggy. [13]

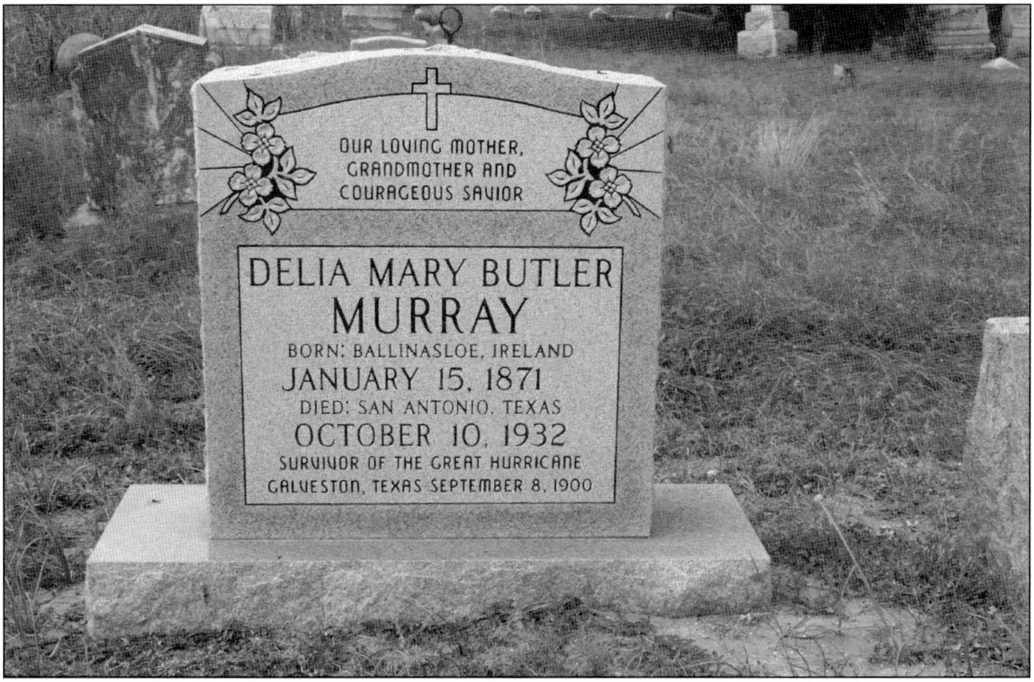

Delia Mary Murray was born in Ireland in 1871 and, later, settled in Galveston for a time. She moved to San Antonio about 1913, not long after the great hurricane of September 1900, which devastated Galveston. Loss of life totaled between 6,000 and 12,000. Delia was one of the lucky survivors. [13]

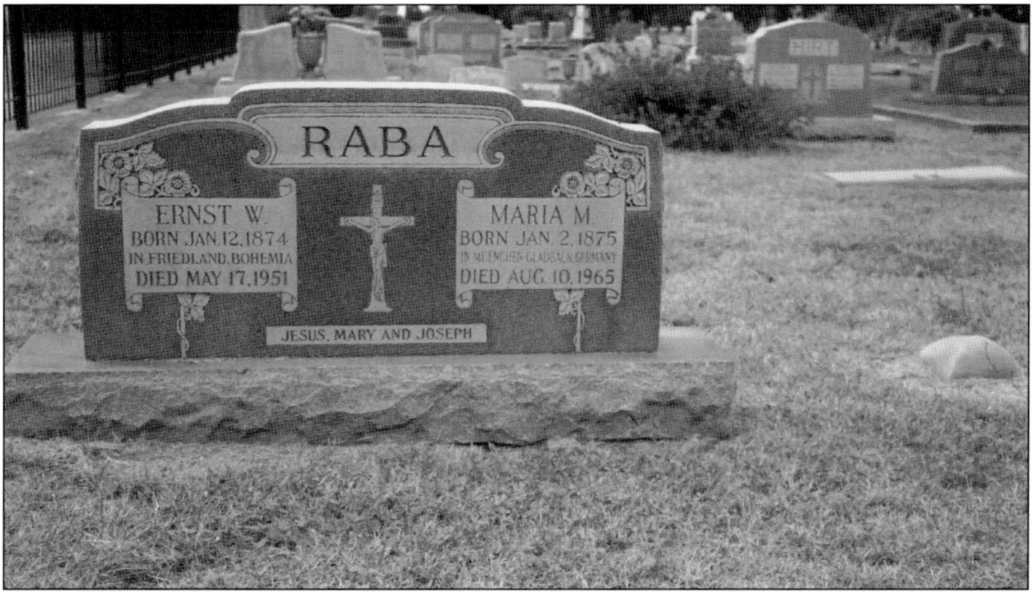

Ernst Wilhelm Raba was the second photographer to open a business in San Antonio. Ernst Raba not only took many pictures of San Antonio and its citizens but also of its visitors, such as the Rough Riders. When the first Battle of Flowers parade was held, he was an official of the parade. He painted landscapes and portraits and also restored paintings. During World War I, he organized a relief group for Austrians. [14]

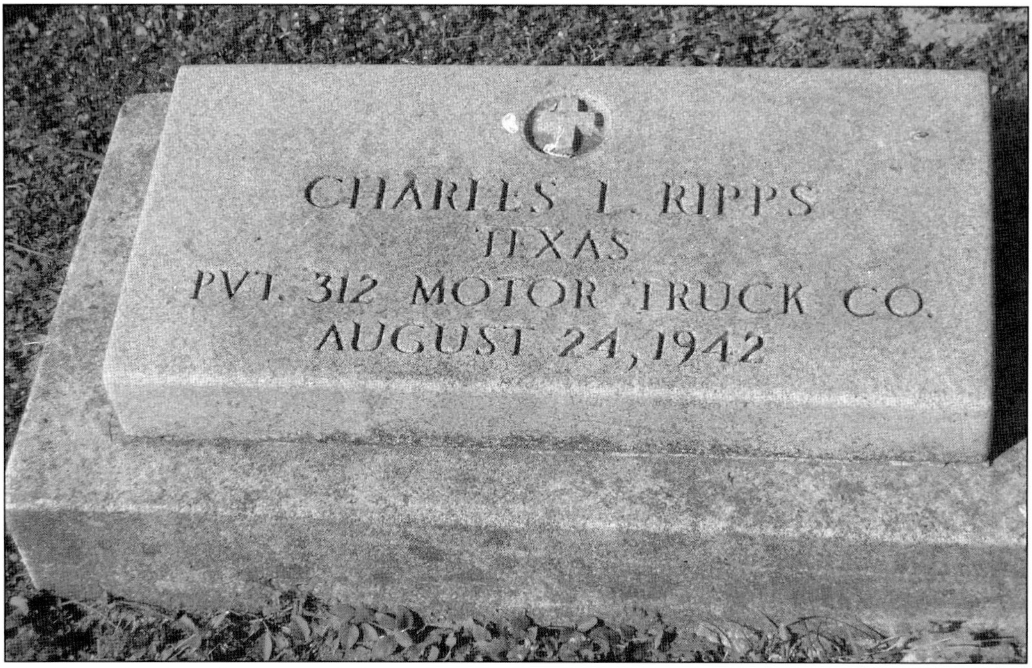

The Ripps brothers both served their country during World War I. Before the war they worked for their father Emil in his grocery and butcher business. After the war, Charles worked at the store his father owned and remained there until he retired. Shortly after the war, Robert Anthony opened a restaurant known as Bob's Place. After his death, his wife, Eliza, continued Bob's Place. The two brothers were buried next to each other with simple gravestones provided by the US government in honor of their service during World War I. [14]

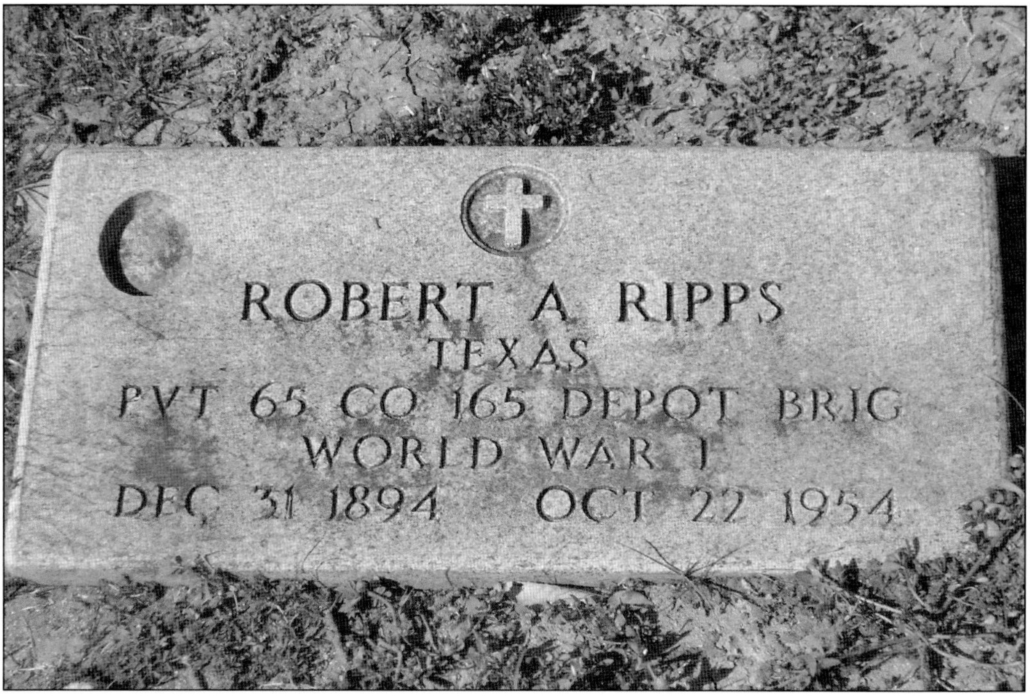

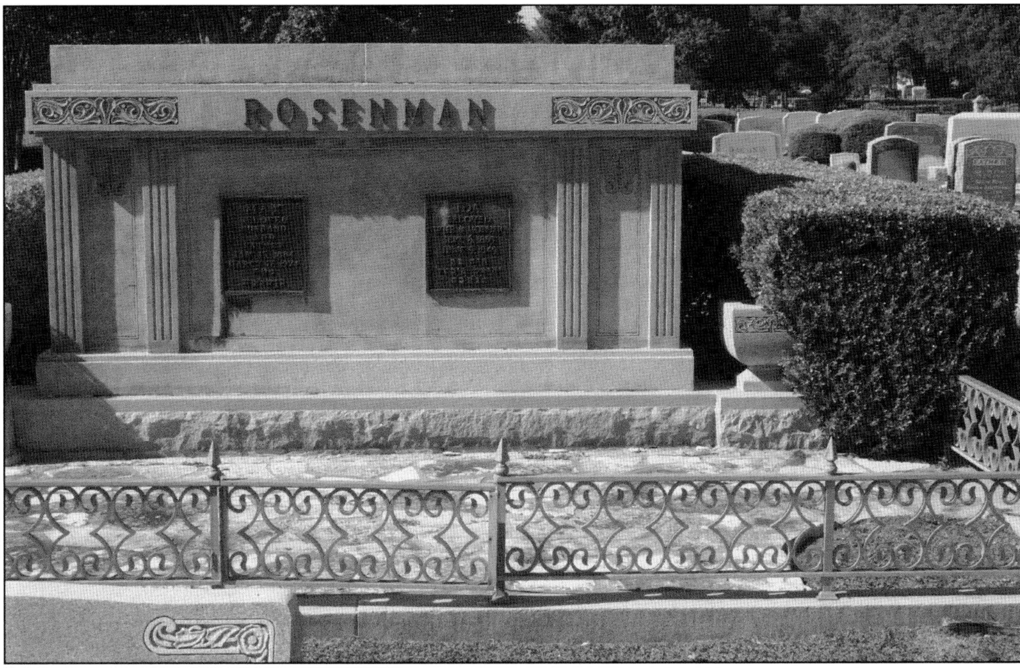

Max Rosenman was married to Ida Milgrom Rosenman. Ida passed away on June 9, 1949, after being involved in an automobile accident. Max was the owner of Max & Meyer Rosenman Men's Wear, Reliable Loan Company, and M&M Rosenman Co. He actively participated in Temple Bethel, Agudos Achim Synagogue, Ancient Free and Accepted Masons Community Lodge No. 1201, Alzafar Shrine Temple, Jewish Social Service Federation, and B'nai B'rith. [10]

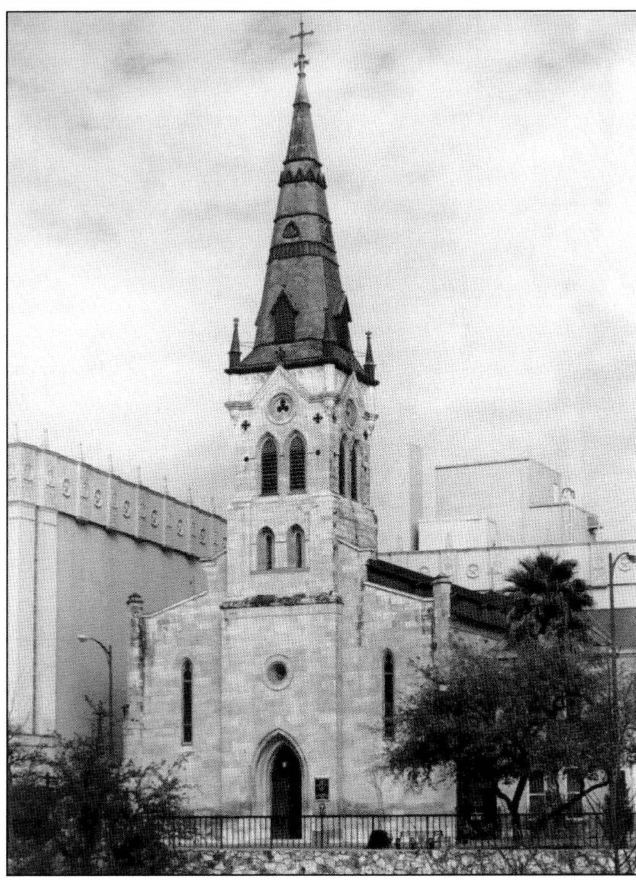

In the heart of downtown, surrounded by the former Joske's Department Store, is St. Joseph's Catholic Church. The Gothic Revival church was completed in 1871 to serve the city's large German-speaking population. The site is believed to be the location of the Alamo mission before it moved to its present location in 1724. The steeple was added in 1898, and stained-glass windows were installed in 1902.

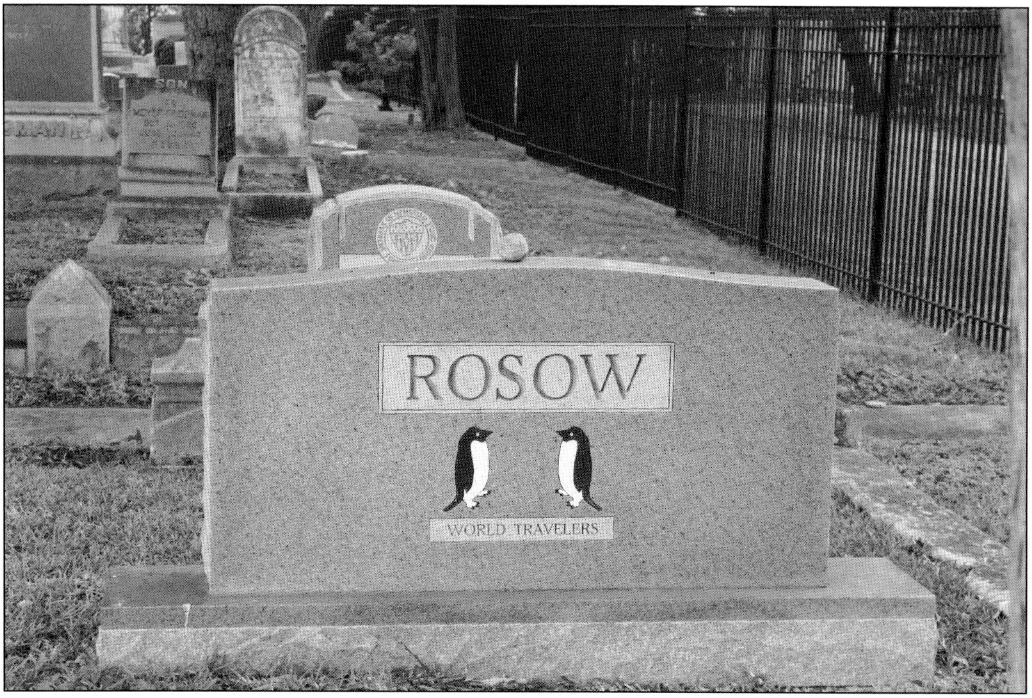

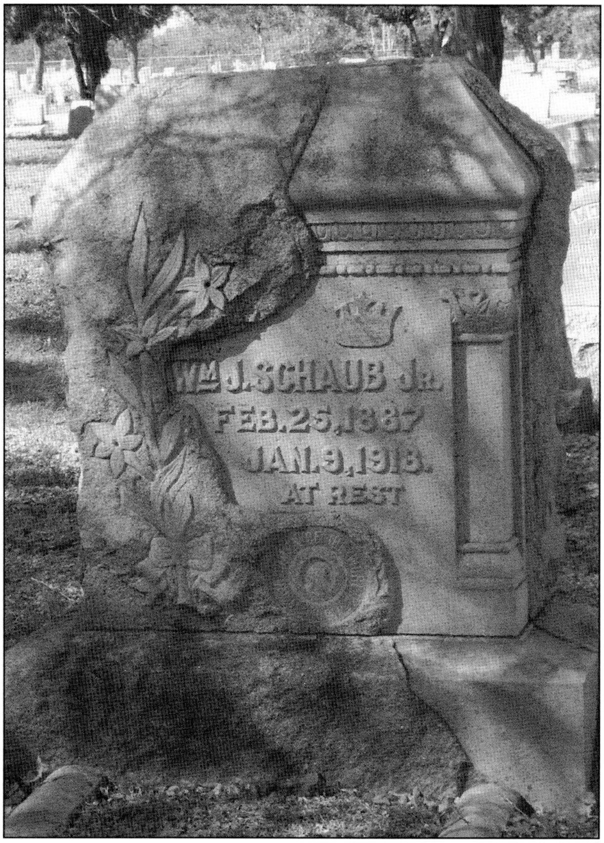

The colorful penguins on this unique but simple stone are eye-catching. Robert Stuart Rosow's parents, who never got past the sixth grade, insisted he get an education. After graduating from St. Mary's University in 1945 with a degree in commerce and economics, he taught there. Later he went into business working as an independent certified public accountant for Ramada Inc. and board member of Aztar Corporation. [9]

William J. Schaub Jr. was a captain for the No. 3 Engine Company of the San Antonio Fire Department. He was a fireman for nine years before he resigned. Schaub held membership with the Fireman's Relief Fund, Eagles, and Woodmen of the World. [14]

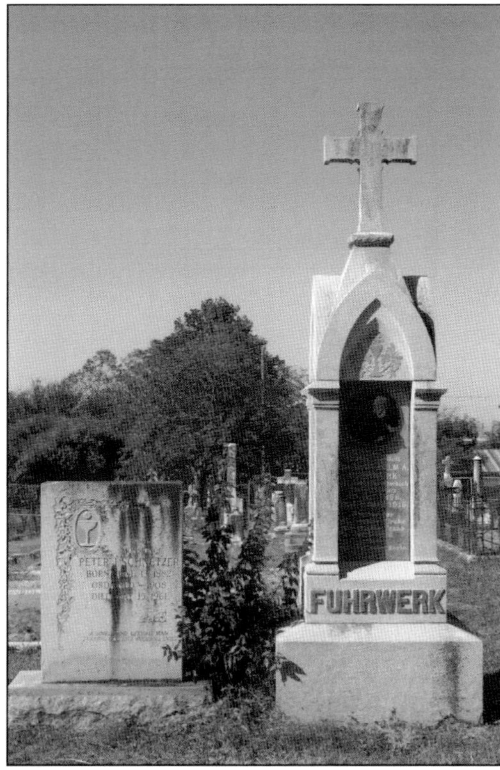

Right Reverend Msgr. Peter J. Schnetzer spent 40 years as pastor of St. Joseph's Catholic Church. Monsignor Schnetzer arrived from Bavaria in 1895. He went to Pontifical College in Columbus, Ohio, and was ordained in 1908. Rev. Fr. William Fuhrwerk was rector of St. Joseph's Catholic Church. [15]

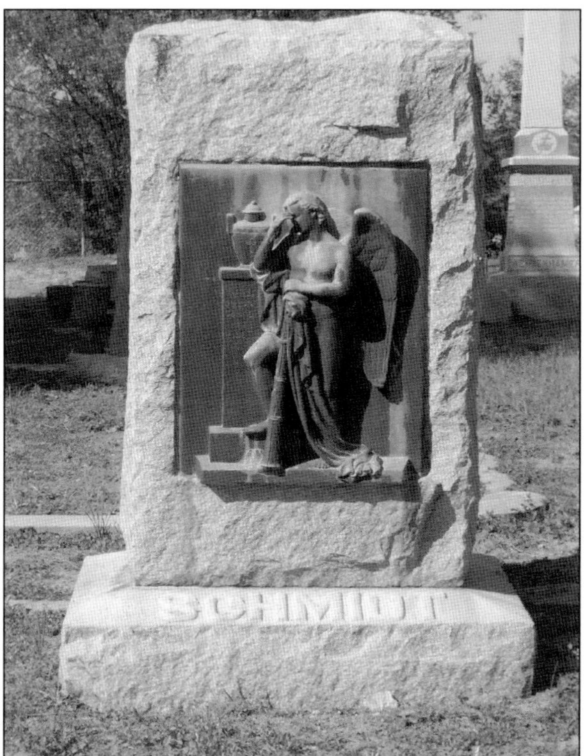

Theresa Simmang married Bart F. Schmidt on December 18, 1895, at St. John's Lutheran Church. They lived at 213 South Sabinas Street. Bart was a farmer. Before her death in 1907 of pneumonia, Theresa had at least four children, one of whom died in childhood. Bart remarried and lived until 1935, when he died while painting his back porch. [14]

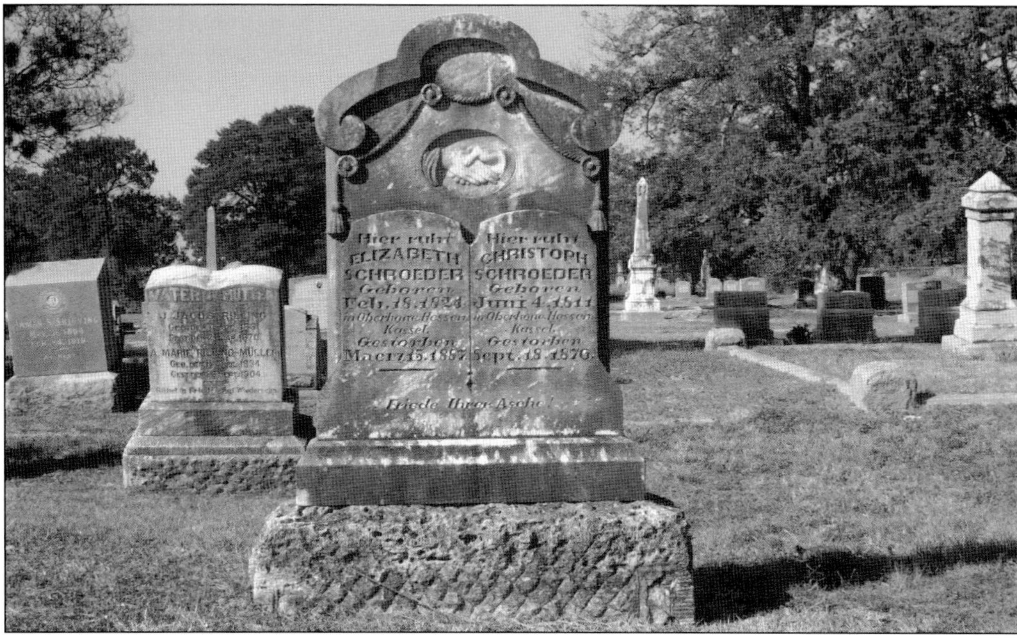

Christoph Schroeder arrived from Germany somewhere between 1855 and 1858 and was naturalized November 20, 1869. He was married to Elizabeth, and they had six children. They were members of St. John's Lutheran Church. Christoph died on September 18, 1876, and Elizabeth died on March 15, 1887. [21]

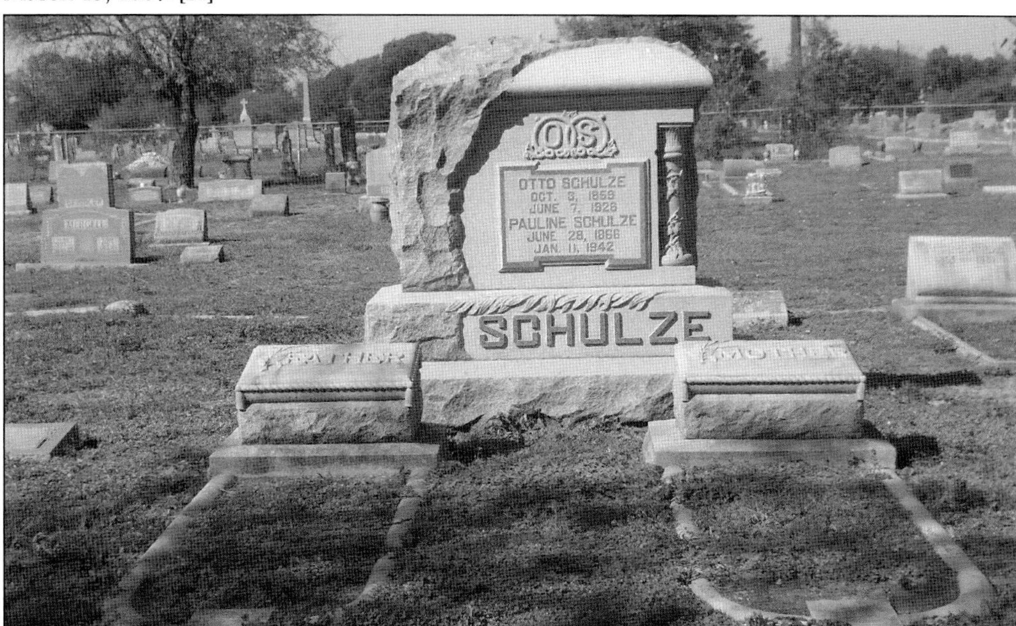

Otto Schulze was born in Germany in 1859. He and his brothers came to San Antonio as cabinetmakers but soon began Schultze Bros., a planing mill and wood manufacturing plant. It became the largest such plant in the city. For 37 years, Schulze was a major member of commercial, fraternal, and civil organizations promoting the city's development. In 1891, he married Pauline Jenner from a family of Texas pioneers. [10]

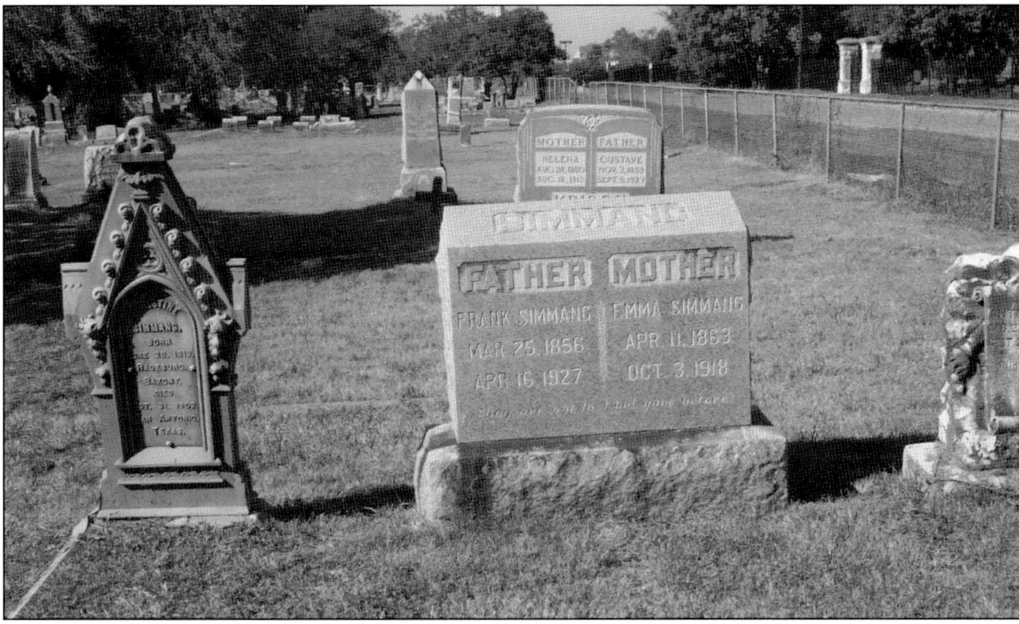

Emma Simmang was married to Frank for over 35 years and had six children. Frank's family came to this country in 1878 and was naturalized on February 6, 1889. They owned Simmang Mattress Factory. According to the 1910 census, Frank Simmang ran the mattress company while his sons Oscar and Albert were mattress makers. Emma passed away October 3, 1918, and Frank died in 1927. [15]

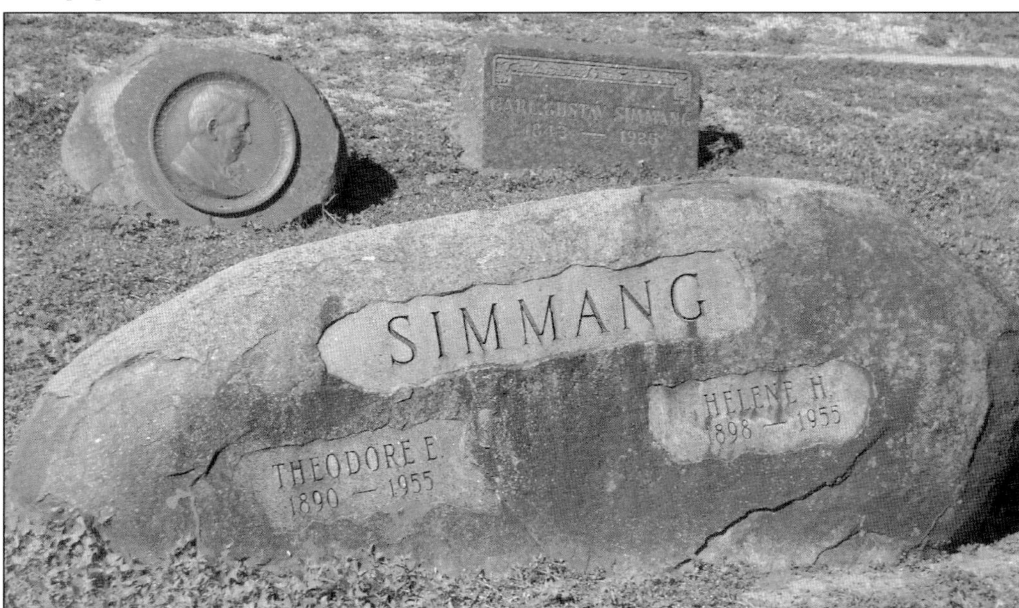

Theodore and Helene Simmang died in a head-on collision in their automobile on January 1, 1955. Theodore was a lawyer while Helene was a housewife. Theodore Simmang was in the US Foreign Service from 1917 to 1920. For seven years he practiced international law, and then he practiced law in San Antonio and held a position as assistant district attorney. Helene Simmang was an active member of Adah Chapter No. 49. [14]

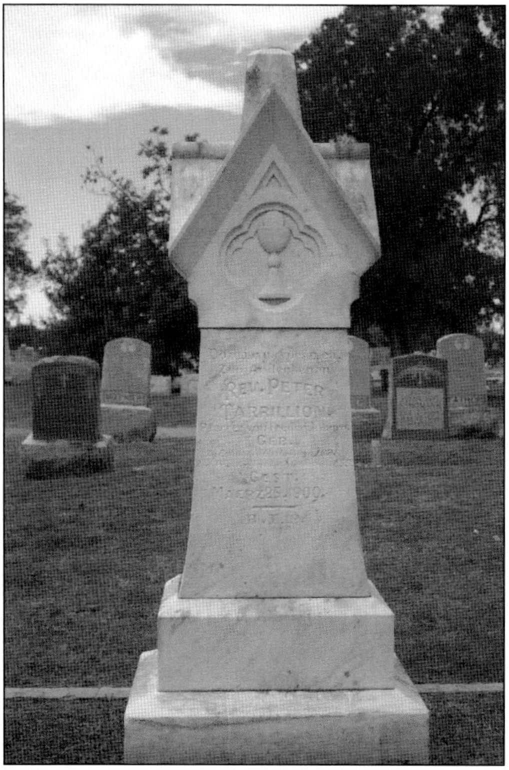

The Rev. Peter Tarrillion was a native of Lorraine. He came to America in the 1850s, studying in Missouri, and was ordained in Galveston on March 25, 1855. His first district as a priest stretched from the Brazos to the Guadalupe, to Austin in the north and Hallettsville to the south. All of this was traveled on horseback. By 1894, there were 20 priests serving the same district.

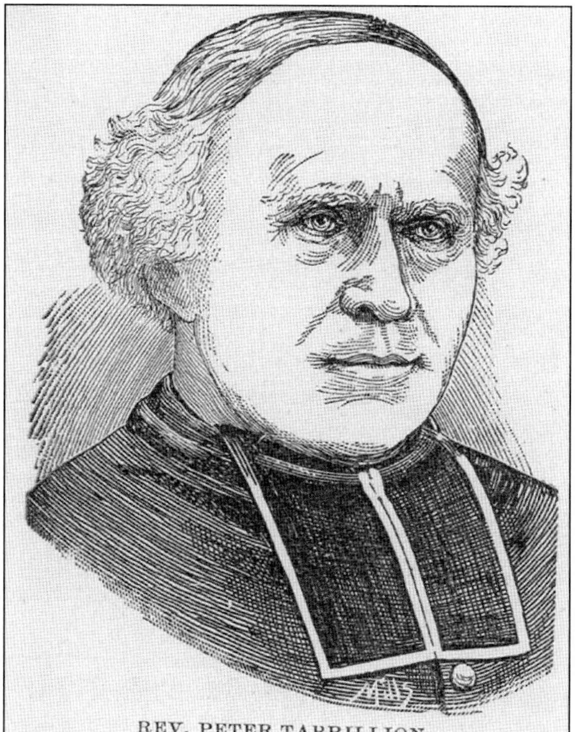

REV. PETER TARRILLION.

Father Tarrillion had many trades. He was an organ builder, watchmaker, locksmith, blacksmith, tinsmith, and carpenter. His parishioners would bring him a watch or a tin utensil on one Sunday; he would repair it and return it the next Sunday. The clock in the steeple of the church at Fredericksburg was once at Galveston, but because it would not work, Bishop Dubois sent it to Father Tarrillion, who repaired it for his church. For special celebrations, he would make fireworks. He served Fredericksburg for 30 years before retiring shortly before his death in 1900. [15]

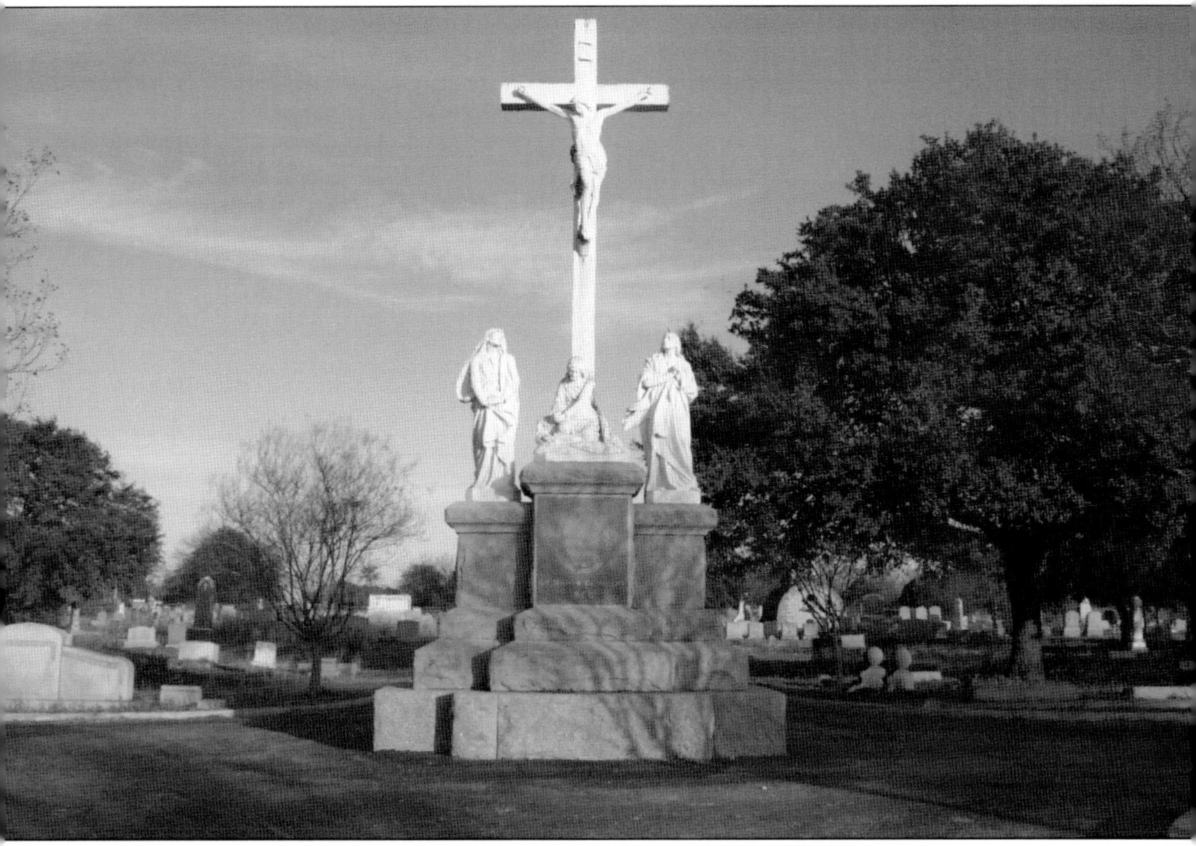

St. Mary's Catholic Church was founded in 1852 to serve the growing English-speaking population of the city. The first church structure was dedicated in 1858, but the flood of 1921 did so much damage to it that it was razed in 1923. The current church is on the original site. Fr. T.P. Johnson, pastor of the church, requested land for the cemetery from city council and received approval in 1884. The church is served by the Oblates of Mary Immaculate. [13]

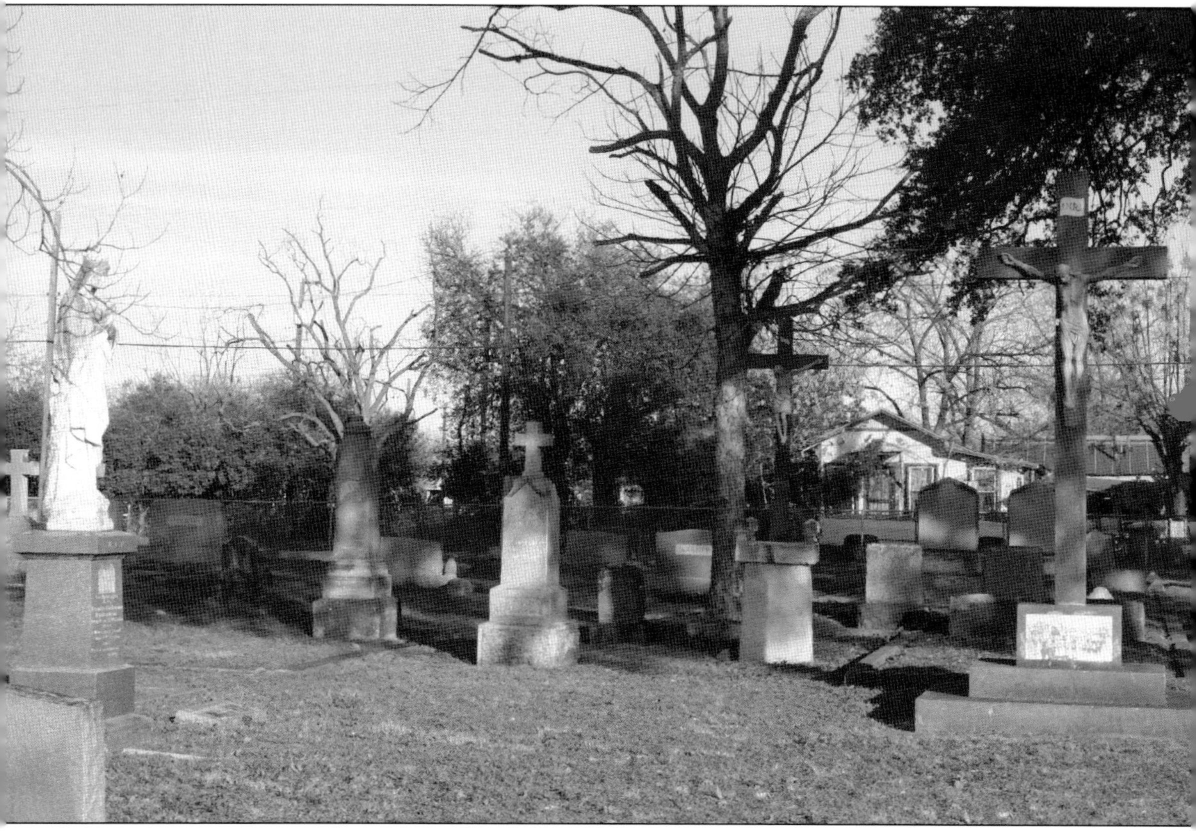

St. Michael's Polish Catholic Church was founded in 1866 to serve Polish immigrants. Fr. Louis Dombrowski served from 1886 to 1912 and Fr. Thomas J. Moczygemba from 1912 to 1950. In 1965, the church property was purchased by the Urban Renewal Agency for Hemisfair. St. Albert's Benevolent Society was organized in 1871. It assessed monthly fees and paid sick and death benefits to families. The city council approved land for the cemetery in 1877. [23]

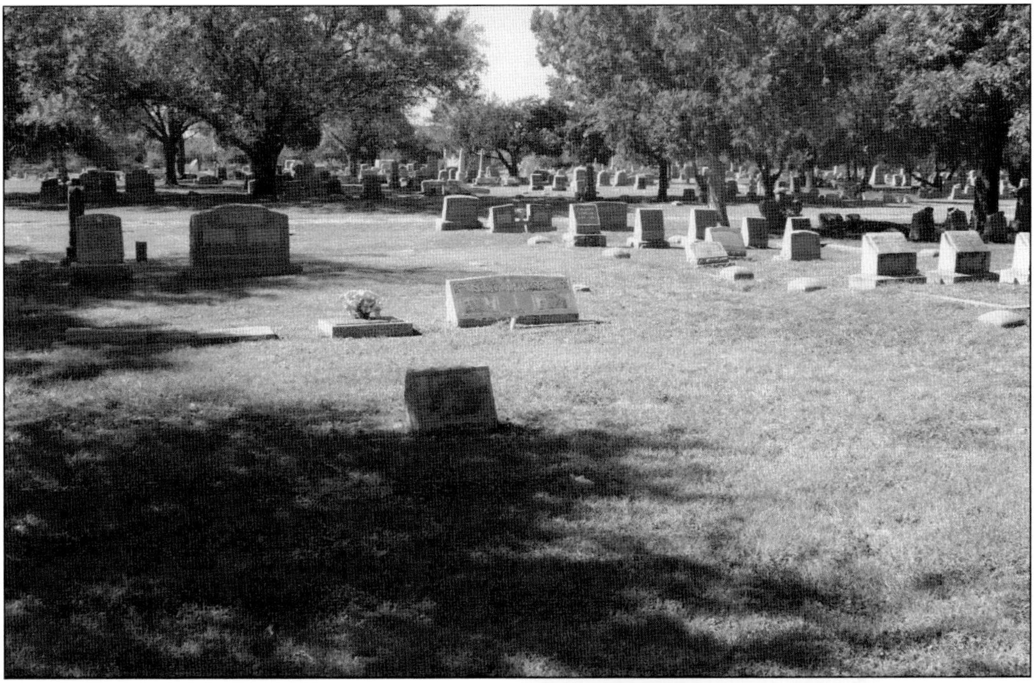

St. John's Evangelical Lutheran Church was organized in 1857. Its first cemetery, shown here, was established in 1866 (Old Lutheran). In 1874, a new cemetery was opened as St. John's. A second congregation, Immanuel Lutheran Church, had a cemetery next to St. John's. In the early 1900s, the two congregations merged. The current St. John's Evangelical Lutheran Church is in its third structure on the same site, 502 East Nueva Street. [14]

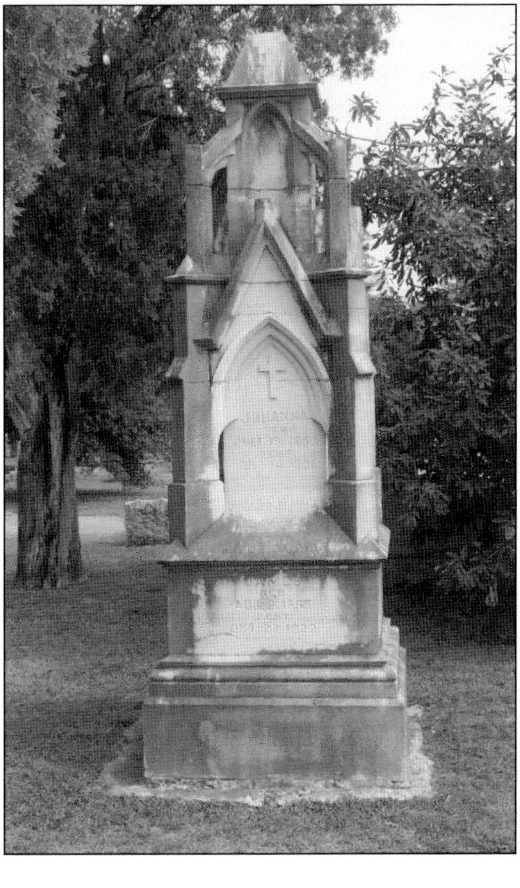

James Wahrenberger's family came to Texas while it was still a republic. While he was young, his family moved to a farm called Bear Creek. He was sent to West Penn Square Academy in Philadelphia and then to Germany and Switzerland to attend universities. Wahrenberger then moved to Austin and later to San Antonio. He participated in the development of many buildings. He was the first city building inspector. [14]

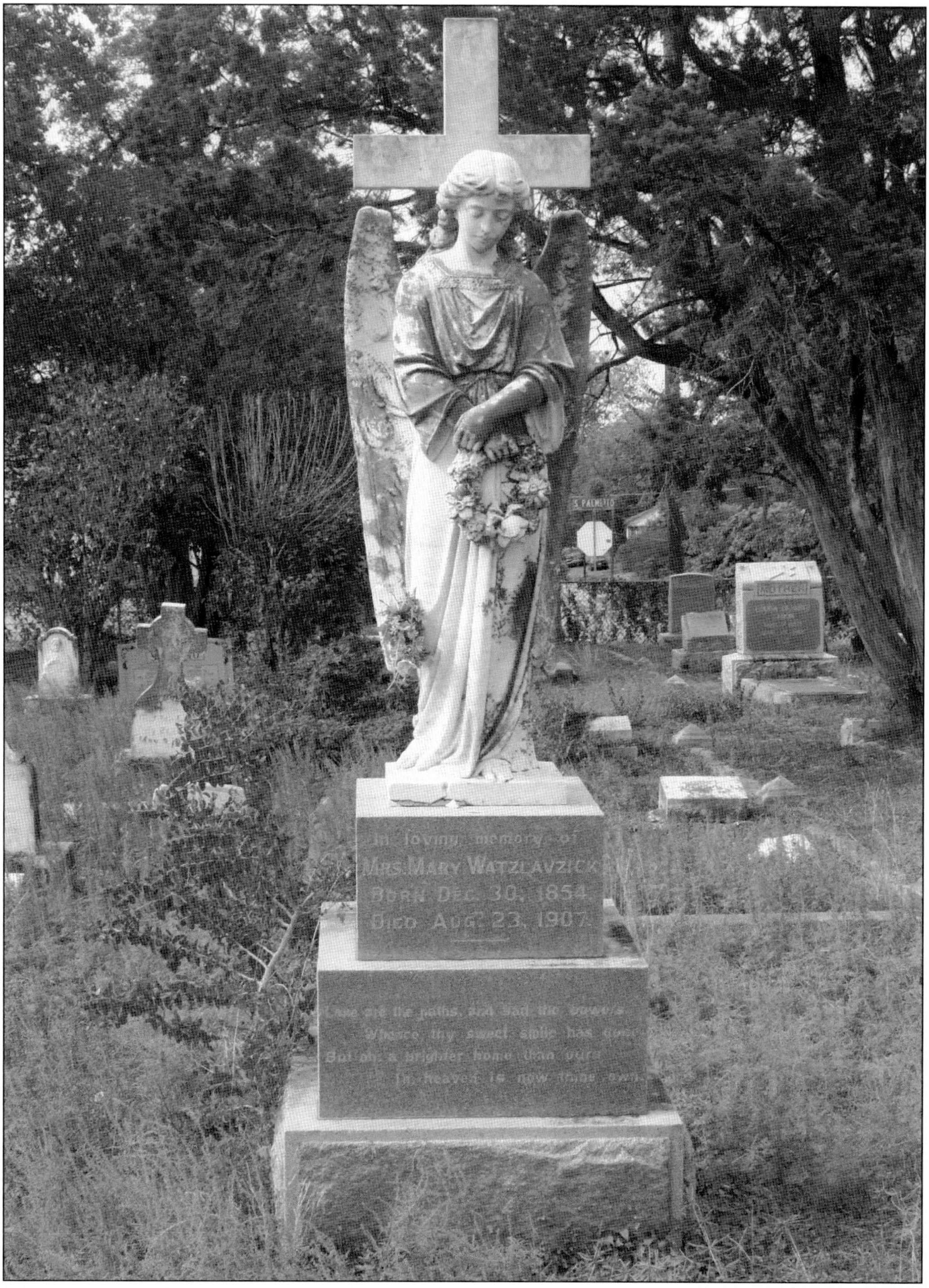

John and Mary Watzlavzick were Polish ranchers in La Salle County. In 1907, they traveled to Germany. Mary passed in 1917, leaving an estate with interesting conditions for rural ranching folk. At the time of her death, World War I was ravaging Europe, so Mary left money to repair church altars in Cestohowa in Germany and the Holy Sepulchre and St. Michael's in San Antonio. [13]

This interesting stone marks the grave of Mae Delespine Winters. She was the wife of Charles H. Winters. Charles and Mae moved every few years. Charles's occupation also changed over time. He was a hackman and a chauffeur for A. Morse (Morse Auto Livery) and also worked for the US government and as a well driller. [13]

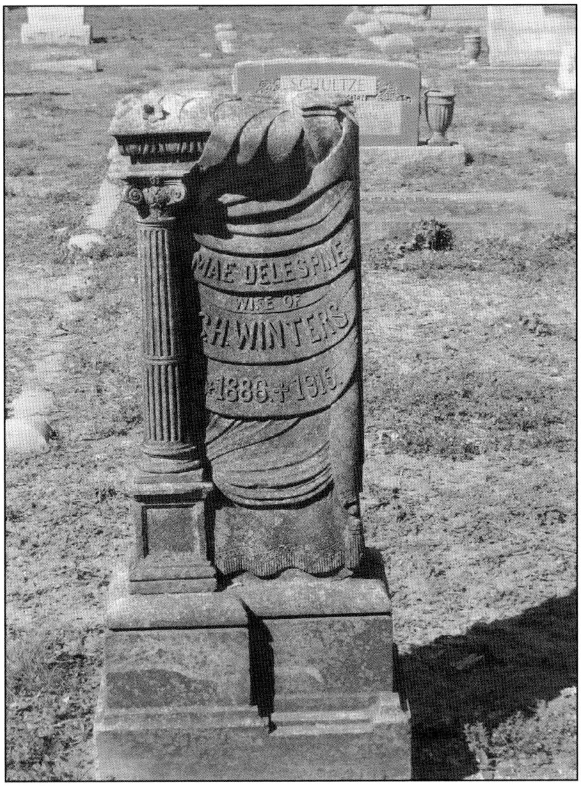

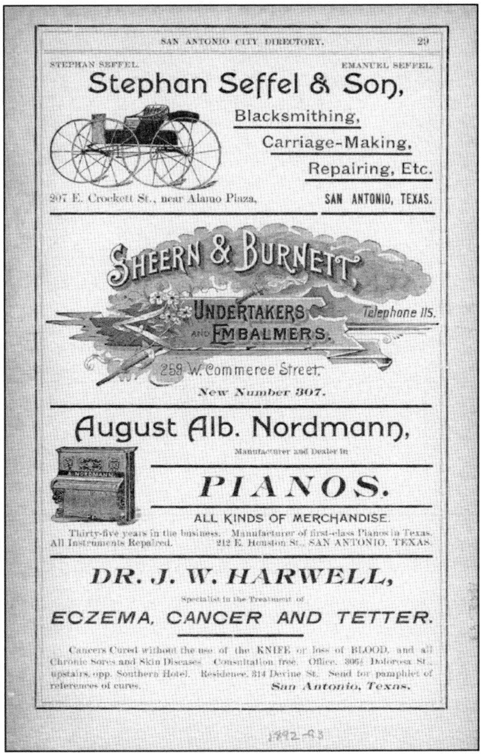

SAN ANTONIO CITY DIRECTORY. 29

STEPHAN SEFFEL. EMANUEL SEFFEL.

Stephan Seffel & Son,

Blacksmithing,

Carriage-Making,

Repairing, Etc.

207 E. Crockett St., near Alamo Plaza, SAN ANTONIO, TEXAS.

SHEERN & BURNETT,

UNDERTAKERS AND EMBALMERS.

Telephone 115.

259 W. Commerce Street.

New Number 307.

August Alb. Nordmann,

Manufacturer and Dealer in

PIANOS.

ALL KINDS OF MERCHANDISE.

Thirty-five years in the business. Manufacturer of first-class Pianos in Texas. All Instruments Repaired. 212 E. Houston St., SAN ANTONIO, TEXAS.

DR. J. W. HARWELL,

Specialist in the Treatment of

ECZEMA, CANCER AND TETTER.

Cancers Cured without the use of the KNIFE or loss of BLOOD, and all Chronic Sores and Skin Diseases. Consultation free. Office, 306½ Dolorosa St., upstairs, opp. Southern Hotel. Residence, 314 Devine St. Send for pamphlet of references of cures. *San Antonio, Texas.*

1892-93

In 1891 or 1892, Joseph Sheern and James T. Burnett began a partnership as undertakers. It lasted until 1897, when Sheern died during a dengue fever epidemic. The following year, in 1898, Burnett died after an operation for appendicitis. He was only 38 years old. Burnett was a member of numerous organizations, including Masons, Knights of Pythias, Elks, and others.

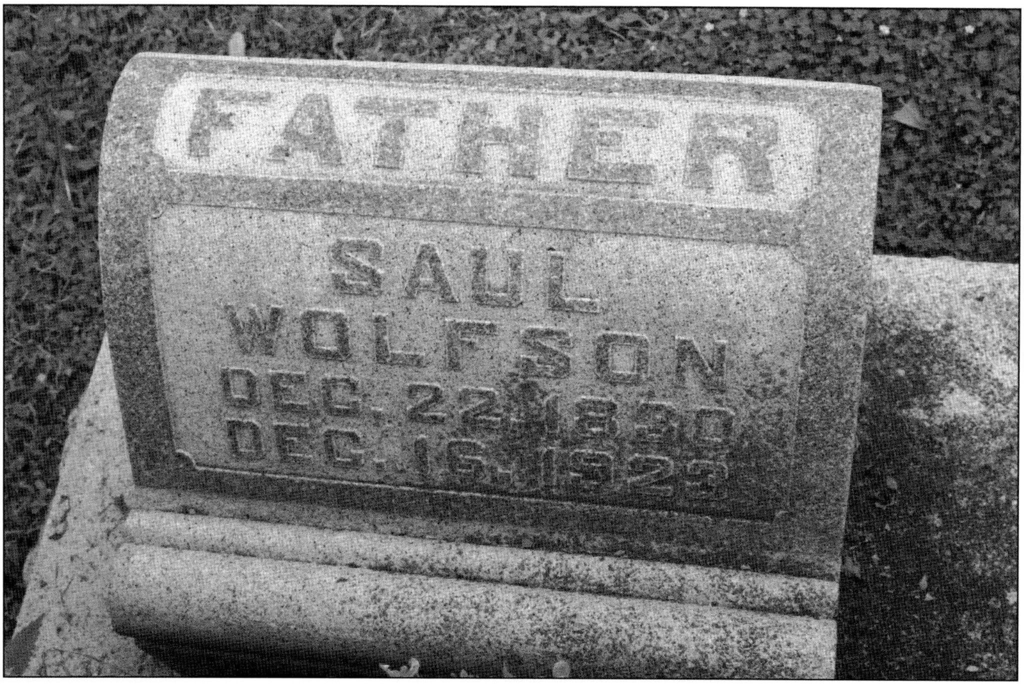

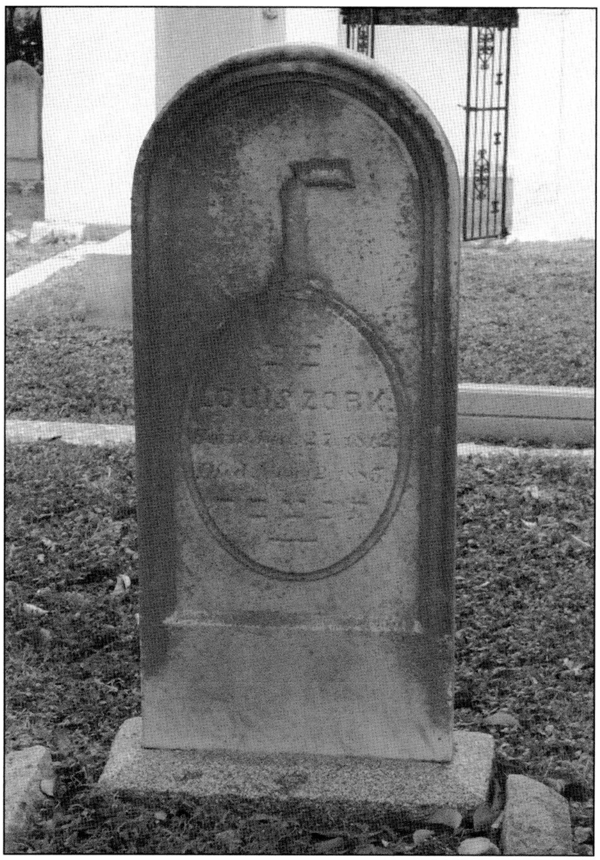

Before coming to San Antonio, Saul Wolfson started developing his talent for business as a foreman in his uncle's wood industry in Germany. He then moved to Connecticut, working as a clerk. Before coming to San Antonio, he served with a Connecticut infantry unit during the Civil War. His first business in San Antonio was an auction house. He is best known for his store, Wolfson Dry Goods Company. [9]

In the 1840s, Louis Zork emigrated from Prussia to San Antonio. He was one of the first Jewish settlers in San Antonio and had several business ventures. Zork had real estate interests as well as a department store. He was welcomed in a group of German Catholics who met at Dosche and Riche's Buckhorn Bar. Louis Zork held several public offices including city alderman and treasurer of Bexar County. [9]

Four

MILITARY

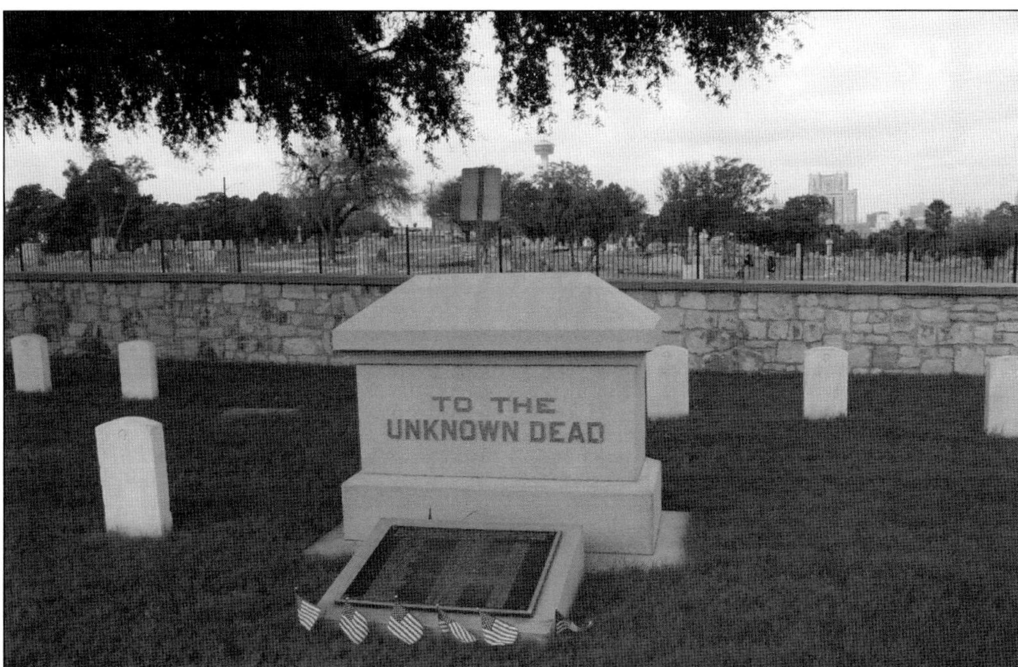

From 1867 to 1899, Fort Concho at San Angelo protected part of the Texas frontier. In 1884 and 1898, over 125 soldiers and dependents buried there were disinterred and reburied at the San Antonio National Cemetery. Over the years, 25 soldiers were identified; 20 of them had been members of the 10th Cavalry. This unit consisted of black soldiers, called Buffalo Soldiers by the Indians because of their short, dark hair, which they thought resembled the buffalo. The 10th Cavalry was proud of the comparison and used a buffalo on its regimental crest. [19]

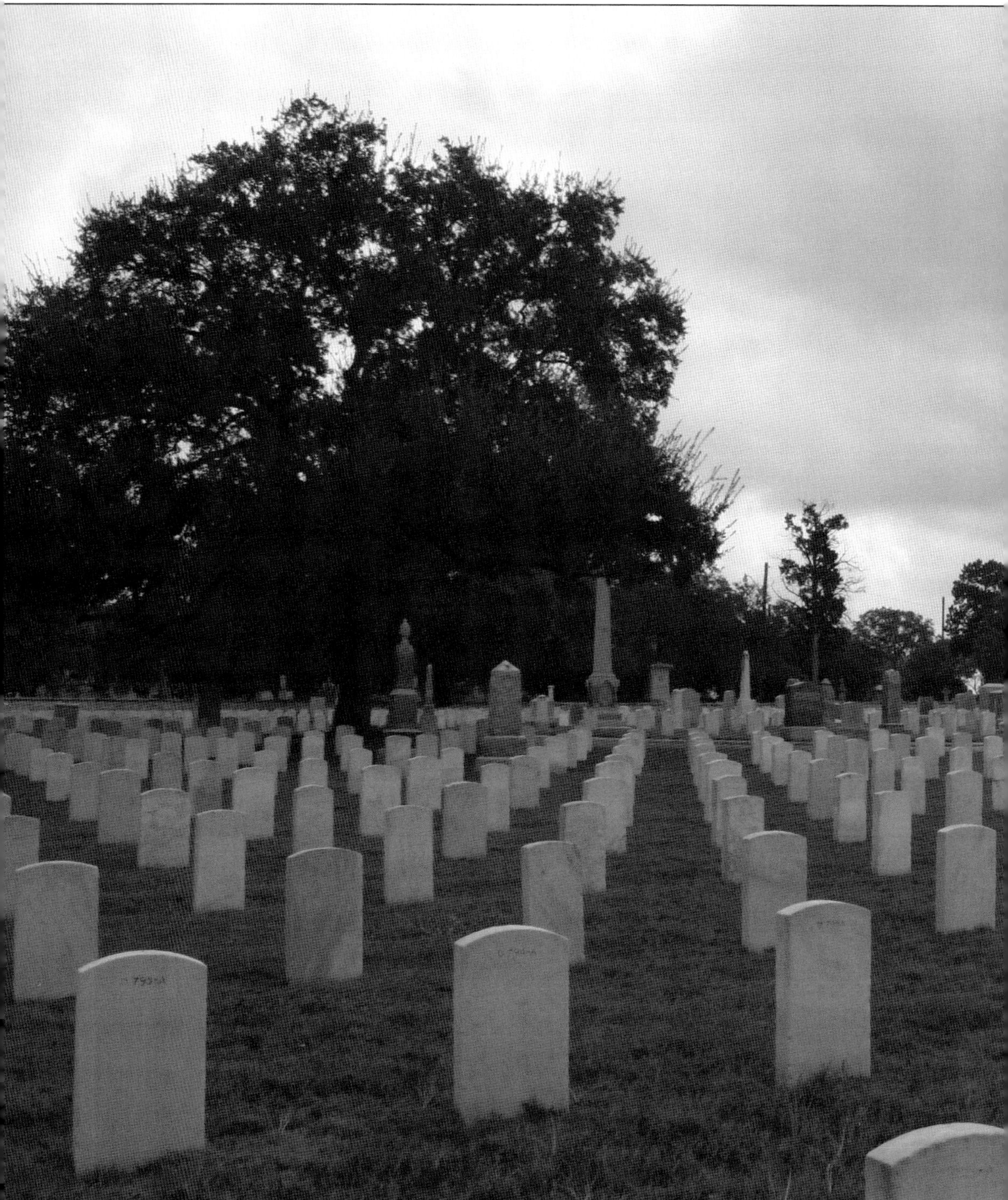

The San Antonio National Cemetery was established in November 1867. Originally consisting of two acres, it has been expanded several times; now, it contains 3.7 acres. Among the numerous government-issued monuments are 250 private gravestones. The earliest grave dates from 1853.

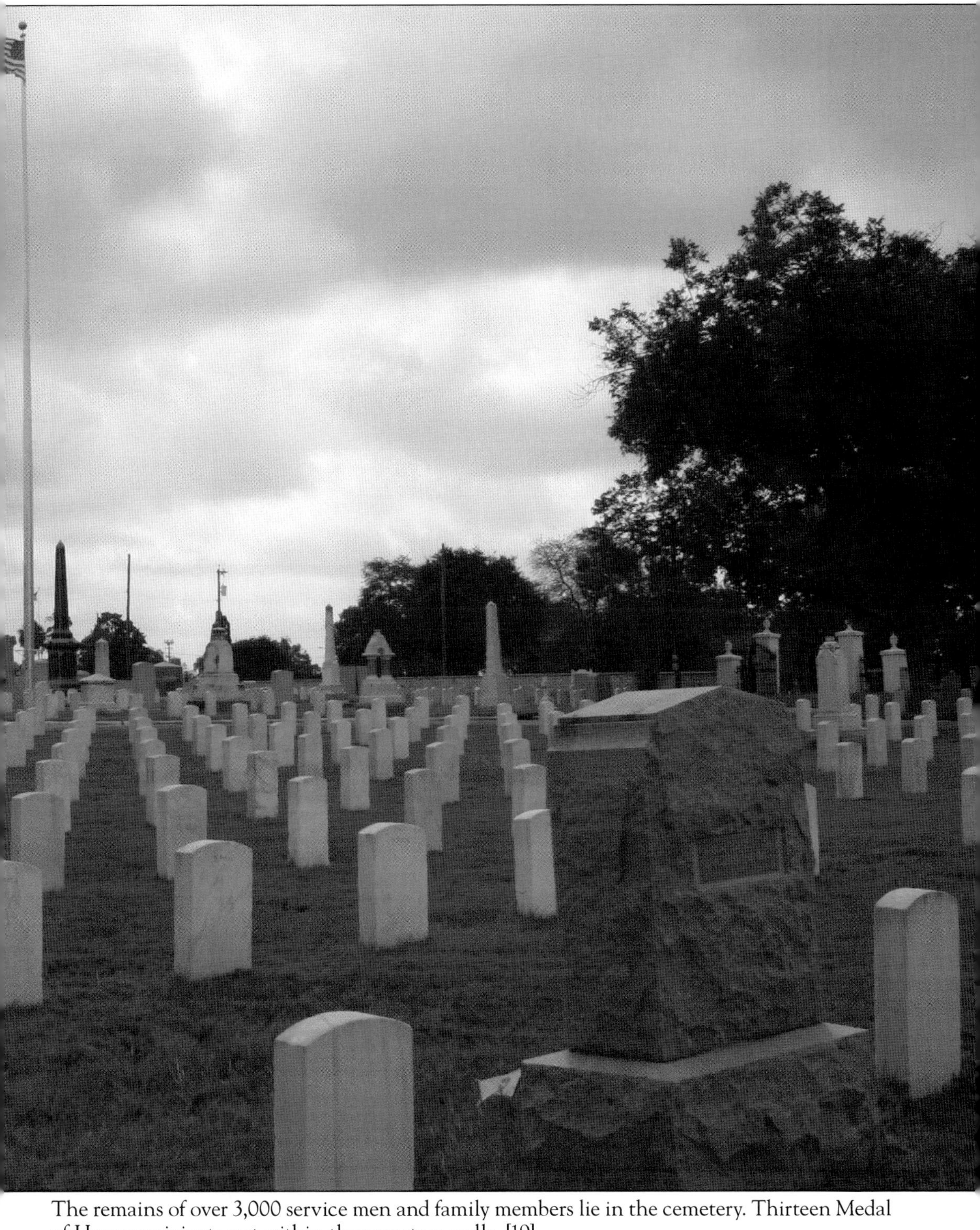

The remains of over 3,000 service men and family members lie in the cemetery. Thirteen Medal of Honor recipients rest within the cemetery walls. [19]

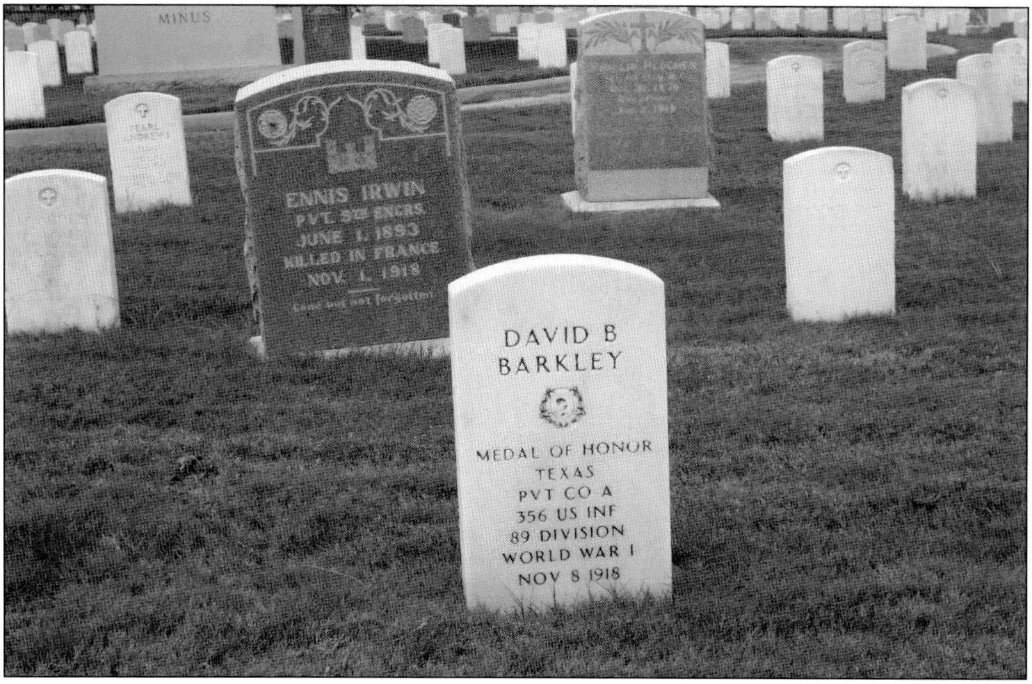

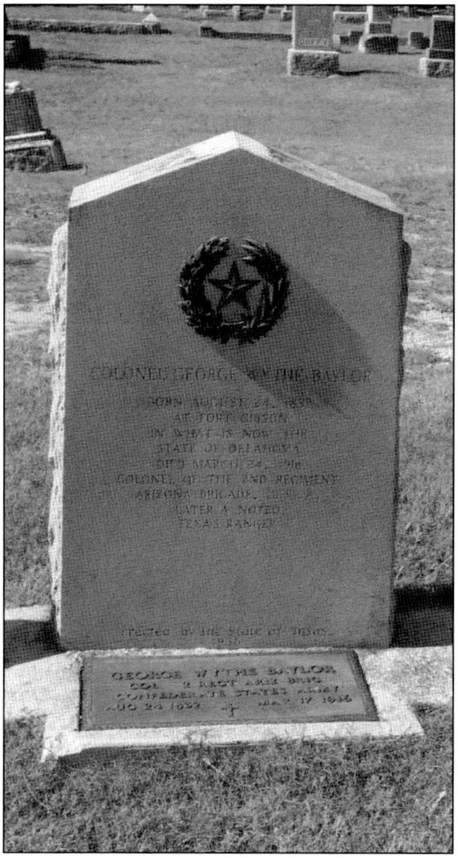

David B. Barkley is known today as the first Hispanic to receive the Congressional Medal of Honor and the only Texan to receive one during World War I. Barkley drowned in the Meuse River while returning under fire from a scouting mission against the enemy. His mother was Antonia Cantu, and his father was Josef Barkley. He had attended Brackenridge High School, and now, he has an elementary school named after him. [19]

Born in 1832, George Baylor was an ardent secessionist. He served on Gen. Albert Sidney Johnston's staff and was with him when he died at the Battle of Shiloh. He later served with the Arizona Brigade. After the Civil War, he was commissioned a Texas Ranger, living in Mexico from 1898 until 1913. When the Mexican Revolution came, he returned to Texas. [18]

Hamilton Bee and his parents arrived in Texas in 1837. He served as secretary to the United States–Texas Boundary Commission. During his military career he served with Ben McCulloch during the Mexican War and in Texas, Louisiana, and Oklahoma during the Civil War. After the latter, he stayed in Mexico until 1876. Between the two wars, he was in the Texas legislature representing the Laredo District. [18]

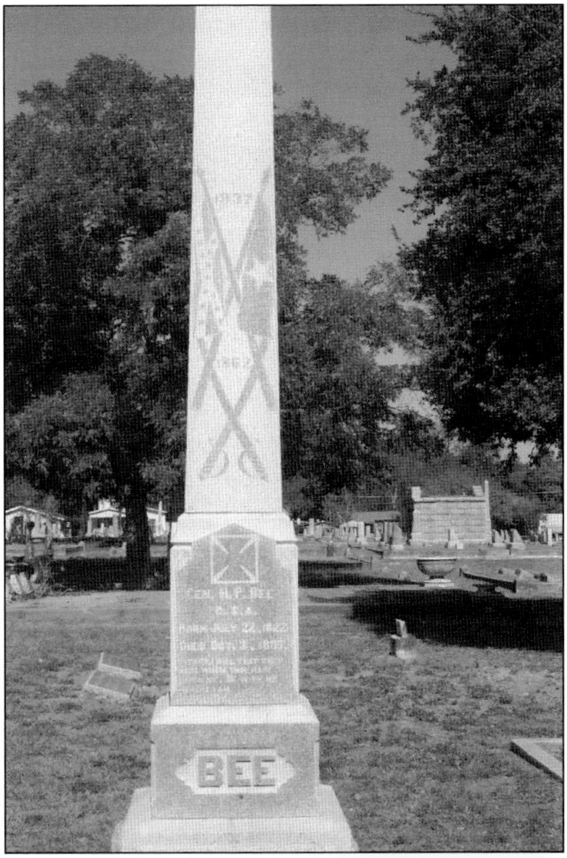

Sgt. Edward Bolger, 15th Field Artillery, was born in Connecticut in July 1891. At the age of 22, his life was cut short, but not in combat. While stationed at Camp Travis, he and some Army friends hired a car and driver to go to Camp Stanley. On the return trip, the driver was speeding when the car overturned near Nine Mill Hill, pinning Bolger underneath. He died a few days later. [19]

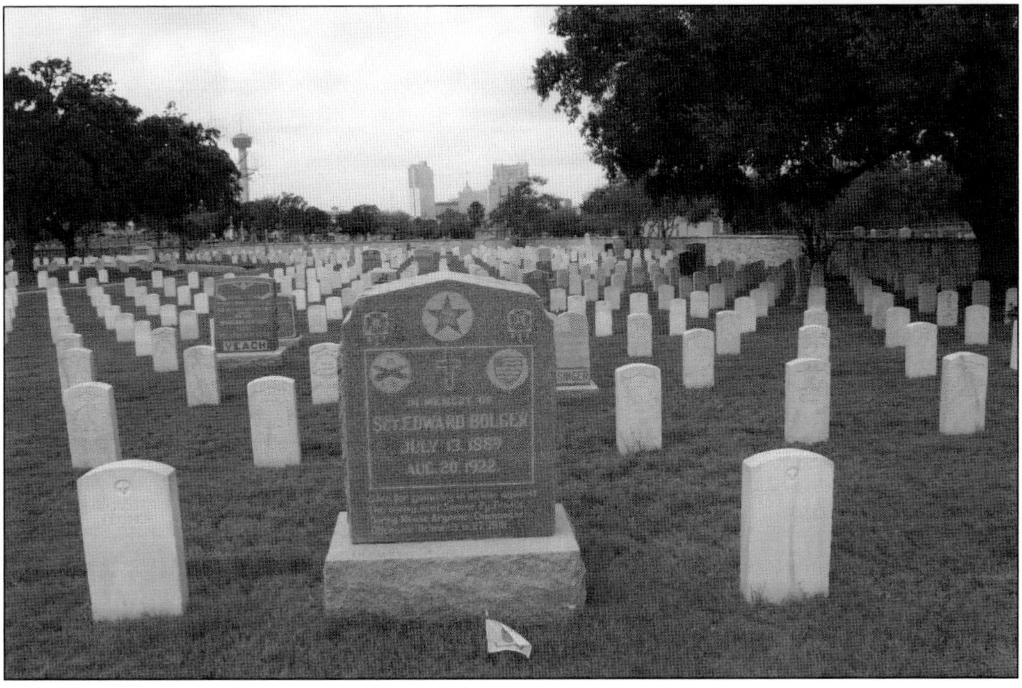

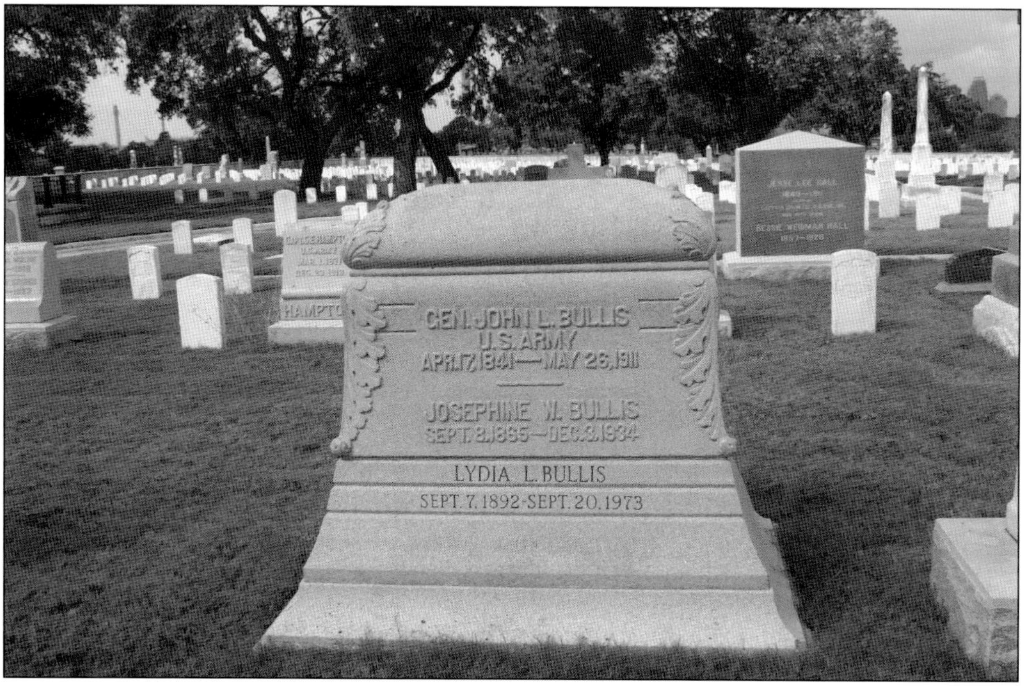

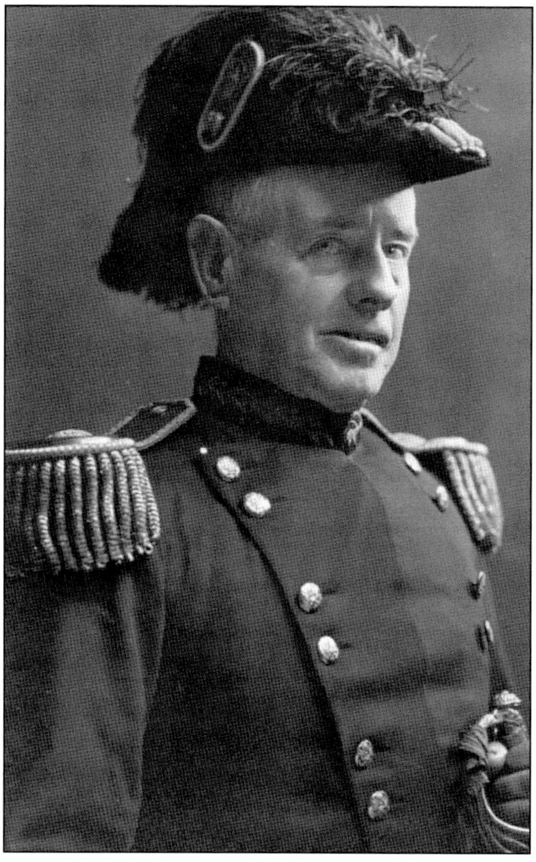

After serving in the 126th New York Volunteer Infantry during the Civil War, John Bullis, the son of devout Quakers, transferred to Texas where he commanded the Black Seminole Scouts of the 24th Infantry and fought Indians and cattle rustlers. In 1872, he married Alice Rodriguez, and after her death, he married Josephine Withers, both of San Antonio. [19]

Just before World War I, an Army training facility was created some 17 miles northwest of San Antonio and named for John Bullis, pictured here. Camp Stanley, named for Brig. Gen. David Sloane Stanley, lies adjacent to Camp Bullis. They have served as training grounds for thousands of troops to the current day.

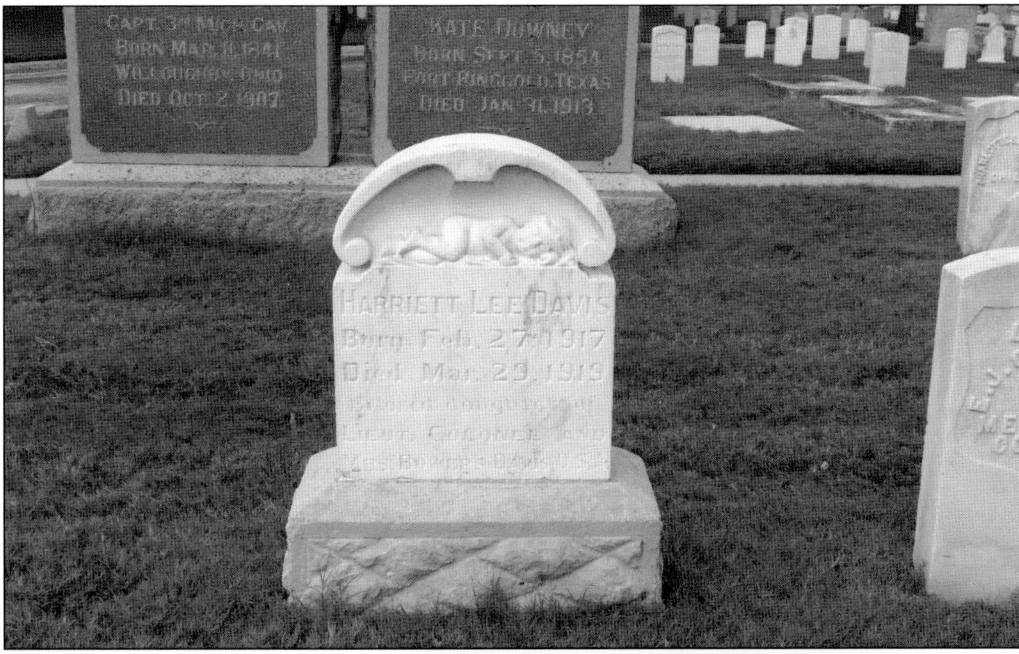

The National Cemetery is not just for military personnel but also for their families. Such is the case with Harriett Lee Davis. She was just over two years old when she died. Her parents were Lt. Col. Bowers Davis of Michigan and Elizabeth Galbraith of Montana. Bowers Davis, 30th Infantry, died in 1933 and is buried in the San Francisco National Cemetery. [18]

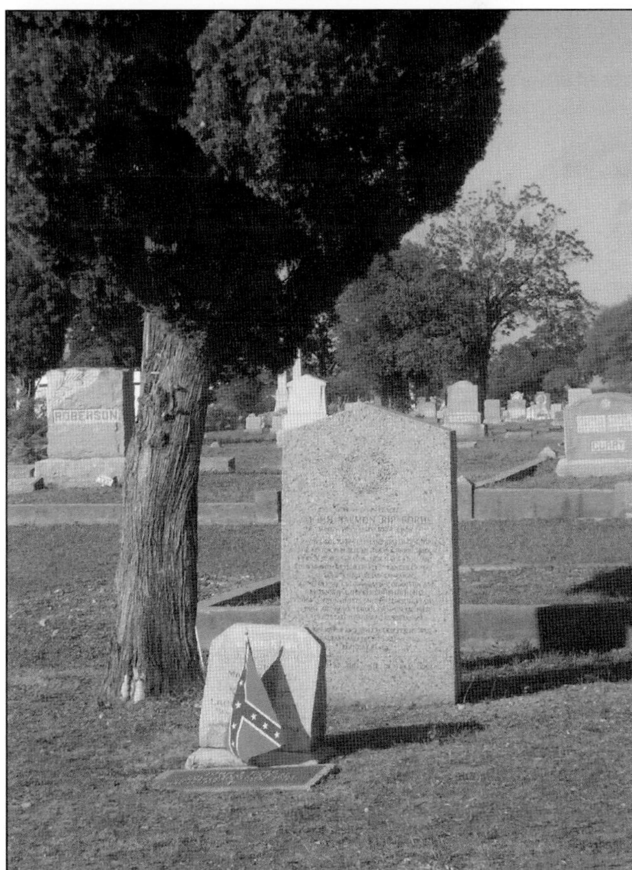

John S. Ford arrived in Texas in 1836. The nickname "Rip" was acquired because he ended letters concerning the deaths of soldiers during the Mexican War with "Rest in Peace." He commanded the 2nd Texas Cavalry during the Civil War, was mayor of Brownsville, served in the Texas Senate and the Texas Constitutional Convention of 1875, and was a charter member of the Texas State Historical Association. [18]

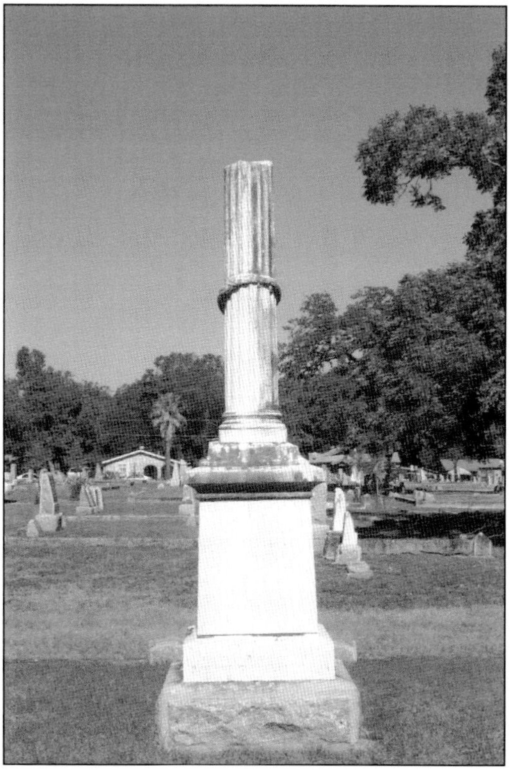

Robert B. Green only lived for 42 years, but in that time, he accomplished much. After going to Texas A&M College and then Lebanon Law School, he became a lawyer. In November 1895, he became district judge in the Thirty-seventh District Court. Green was elected twice as a county judge in Bexar County. He was considered a fair and trustworthy judge, and his decisions were used as examples for other judges to follow. In November 1906, he was elected as a Texas senator. Green is credited with organizing the San Antonio Belknap Rifles. [18]

The Albert Sidney Johnston Camp of the Sons of Confederate Veterans purchased the first piece of the Confederate Cemetery in 1885. Over the years, additional deeds were granted to them and the United Daughters of the Confederacy so that the cemetery now contains 10.5 acres surrounded by City Cemeteries Nos. 4 and 6. [18]

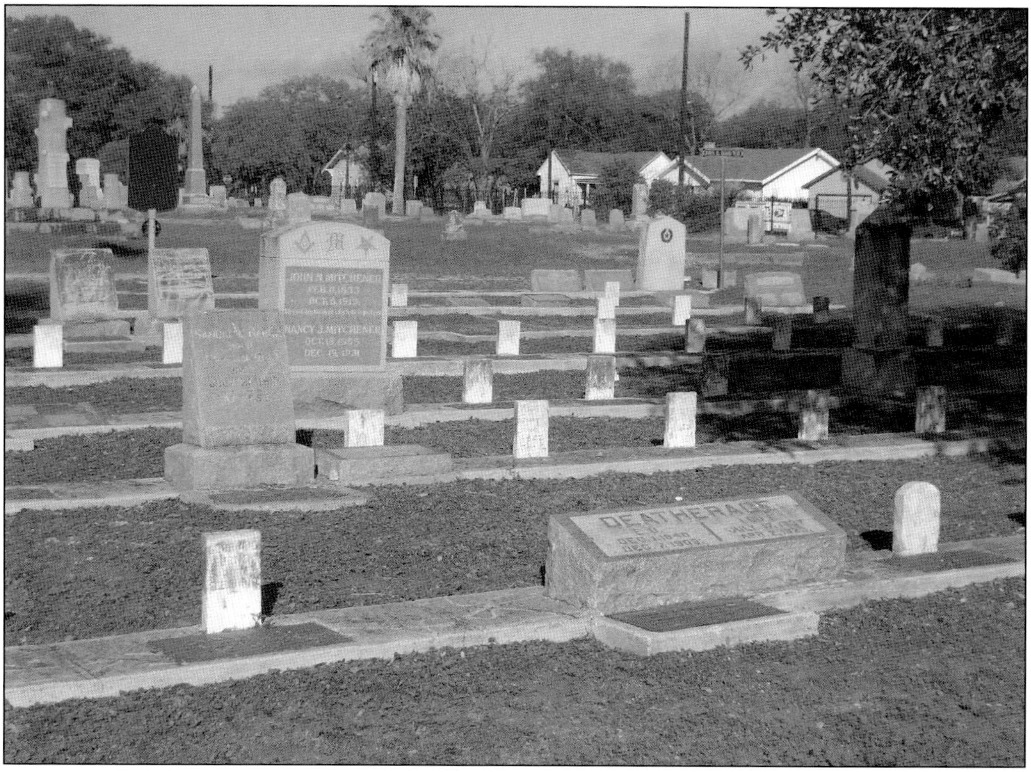

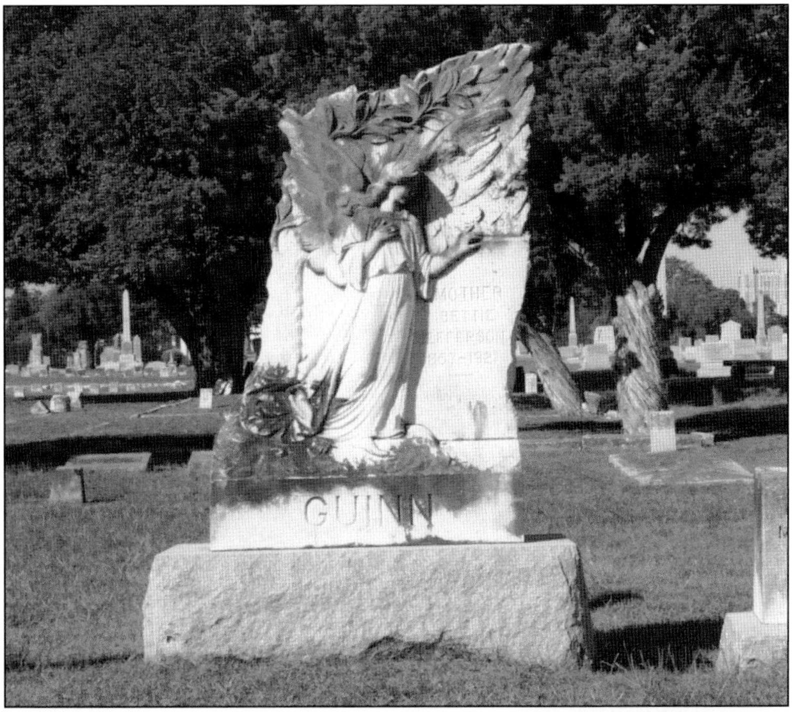

The subject of this beautiful grave marker, located in the Confederate Cemetery, is Mrs. John David Guinn (Bettie). She was a member of the United Daughters of the Confederacy, Tuesday Musical Club, Daughters of the Republic of Texas, and other organizations. She was the daughter of John Robertson Jefferson, a cousin of Pres. Thomas Jefferson. [18]

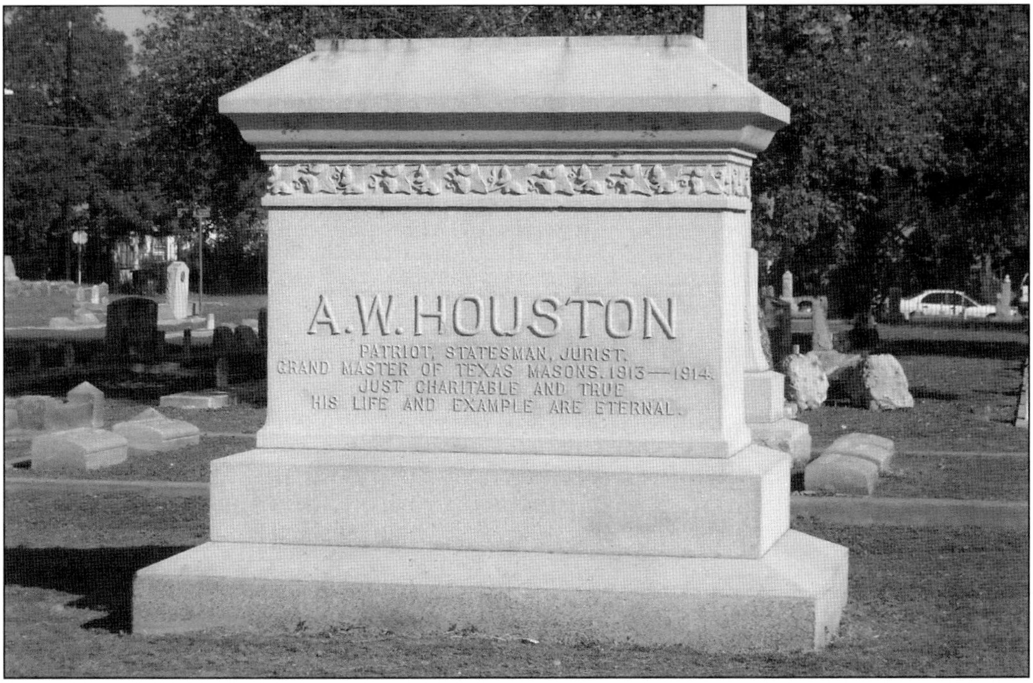

Judge Augustus Weyman Houston's monument befits the dean of the San Antonio Bar and the "greatest lawyer of all of its [San Antonio's] history." He served as general counsel for the San Antonio & Aransas Pass Railroad and Belknap's street railway company. In the Texas Senate, he introduced the bill to purchase the Alamo for the state and an equal rights bill allowing women to work in state government offices. [18]

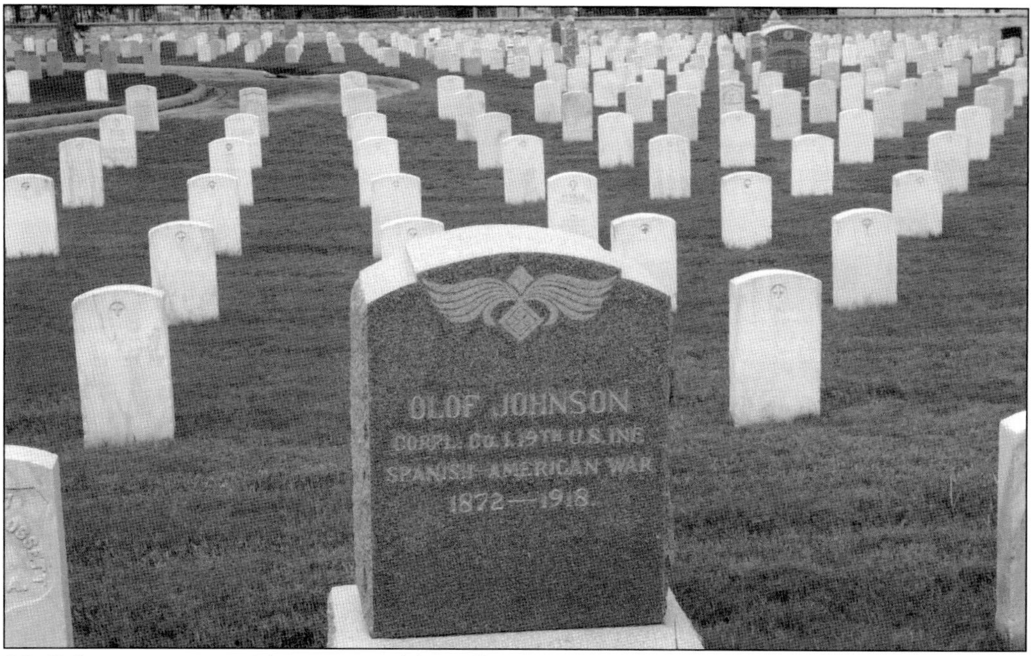

Olof Johnson was one of the victims of the influenza epidemic in 1918. Born in Sweden in 1872, he immigrated to the United States and enlisted in the Army in 1894. During the Spanish-American War, he served as a corporal in Company I, D Regiment, 19th US Infantry. During this war, the unit was stationed in Puerto Rico and, later, was sent to the Philippines. [19]

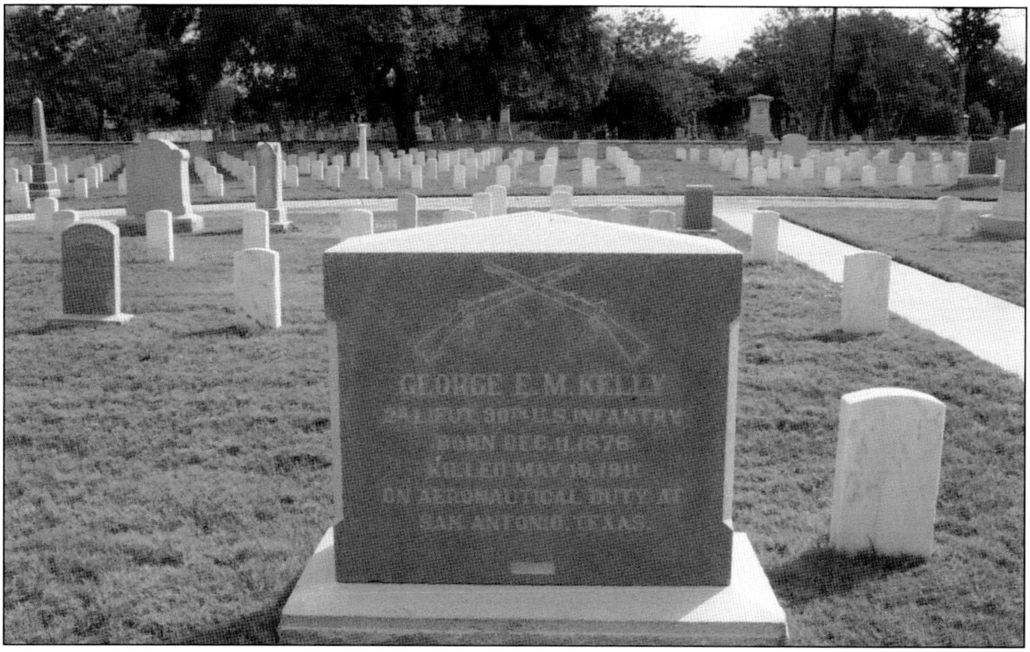

Lt. George E.M. Kelly died in May 1911. As a member of Fort Sam Houston's fledgling aero squadron, Kelly made a brave decision. Kelly took his Curtiss airplane up, circled a few minutes, and decided to land. Unfortunately, the plane dipped downward heading toward staff tents. Kelly was able to maneuver his machine away from the tents but died after the crash. [19]

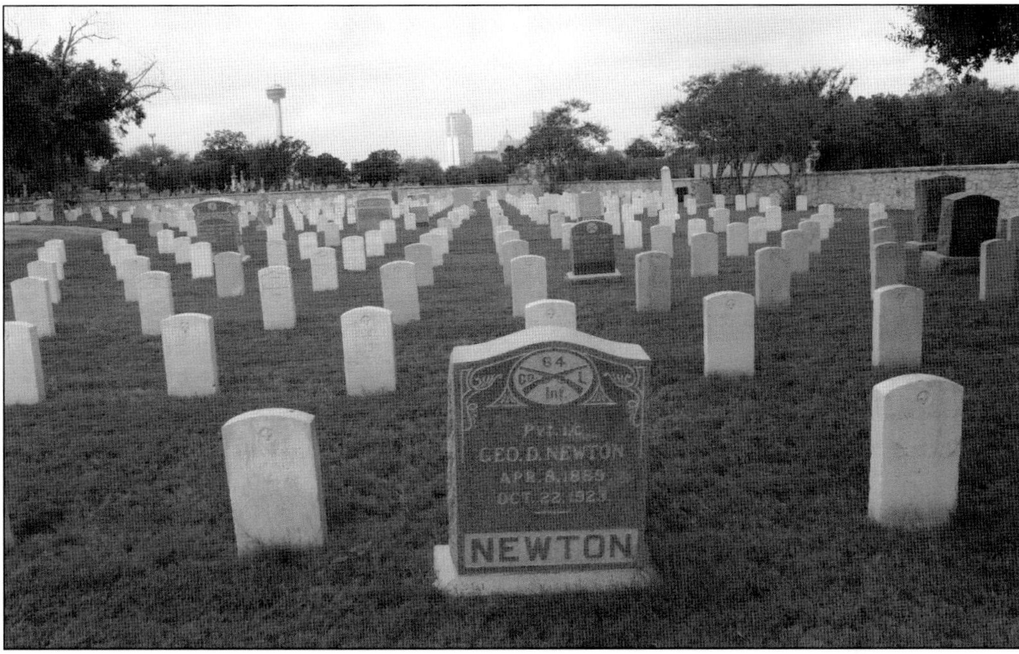

George D. Newton was a typical young man from San Antonio. His father, George W., was from New Orleans; his mother, Isabel Delgado, had been born in Mexico. George D. served in Company L, 64th Infantry, during World War I. Both before and after the war, he was a mail carrier for the US Post Office. He died of pulmonary tuberculosis at age 34. [19]

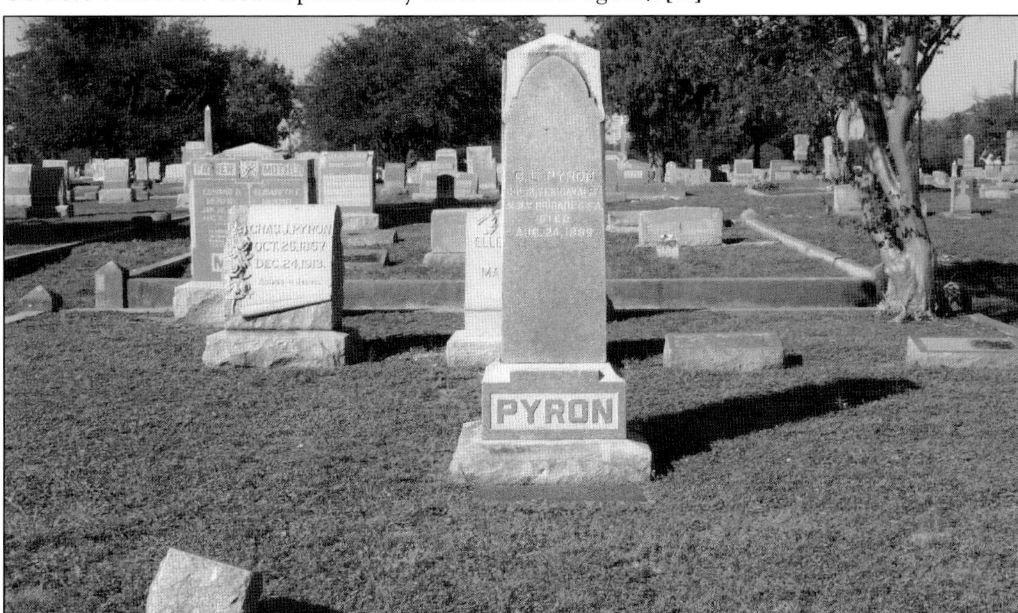

Col. Charles Lynn Pyron enlisted in the Confederacy at a young age. In the many battles he fought in the Civil War, he showed many acts of bravery. He became a resident of Texas in 1848, where he eventually bought a ranch six miles from San Antonio. Since he raised high-quality cattle, he was a very successful rancher. He was an active member of the Masonic lodge and Anchor lodge. [18]

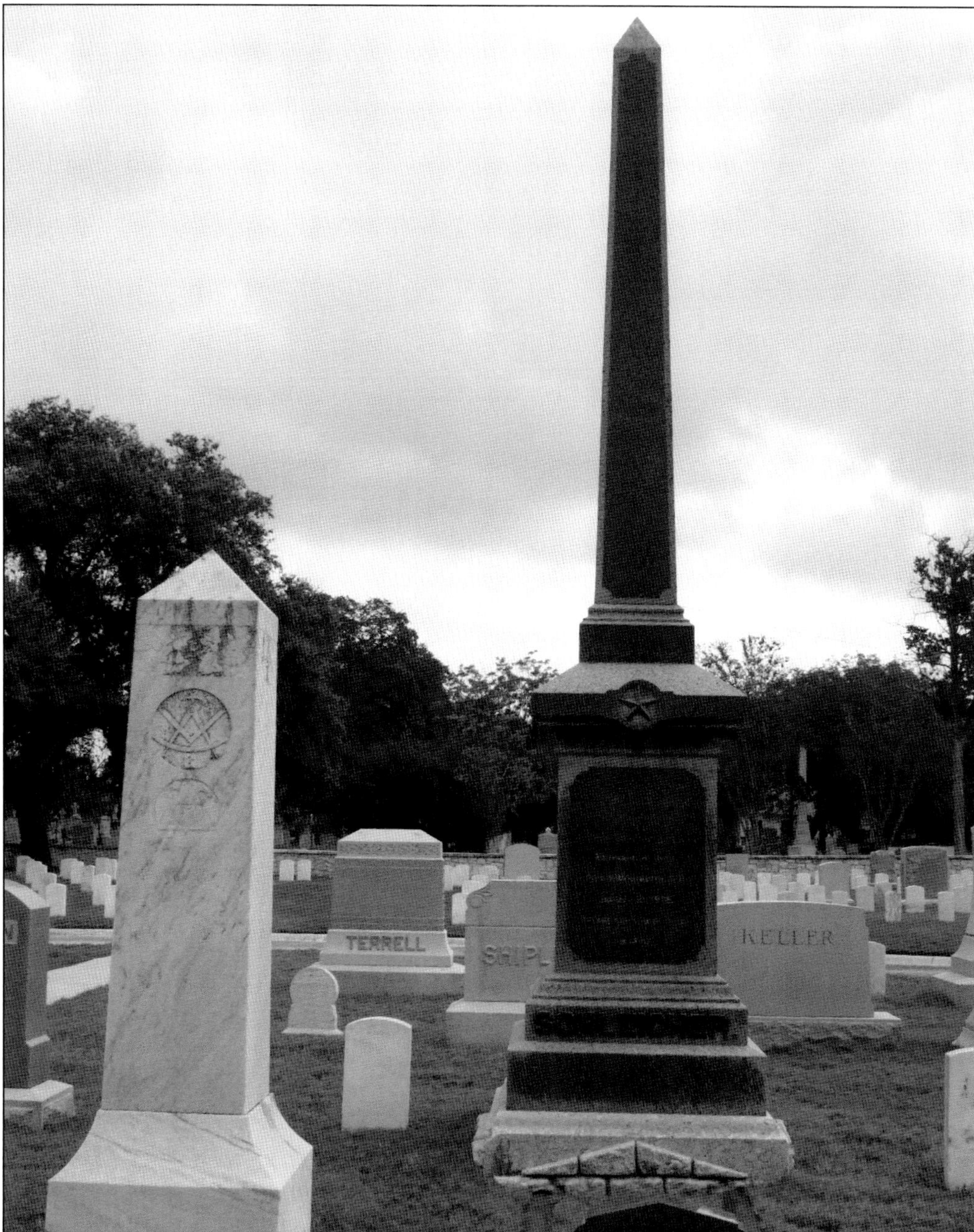

Gustav Schleicher studied engineering and architecture in Germany before coming to Texas as one of the founders of Bettina, a communist settlement venture. He opened a shingle mill before becoming a surveyor for the Bexar Land District. In between, he served in the Texas House of Representatives and, later, the Texas Senate for two terms. During the Civil War, he served in the Confederate Engineer Corps. After the war, he practiced law and engineering. He served in the US House for two terms, dying in office. His remains were returned to San Antonio and laid in state at the Literary Hall. He is buried in the San Antonio National Cemetery by the flagpole. Schleicher County is named for him. [19]

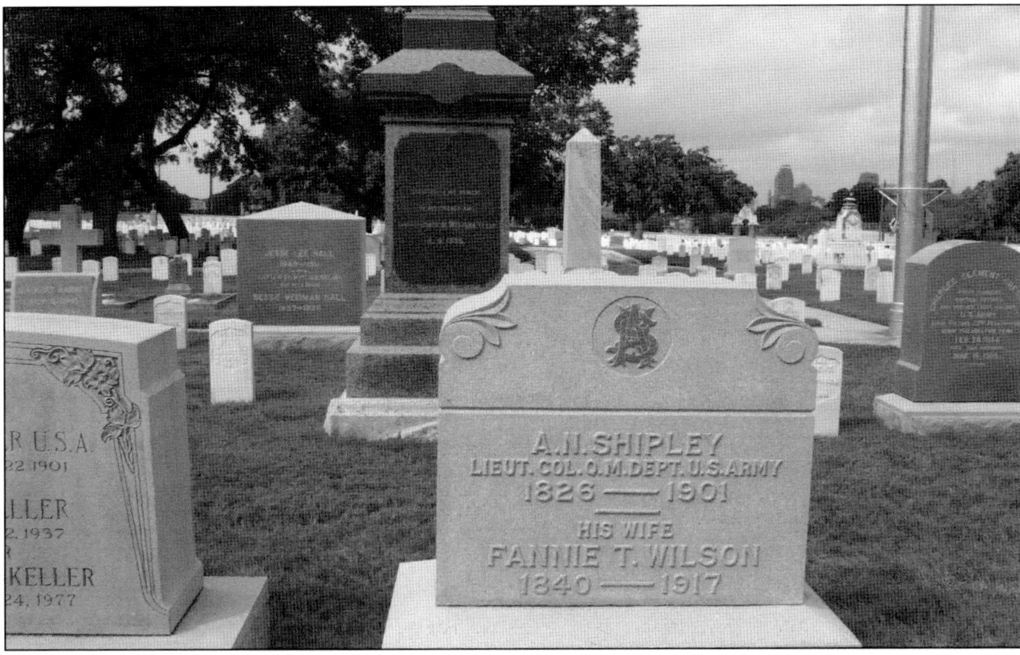

Pennsylvanian Alexander N. Shipley began his military career as an infantry private in 1848. In 1862, during the Civil War, he became a captain in the Quarter Master Corps. He passed away in 1901 while a lieutenant colonel in the Pension Office in Austin and was originally buried there. Perhaps it was when his widow, Fannie T. Wilson, passed in 1917 that they were buried in the San Antonio National Cemetery. [19]

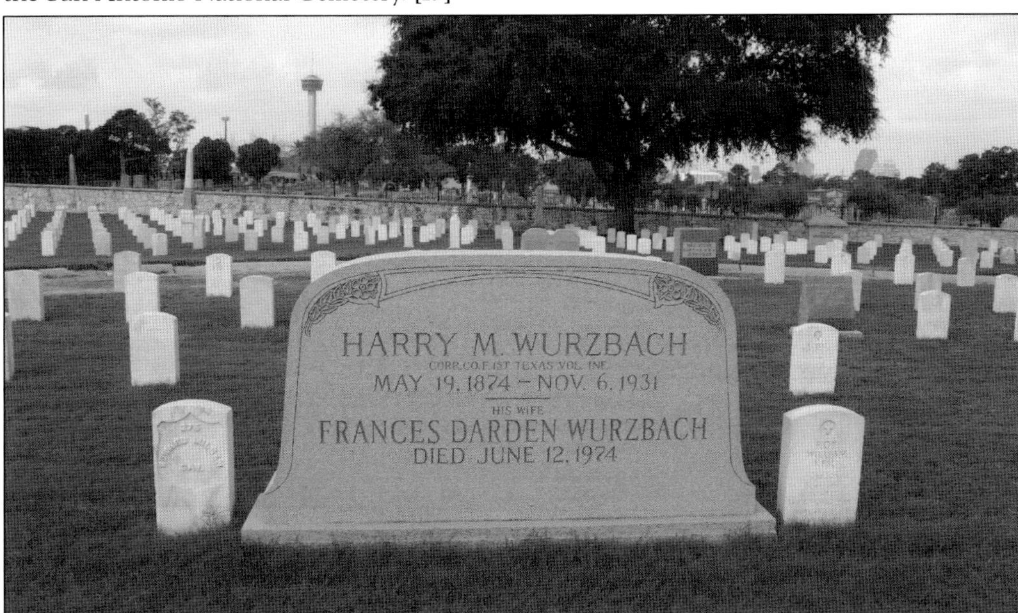

A native of San Antonio, Harry McLeary Wurzbach attended Washington and Lee University and was admitted to the bar in 1896. When the Spanish-American War broke out he enlisted in Company F, 1st Texas Volunteers. In 1900, he was elected Guadalupe County attorney and then county judge for four terms. From 1920 until his death, he served as a US representative. [19]

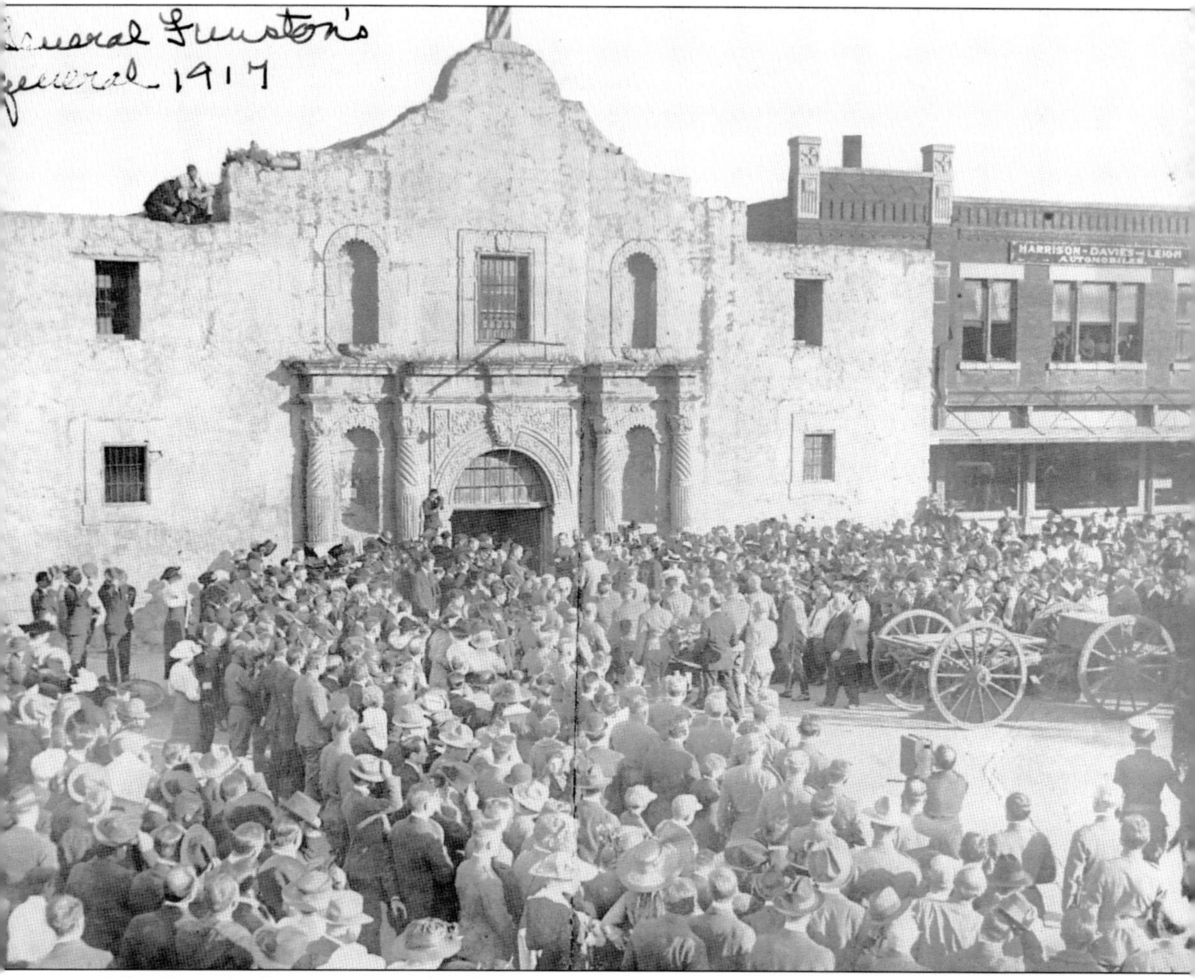

The funeral of Maj. Gen. Frederick Funston in 1917 took place at the Alamo, although he was buried at the San Francisco National Cemetery. General Funston had been President Wilson's choice to lead the American Expeditionary Force in Europe. Ironically, it was Maj. Douglas MacArthur who informed President Wilson of the general's death. Funston had previously worked on the Santa Fe Railroad, as a journalist, and explorer. He fought with the Cuban Revolutionary Army in its independence efforts from Spain. During the Spanish-American War, he served several years in the Philippines. He returned to the United States in time to be in command of the Presidio of San Francisco at the time of that city's 1906 earthquake. He served during the American invasion of Mexico in 1914–1916 and remained in charge of troops in Texas and the border region until his death. He was often considered a controversial figure.

Five

Fraternal

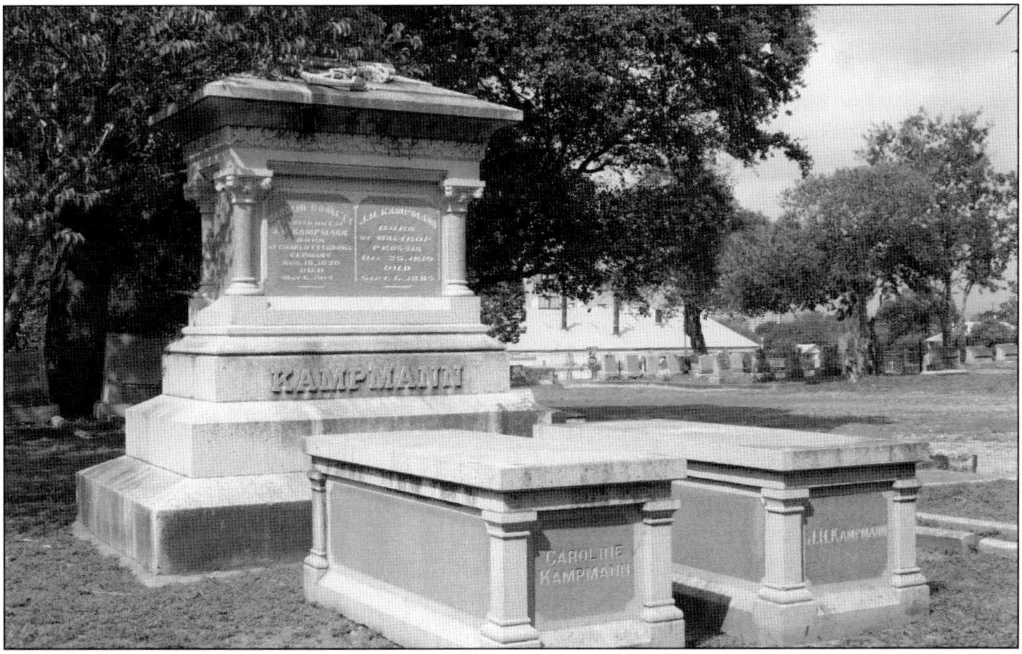

John Hermann Kampmann is a good example of the many Germans who came to Texas. Born in Prussia on Christmas Day 1819, he was from a farming family. He studied architecture at Cologne and was apprenticed at age 14. He served two years in the Prussian army. When revolution broke out in Germany, his sympathies were suspect, and he fled to the United States, eventually coming to San Antonio. Arriving almost penniless, he earned a living as a stonemason. In time, he was recognized as an architect and master builder. During the Civil War, he raised a company of Germans loyal to the South that became part of the 3rd Texas Cavalry. The rest of his life was spent in real estate and construction. After his death, his wife, Caroline Bonnett Kampmann, donated land for the county courthouse and the original Carnegie Library in San Antonio. [11]

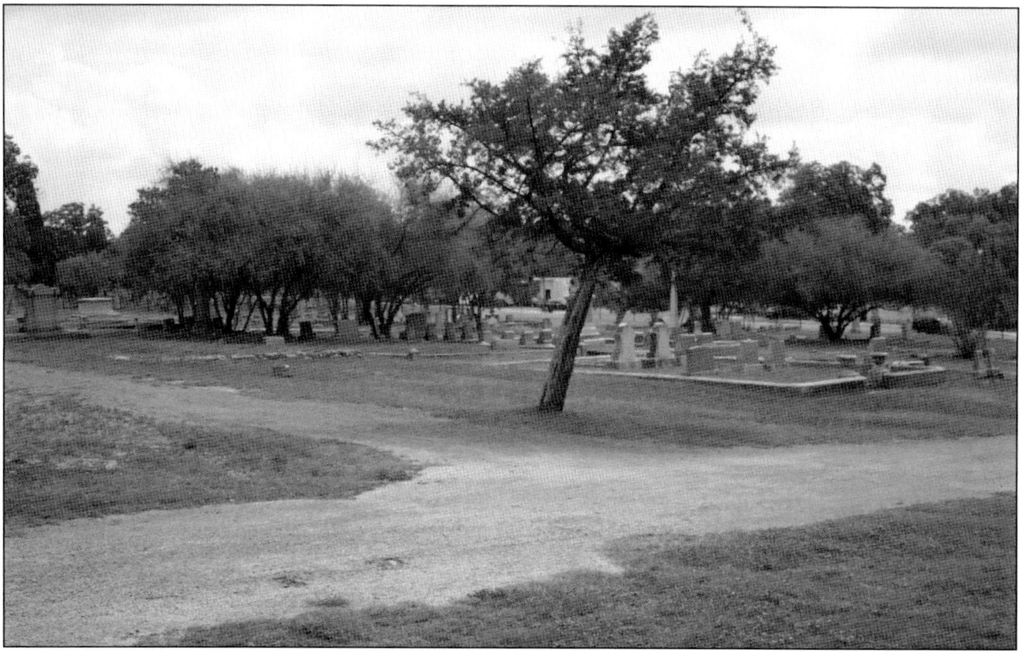

A group from the Army Quartermaster Corps quartered at the Alamo established the Alamo Masonic Lodge in 1847. The charter was approved the next year as Alamo Lodge No. 44, Ancient Free and Accepted Masons. This cemetery was established on November 28, 1853, when the lodge purchased the property from the city. [11]

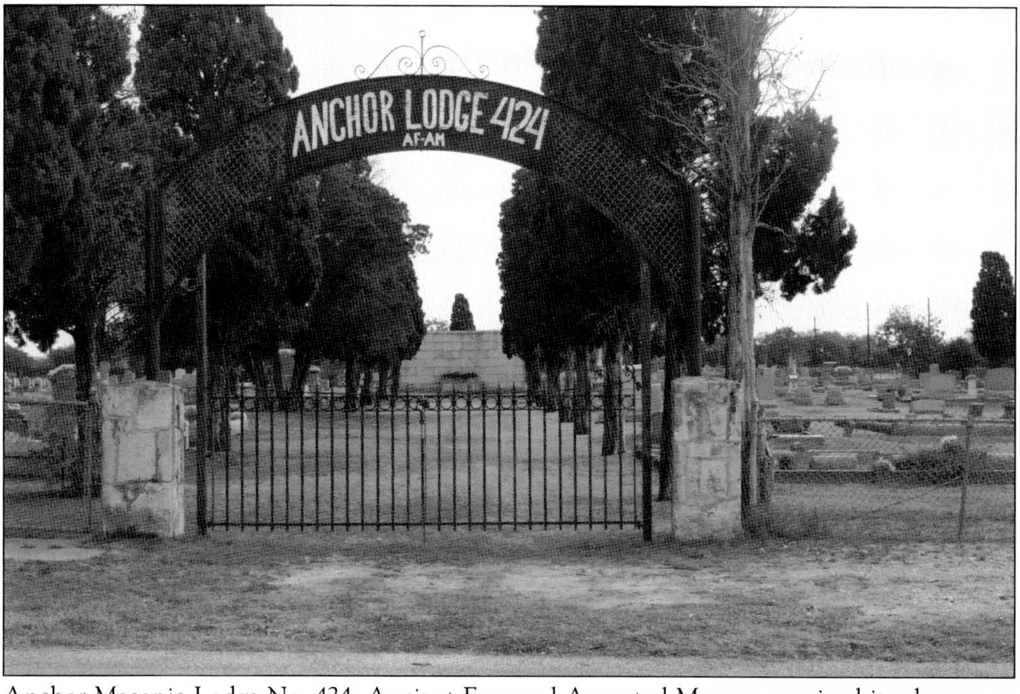

Anchor Masonic Lodge No. 424, Ancient Free and Accepted Masons, received its charter on June 5, 1875. The cemetery property was purchased from the city in 1882 when the lodge asked for land not to exceed two acres. [31]

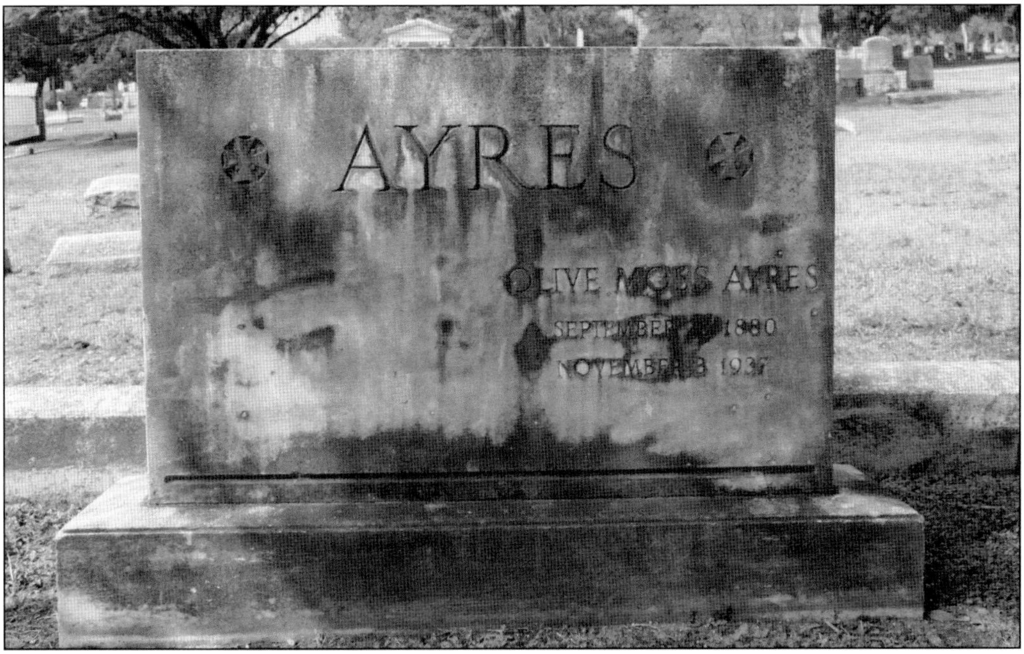

Olive Moss Ayres rests alone in Alamo Masonic Cemetery. Olive was the first wife of Atlee Bernard Ayres, a prominent architect. Atlee and his son Robert designed buildings such as First Presbyterian Church, the Federal Reserve Building, and the Administration Building at Randolph Field. Atlee is buried at Mission Burial Park with his second wife, Amelia. [11]

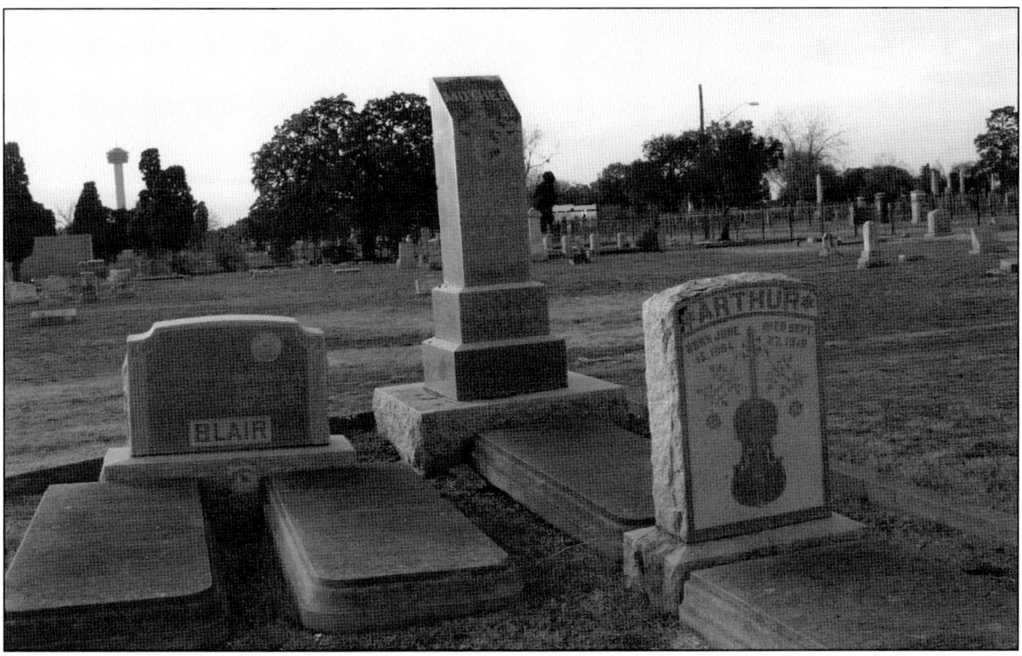

Dr. Henry Blair was born in Hungary, and early on, he lived in St. Louis. After arriving in San Antonio as a doctor of pharmacy, he was the proprietor of Farmers Drugstore at 819 East Commerce Street. His first wife, Jessie, was also a pharmacist and died in 1900. In 1905, he married Henrietta Rosenbaum of Cincinnati. Blair was a member of the Knights of Pythias, Masons, and Elks. [8]

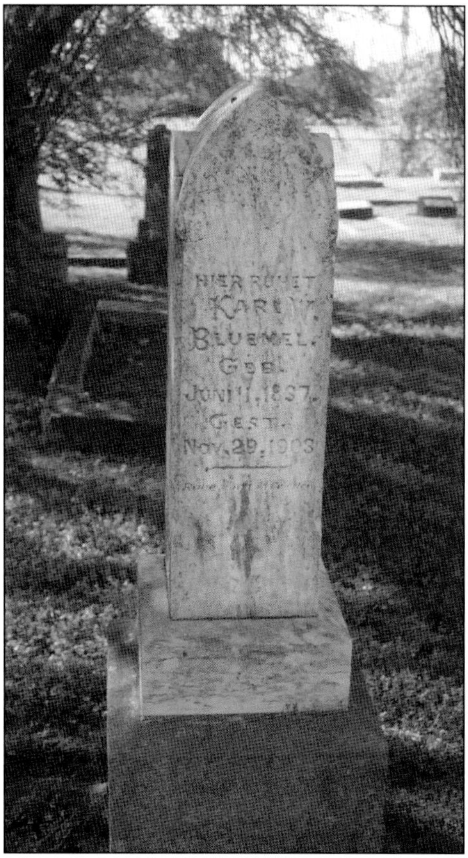

For many years, Bluemel's store, about 10 miles from downtown on Fredericksburg Road, was a gathering place for that area's community. Karl W. Bluemel came to Texas in 1878 or 1879 from his native Austria. He brought his family with him. By 1900, he was living in San Antonio at 314 Alamo Plaza with son Carl Jr., a brewer. [12]

Richard Bluemel, son of Karl, was proprietor of the Alamo Saloon on Alamo Plaza. In 1907, burglars broke into the saloon, stole the safe containing $41, and rode off with it in a wagon. With his wife, Clara Lehman, Bluemel later operated the grocery store on Fredericksburg Road. He was a member of Hermann Sons, Fraternal Order of Eagles, and the Beethoven Maennerchor. [12]

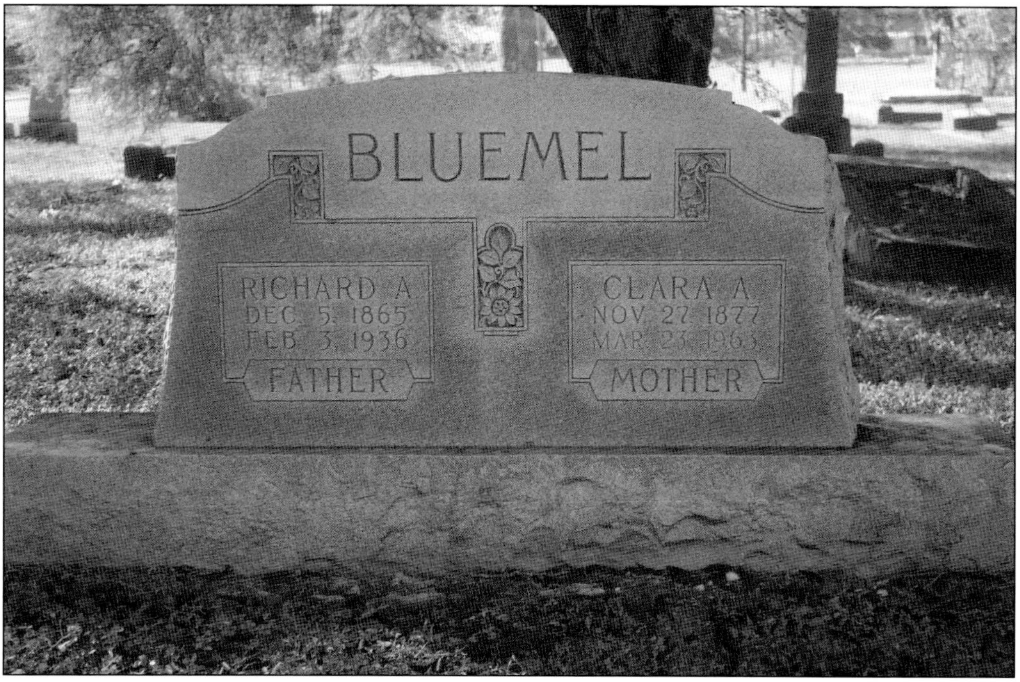

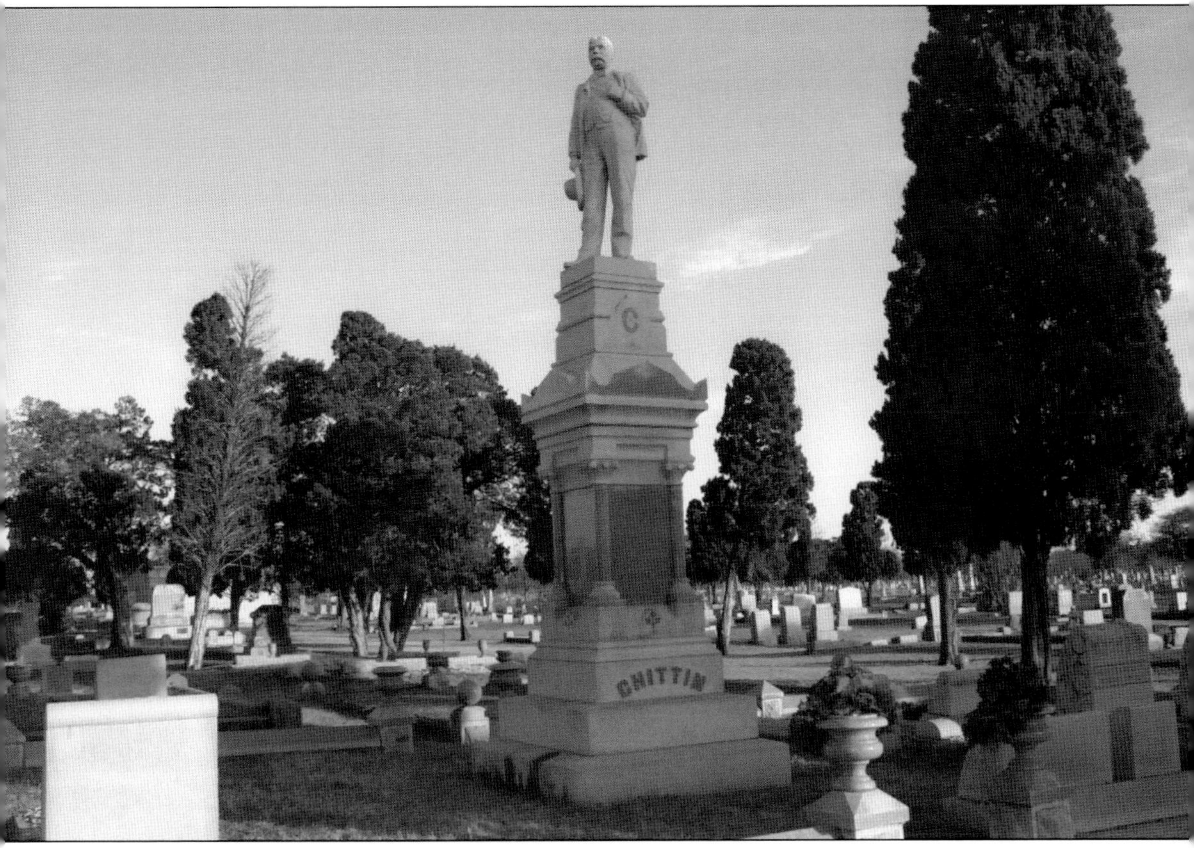

James M. Chittim stands, surveying the Chittim family lot, as he must have supervised his cattle business. Frank Teich created the sculpture. Born in Gentry County, Missouri, in 1858, Chittim later moved to Kansas, beginning his work with cattle. At 25, he married Annie Elizabeth "Betty" Oberle in Memphis and, shortly after, arrived in Texas. They lived in Victoria for a while and then moved to San Antonio. Most of his career was spent buying and selling livestock. He never took on a partner, as he preferred to work with other prominent cattlemen throughout Texas directly. He was a Knight Templar Mason and a member of First Presbyterian Church. James Chittim was active in civic affairs but refused to run for political office. After he passed away in 1911, Betty continued to live in Terrell Hills until her death in 1938. [31]

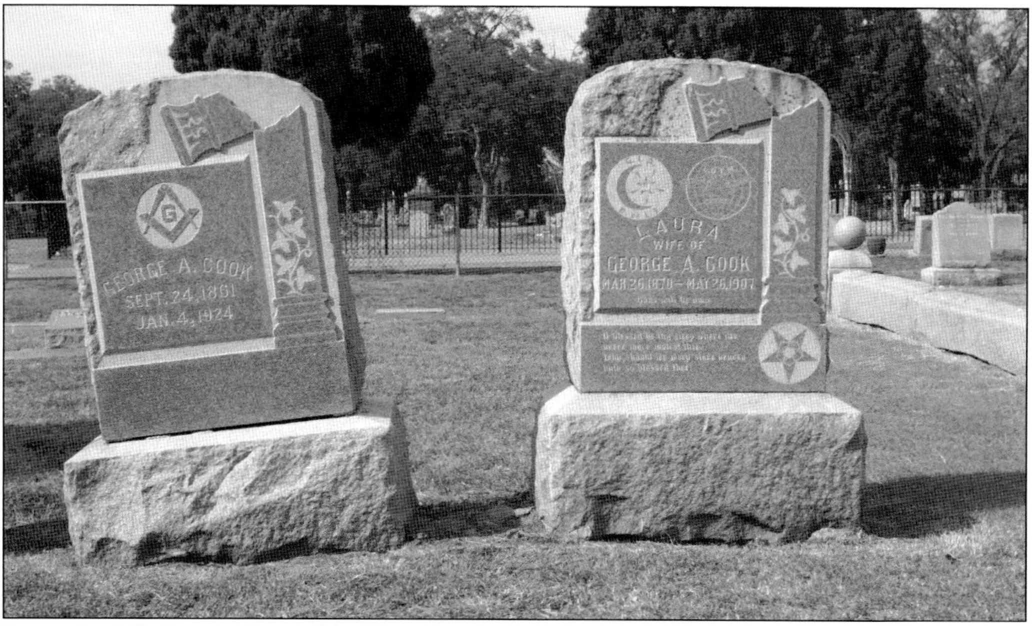

During his life, George A. Cook had been a railway engineer as well as a member of the Brotherhood of Locomotive Engineers. In 1923, he was one of those in charge of conferring degrees during the 23rd reunion of the last consistory held in the Old Cathedral of the San Antonio Scottish Rite. George's wife, Laura, was also involved in various organizations, such as the Ladies of the Maccabees and the Government Hill Literary Club. [31]

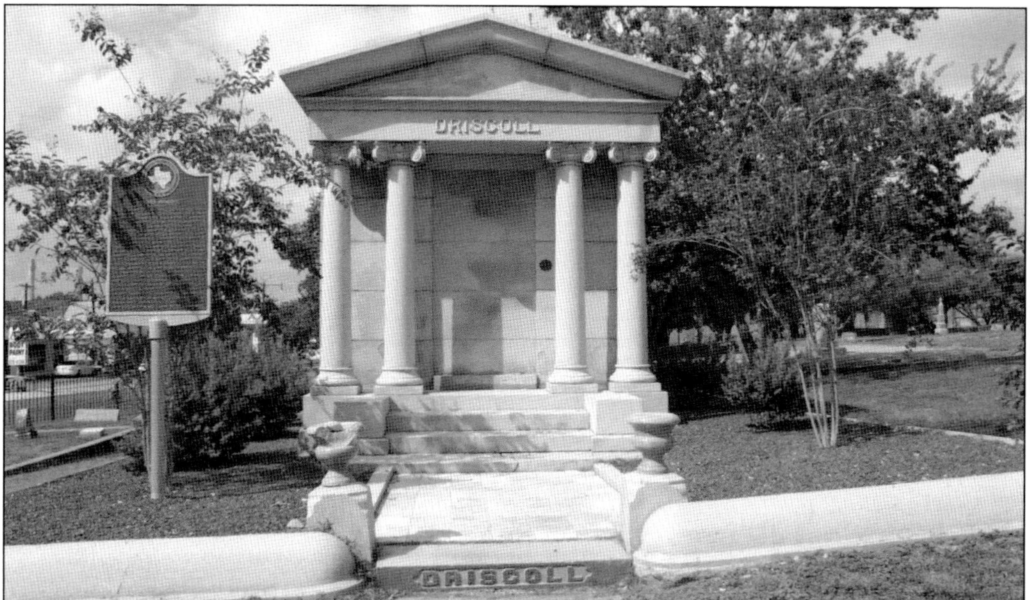

Clara Driscoll, daughter of a wealthy rancher and descendant of early Texas pioneers, was born in Refugio County. As a young woman, she became aware of the impending sale of the Alamo to a private firm. She bought the Alamo property with her own money to save the site. In 1905, the state bought the property from her and turned management over to the Daughters of the Texas Revolution. [11]

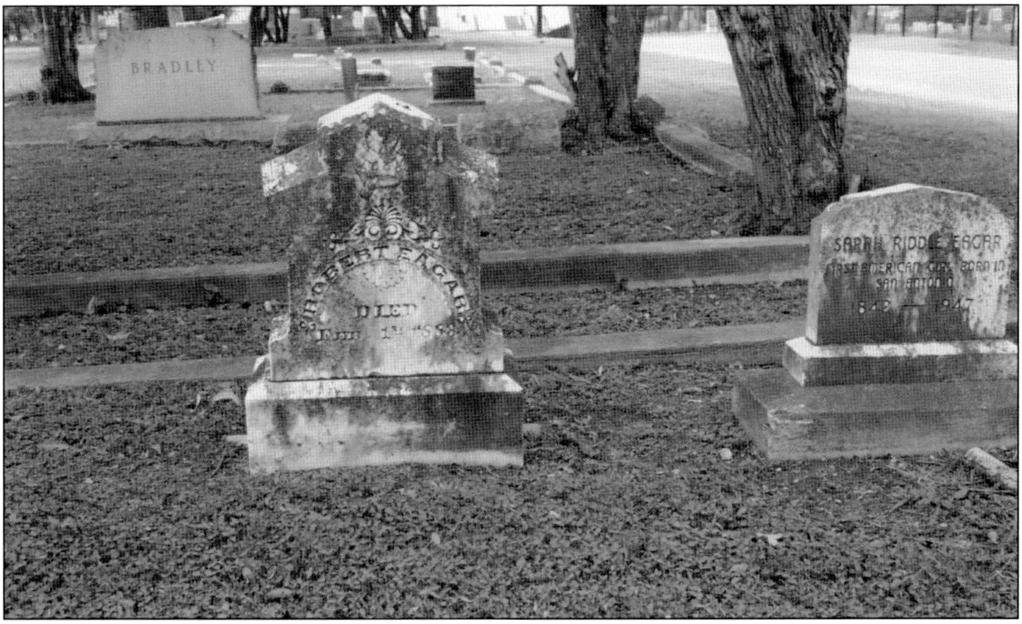

Robert Eagar was born in Halifax, Nova Scotia, on April 1, 1830, and arrived in San Antonio in 1850. He was a bookkeeper for Vance Brothers until he went into business for himself in a commission and brokerage firm. Albert Pike came from Washington to confer the 33rd degree on Eagar, an active Mason. Robert married Sarah Elizabeth Riddle, said to have been the first American girl born in San Antonio. [11]

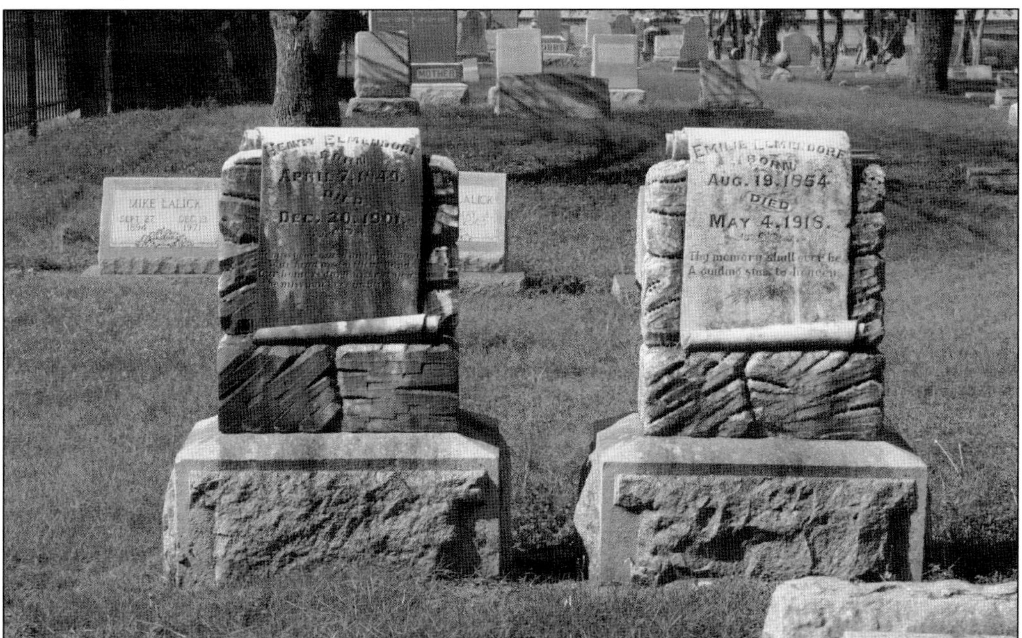

When Mayor George Paschal died in office, Henry Elmendorf succeeded him. He was elected to a following term. One of his major accomplishments was a sewer system, which was completed in 1895. Elmendorf succeeded in the family hardware business, and also had interests in the Alamo National Bank and Lakeview Land Company. [22]

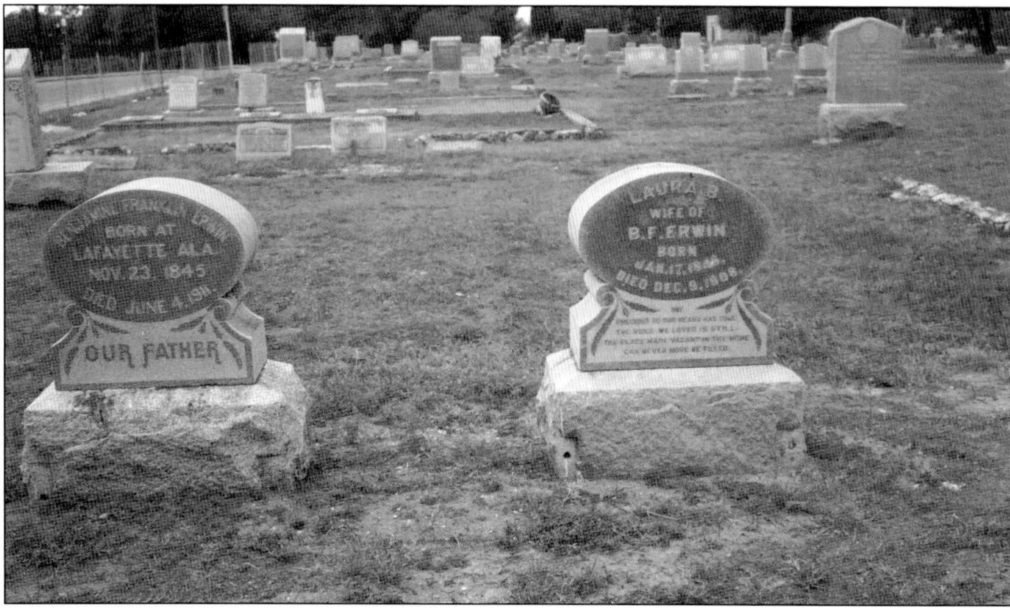

Laura and Benjamin Erwin liked to travel. He was born in Alabama while she was born in Kentucky, and their children were born in Tennessee and Texas. Benjamin was a house carpenter. Laura's inscription reads, "One / precious to our heart has gone / the voice we loved is still. / The place made vacant in thy home / can never more be filled." [8]

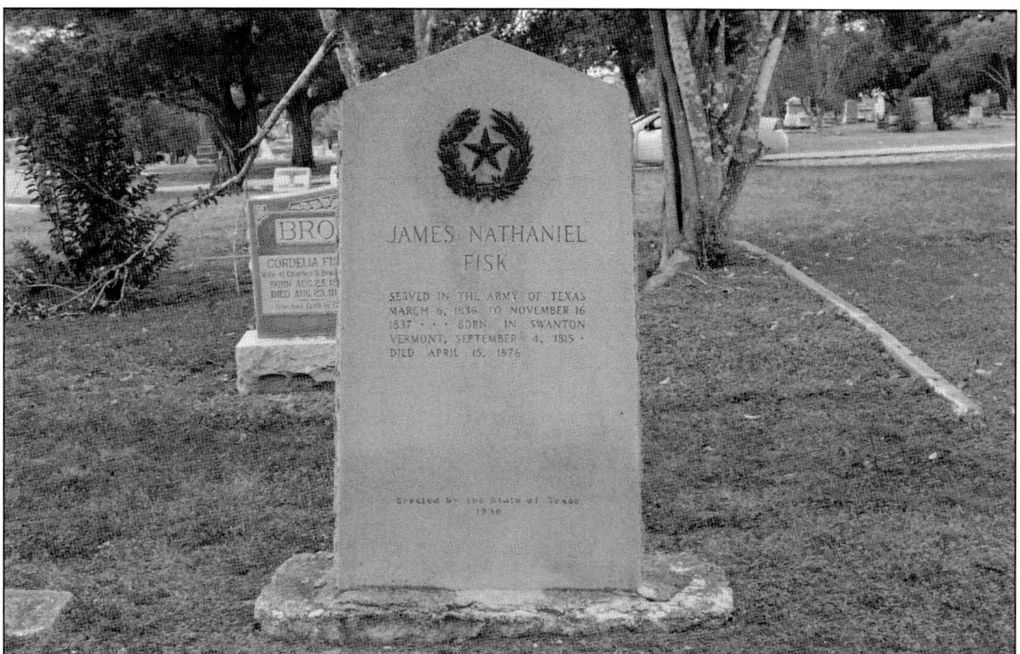

Vermont native James Nathaniel Fisk came to Texas in 1836 and served with Erastus "Deaf" Smith during Texas's fight for independence. In 1839, he married Smith's daughter Susan. When she died, he married Simona, another of Smith's daughters, and they had 15 children. During the Civil War, he served as a Union captain of cavalry in Louisiana. During the 1936 Texas Centennial, markers such as these were erected. [11]

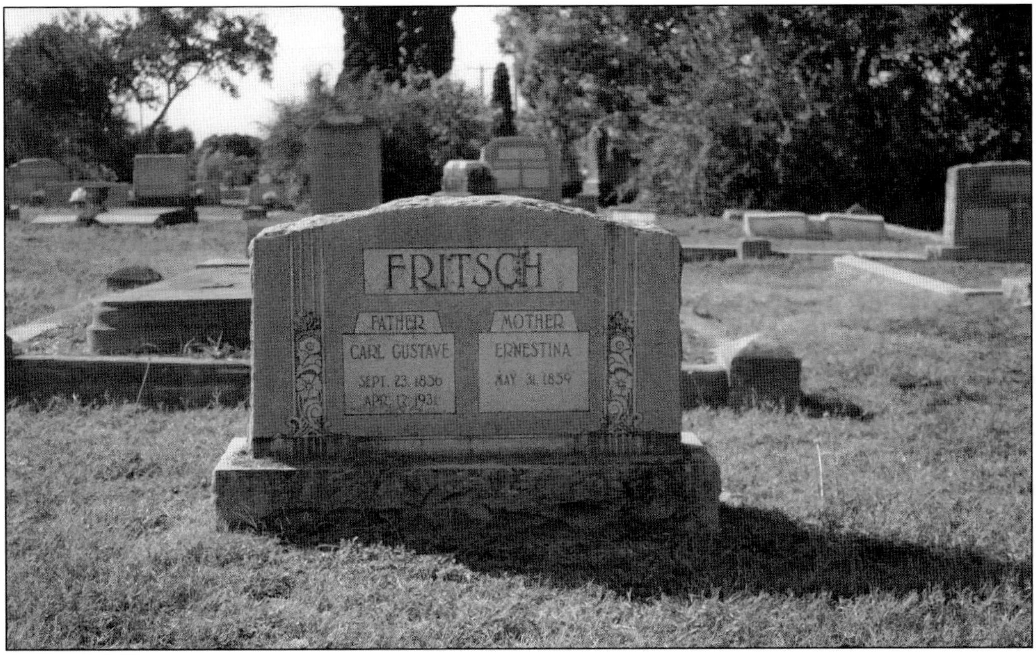

Carl Gustav Fritsch, another native of Germany, came to San Antonio about 1870. He was a pioneer shoemaker in the city. In the 1920s, he operated the San Antonio Shoe Hospital at 236 East Commerce Street. Also a German native, his wife, Ernestina, was the daughter of Carl Gustav Krause and Christina Y. Hoppe. [12]

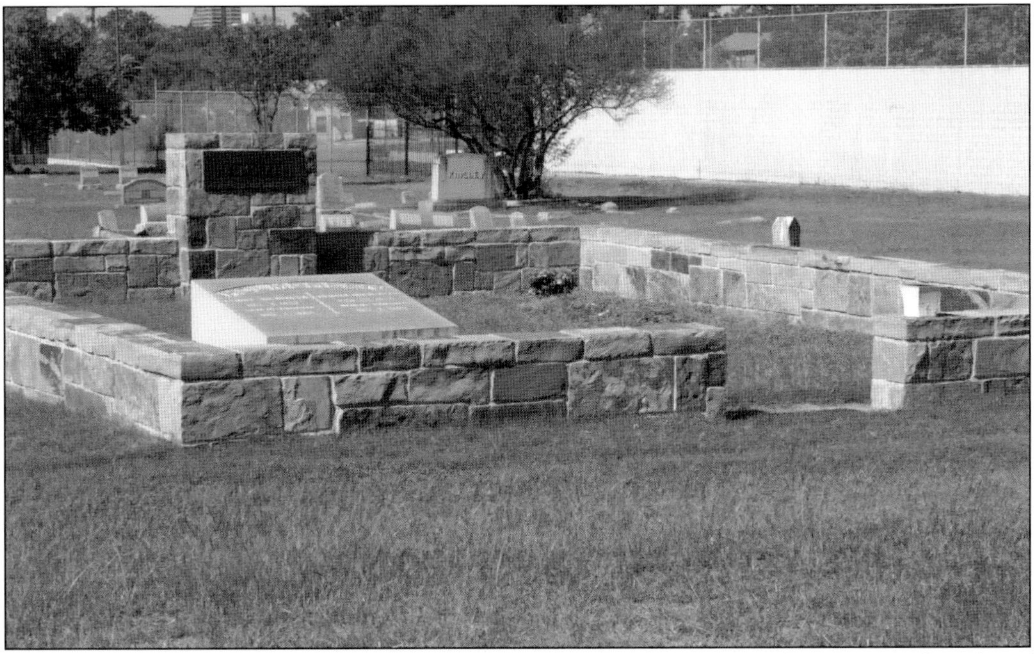

Within the Holmgreen lot in the Odd Fellows Cemetery is George Holmgreen Sr., founder of Alamo Ironworks. George arrived in town in 1878 with a few hundred dollars and the idea for an ironworks and machine shop. Soon, his sons, Eugene and Julius, joined him in Geo. Holmgreen & Sons. Julius designed and built drilling and pumping equipment for wells. [22]

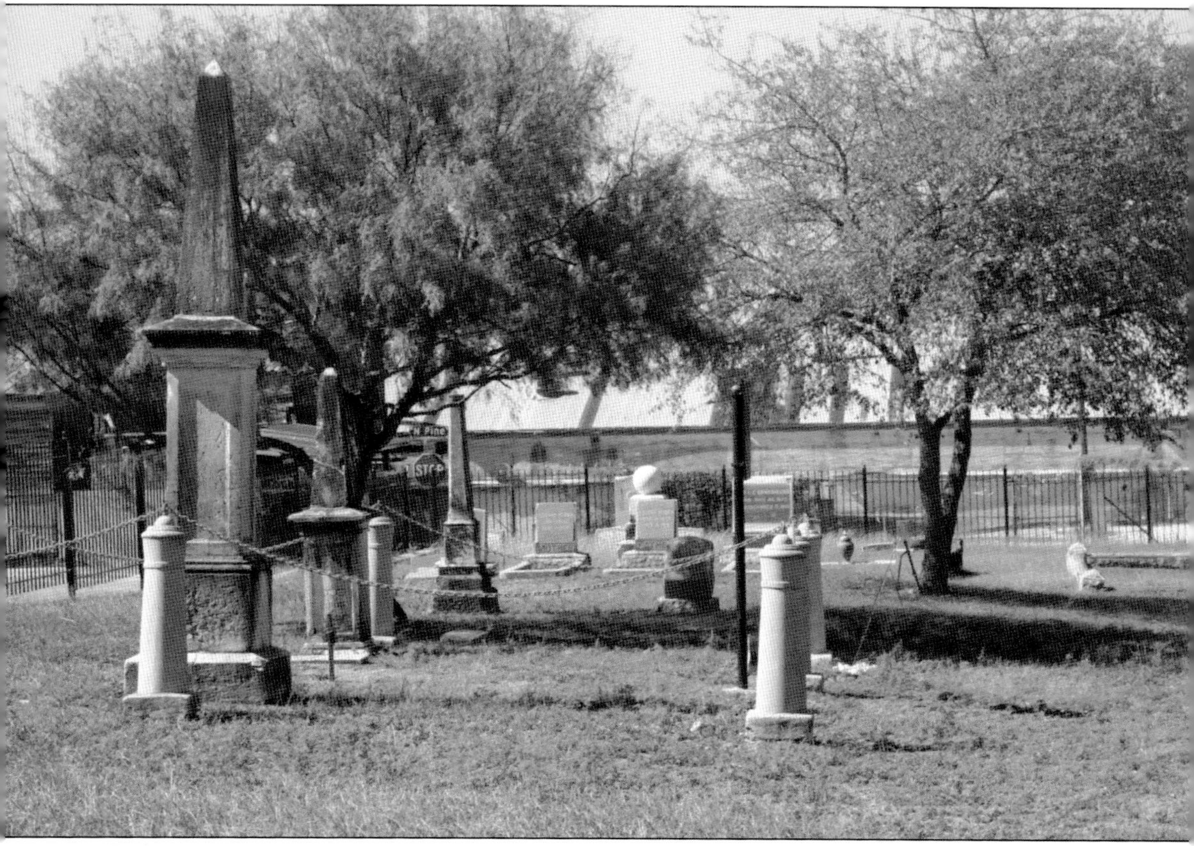

Before arriving in Texas in 1836, Samuel Walker, a Maryland native, fought in the Florida Seminole wars. In 1839 he traveled to New York, met with Samuel Colt, and suggested changes in a pistol, which became known as the Walker Colt. He fought in the Somervell Expedition and was captured and imprisoned in Mexico. Killed during the Mexican War, he and Robert Gillespie were later interred in the Odd Fellows Cemetery. Gillespie and his brothers moved to Texas from Tennessee in 1837 to establish a mercantile business. In 1842, he participated in the Somervell Expedition and then enlisted in John Coffee Hay's Texas Ranger Company. It was there that he met Samuel Walker. They fought Indians together before serving in the 1st Regiment Texas Mounted Riflemen during the Mexican War. Gillespie was killed at the Battle of Monterrey. [22]

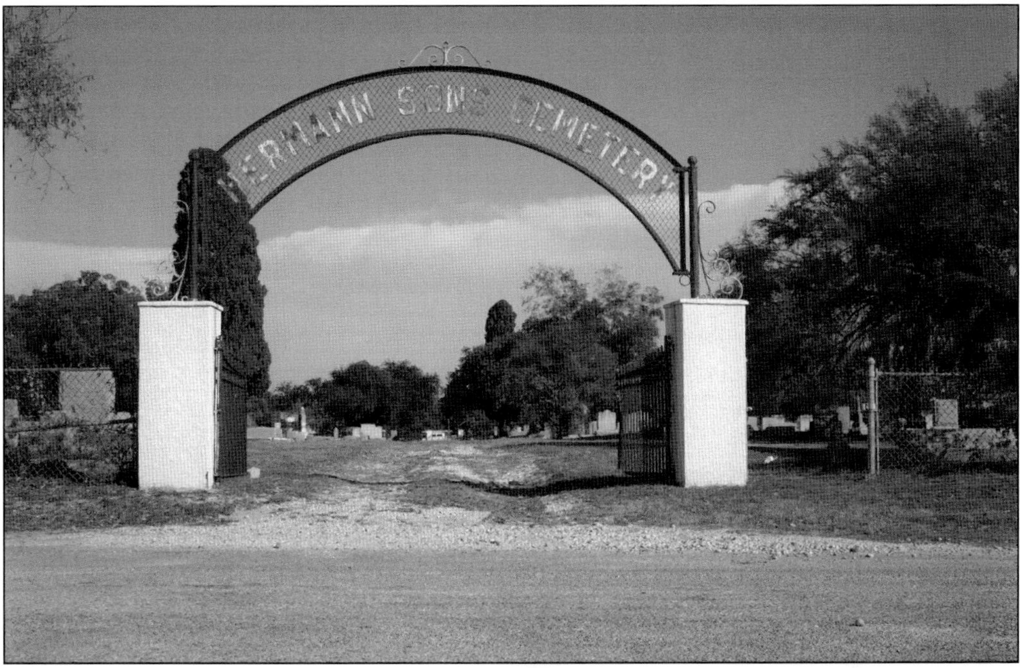

In the Eastside cemetery complex, there are two Hermann Sons cemeteries, the one pictured [12] and Harmonia Lodge No. 1 [28]. Hermann Sons was formed in New York in 1840 by a group of Germans to help other Germans in need. The Texas Order of Hermann Sons formed in 1860 in San Antonio. With the motto of "Friendship, Love, and Loyalty," Hermann Sons continues as a fraternal and service organization. [12]

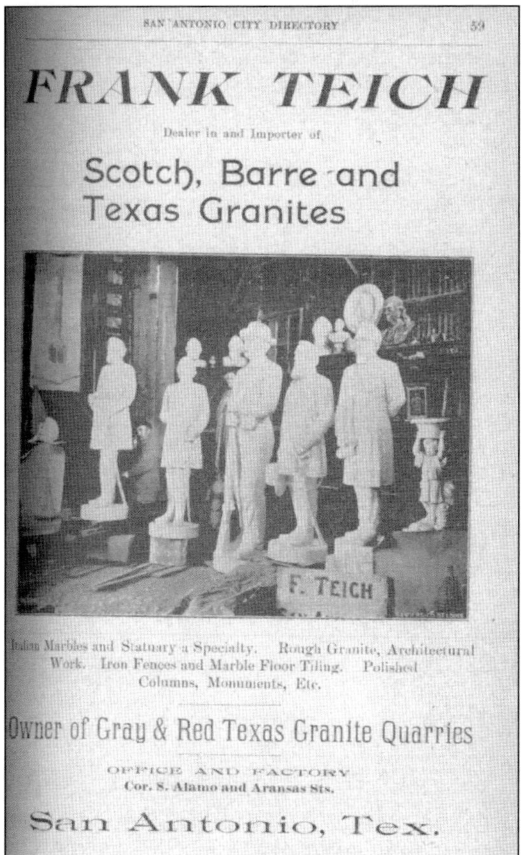

SAN ANTONIO CITY DIRECTORY 59

FRANK TEICH

Dealer in and Importer of

Scotch, Barre and Texas Granites

Italian Marbles and Statuary a Specialty. Rough Granite, Architectural Work. Iron Fences and Marble Floor Tiling. Polished Columns, Monuments, Etc.

Owner of Gray & Red Texas Granite Quarries

OFFICE AND FACTORY
Cor. S. Alamo and Aransas Sts.

San Antonio, Tex.

Born in Germany in 1856, Frank Teich is a well-known sculptor and stonecutter. He arrived in the United States in 1878, reaching San Antonio in 1885. Here, he opened a marble yard across from the Alamo. His works include the Confederate Monument in Austin, San Antonio City Hall, the Kampmann Building, and the altar of St. Mary's Church. He later moved to Llano, where he died.

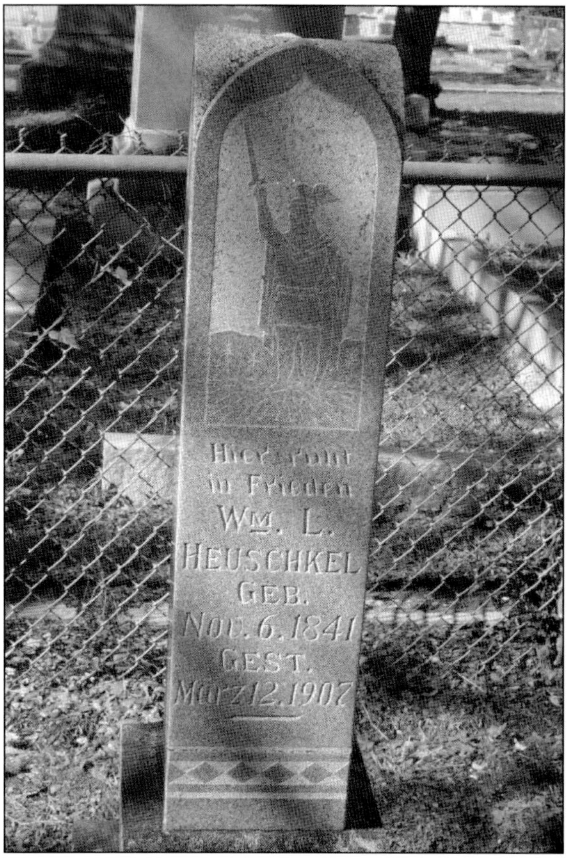

William Ludwig Heuschkel worked as a teamster for the Alamo Cement Company. A teamster at that time was one who drove a wagon and team of horses, mules, or oxen. He was a member of the Frederick Lubing Jahn Lodge No. 172 of the Sons of Herman. William was at one time president of the lodge. Note the image of Hermann on his stone. [28]

The stone at right is of William Heuschkel's wife, Anna Elisa, who died in 1886, and their son Albert, who died in 1887, at just a little less than a year old. Hermann the Cherusker, or Arminius, was an early German hero noted for defeating the Roman army at the Battle of the Teutoburg Forest. [28]

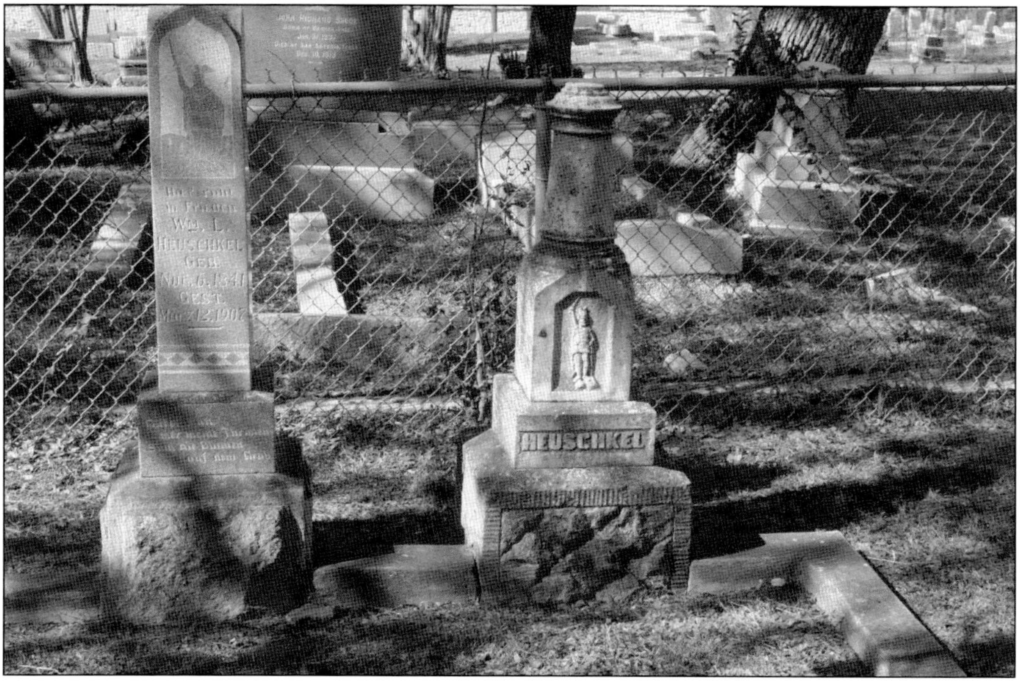

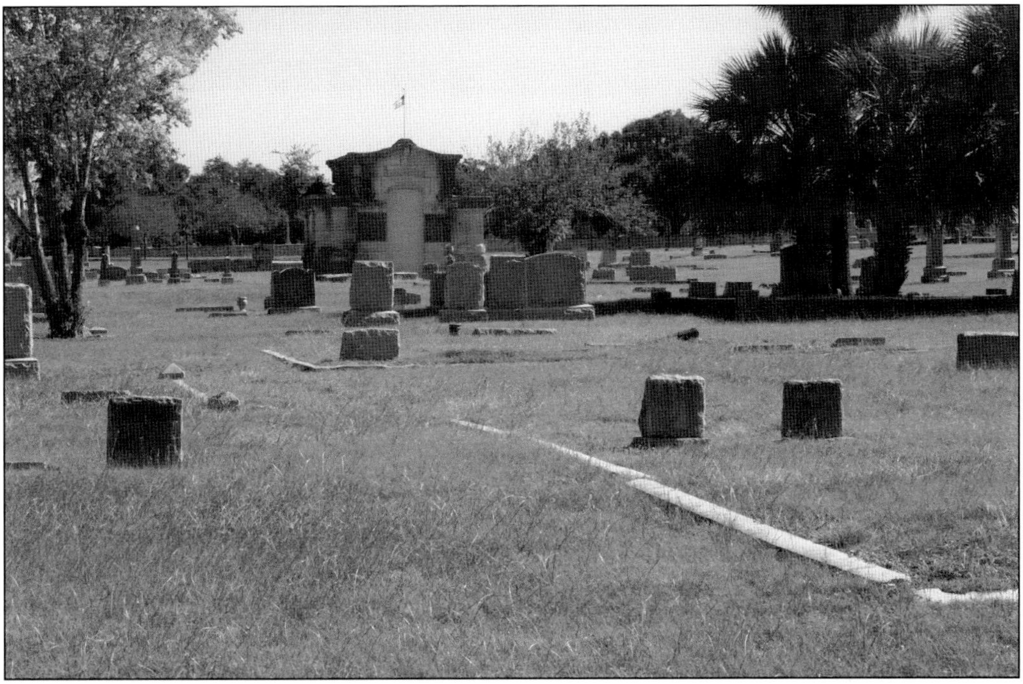

In 1855, San Antonio Lodge No. 11 was established. Later that year, it paid Alamo Masonic Lodge No. 44 for six acres of cemetery land. It was cleared and laid out by Mickle John, who also paved the first brick streets in San Antonio. The first burials were those of Samuel Walker and Robert Gillespie, who had been killed in the Mexican War. The second burial was of a man from Chicago who had sought relief from tuberculosis here. Later, the Odd Fellows operated the Norwood Clinic here. The Odd Fellows are known for "the Three Links of Fraternity"—Friendship, Love, and Truth. [22]

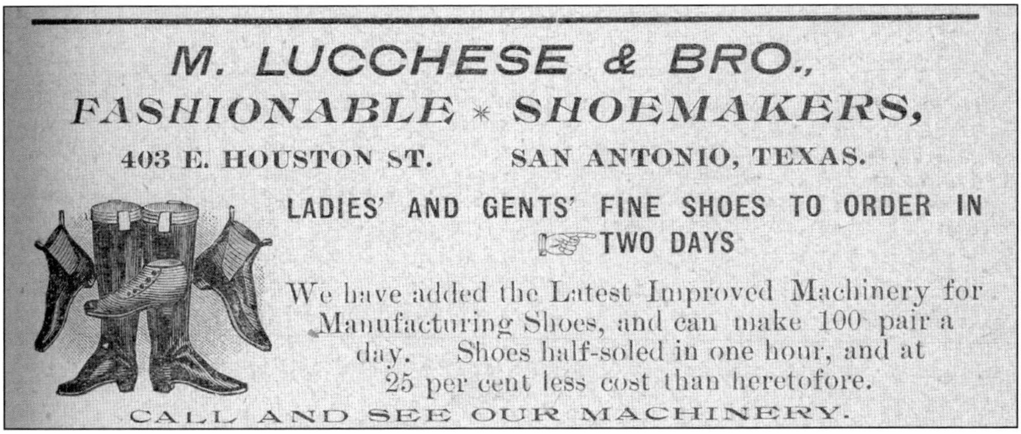

When Gaetano Lucchese and his family arrived in this country, he carried his tools in a sack. He bought a shoe shop from a man named Beckman by the old Southern Hotel on Main Plaza. Next door, Cosimo Battagllia, another Italian, also had a shoe shop. Those were the days before mass-produced shoes and boots, but the late 19th century saw the development of new equipment for making both.

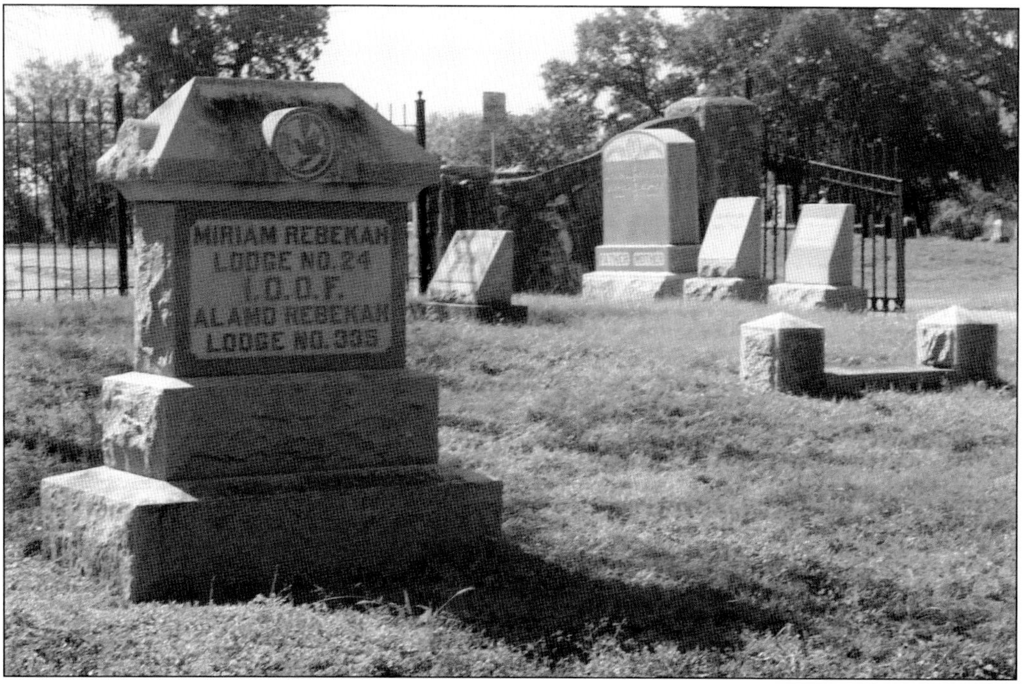

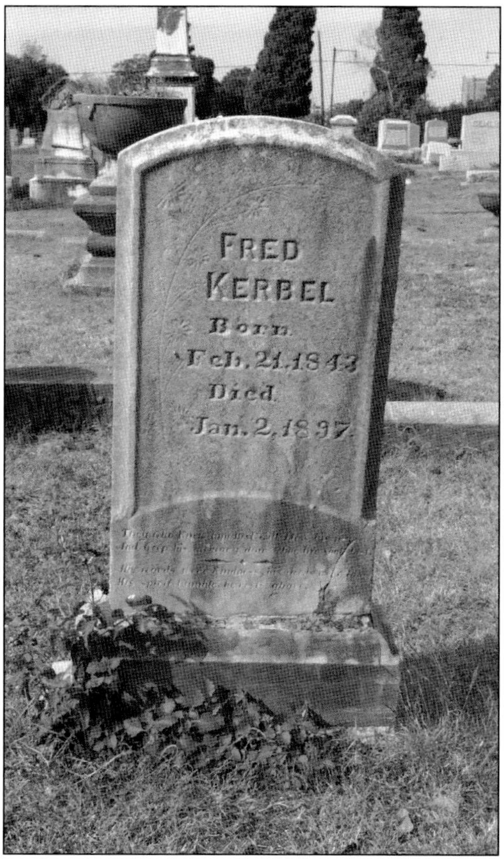

The Independent Order of Odd Fellows recognized the contribution women were making to their organization and communities. In 1851, the Grand Lodge, in session in Baltimore, authorized the Rebekah Degree for women based on the principles of faithfulness, hospitality, purity, and Biblical principles. One example is Miriam, symbolizing zeal and devotion. [22]

Frederick Kerbel, a native of Buffalo, New York, served in the Union army during the Civil War. Afterward, he went to California and then came to San Antonio. From 1882 to 1891, he ran San Pedro Park, making it a popular resort with dancing, rowing, games, entertainment, and more. At the time of his death, he was alderman of the Third Ward and proprietor of the White House Saloon. [31]

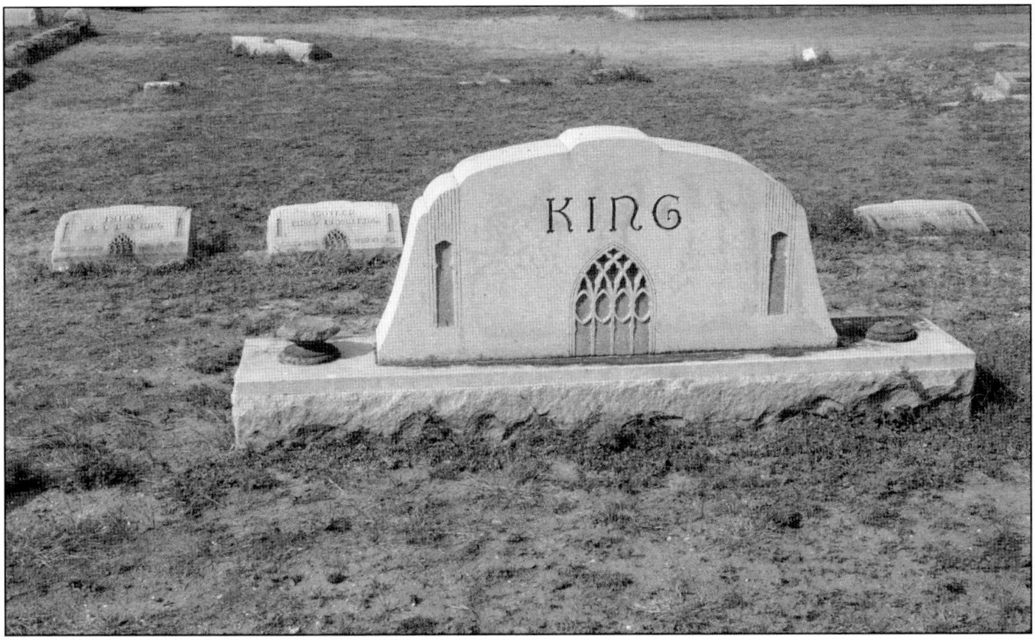

After arriving in Louisiana from England, Claudius Edward Richard King and his family soon moved to Virginia where he studied medicine. During the Civil War, he served in the Confederacy, and once in San Antonio, he became a member of the United Confederate Veterans. He served as the first president of the Texas Medical Society and was a member of St. Mark's Episcopal Church. [31]

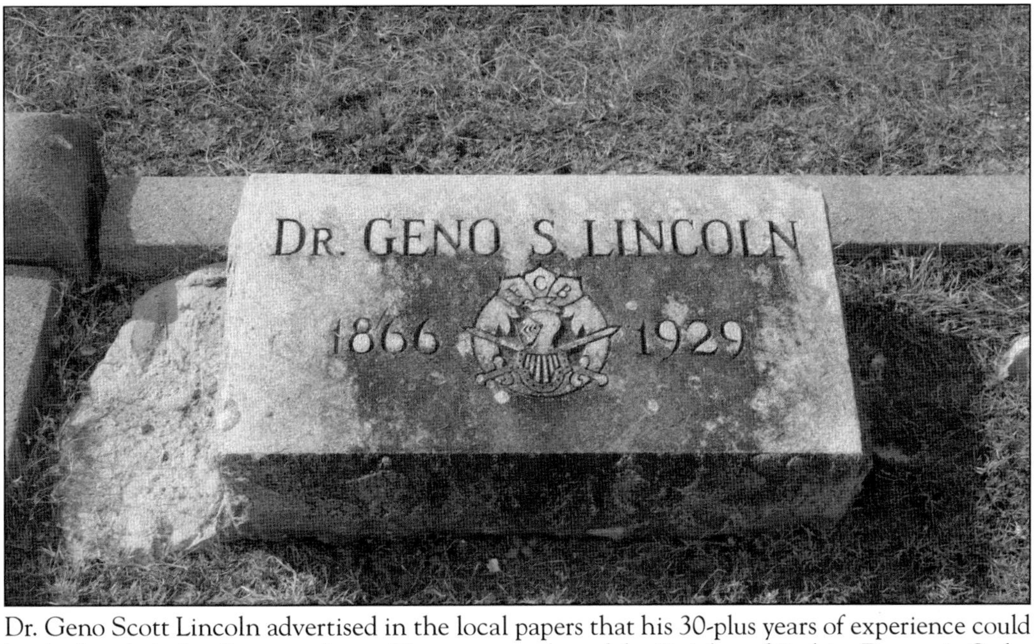

Dr. Geno Scott Lincoln advertised in the local papers that his 30-plus years of experience could be the best help for diseases of men. He was a member of the Knights of Pythias Dramatic Order Knights of Khorassan, El Bexar Temple No. 181. In 1925, he was listed as the organization's secretary. The "F. C. B." on his stone refers to the Knights of Pythias motto "Friendship, Charity, Benevolence." [8]

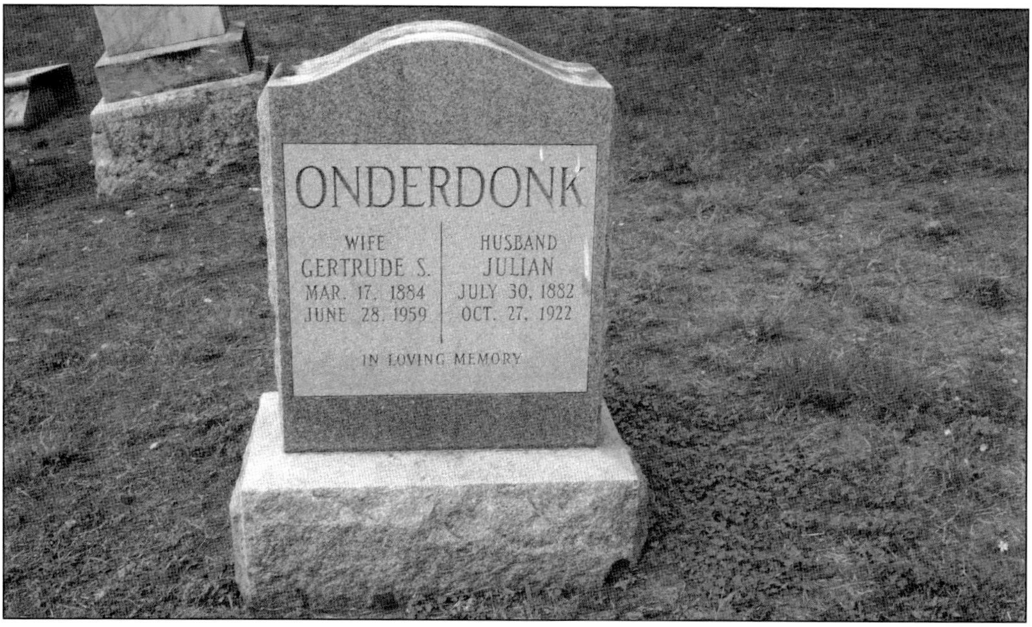

This simple, plain gravestone hides the fact that the inhabitant was in fact an artist. Born in 1882 in San Antonio, Julian Onderdonk studied landscape painting at New York's Art Students' League. He returned in 1909 to paint the bigness of Texas. His works are full of bluebonnets, rivers, valleys, and hills of the Texas hill country and beyond. He passed away at only 40 years of age. [11]

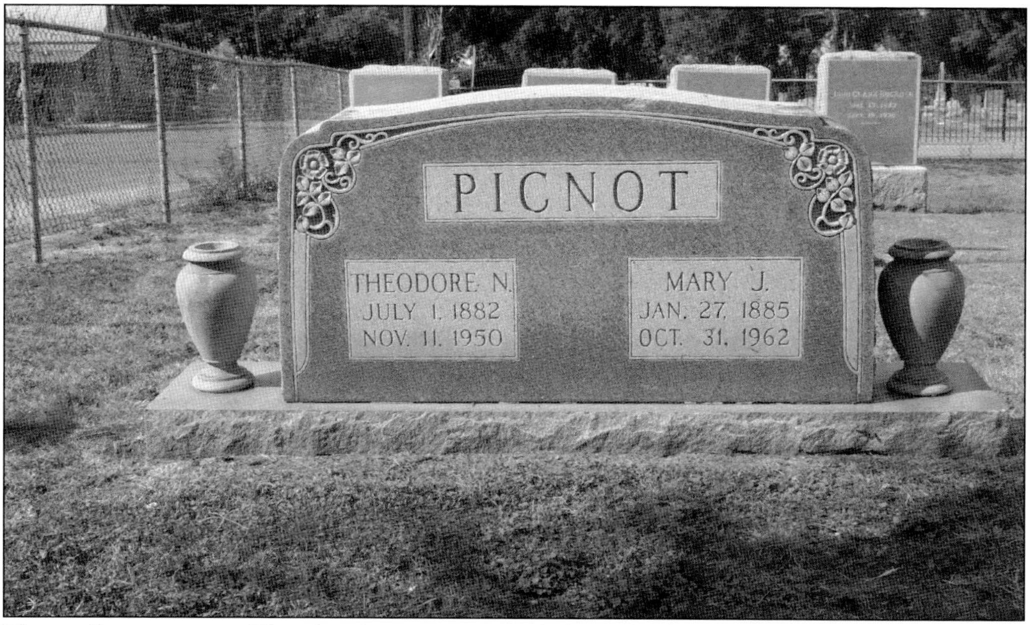

Blanco County native Theodore Napier Picnot's father, Charles, was born in Belgium and his mother, Marie J. Gerritsen, in Holland. A civil engineer by training, most of his active career was spent with City Public Service as an industrial manager. He was active in the Masons and Texas Pioneers. During the 1930s and early 1940s, he led City Public Service efforts to clean up the slums on San Antonio's Westside. [31]

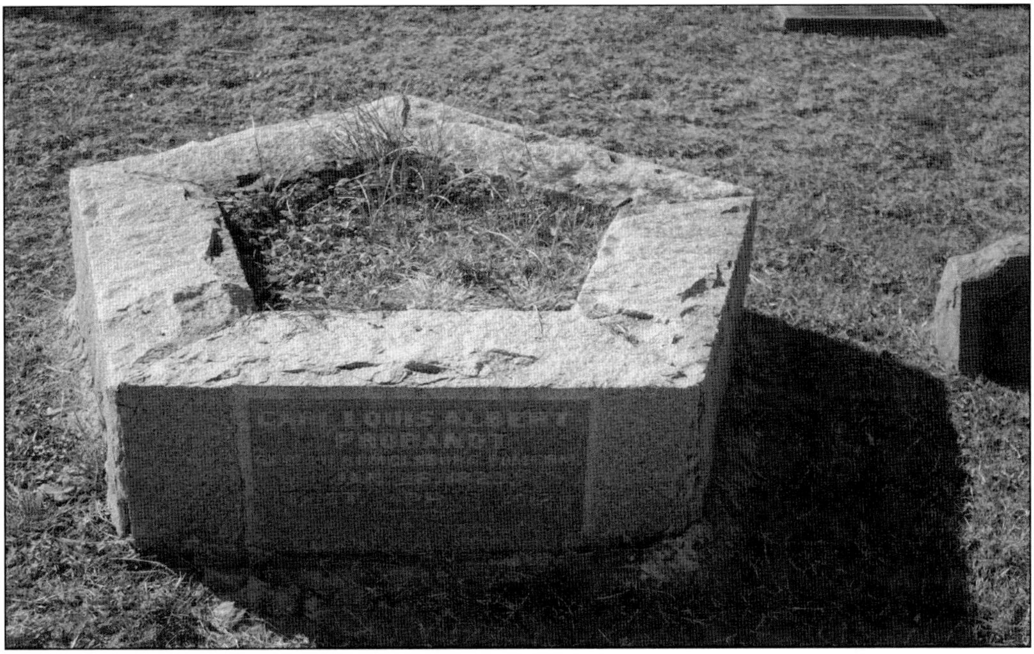

Carl Louis Albert Probandt has an unusual gravestone. Born in Germany in 1823, he arrived in the United States in 1851 and came to San Antonio. By 1880, his wife, Dorothea Mae, was listed as a widow on the federal census. However, note that the gravestone lists his death as 1912. On the 1910 census, he was listed as Louis Probandt, a retired merchant, and divorced. [12]

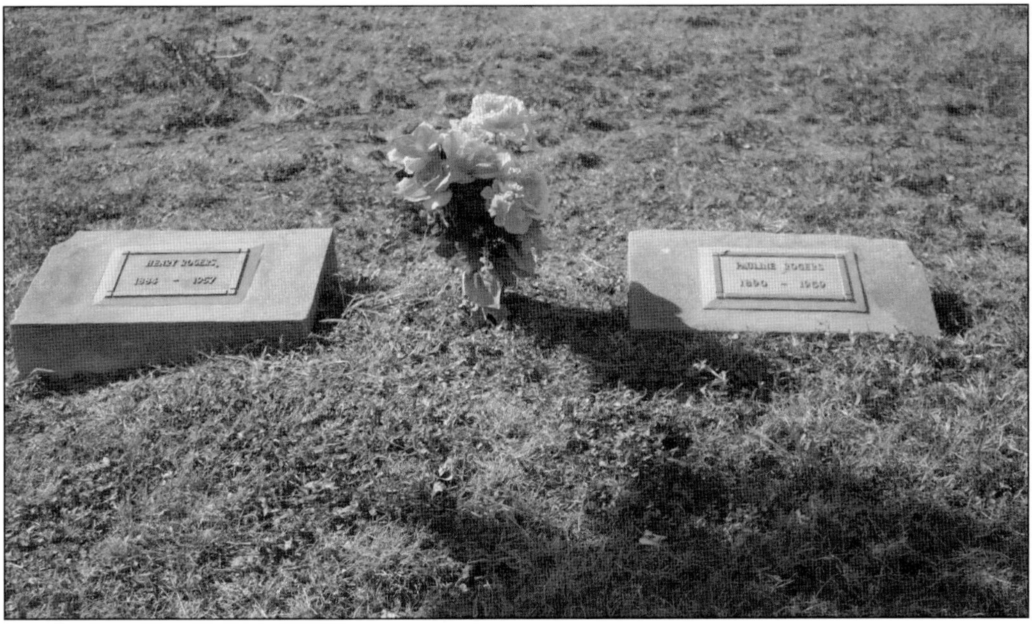

Here are two simple, small bronze markers for Henry and Pauline Rogers, which have been marked by someone with a few pretty artificial flowers. Henry Rogers owned Rogers Bicycle Shop at 407 Fredericksburg Road for a number of years. Pauline was born in Missouri, as was Henry's father, while Henry was born in San Antonio. Death certificates reveal that they were cremated and remembered here. [12]

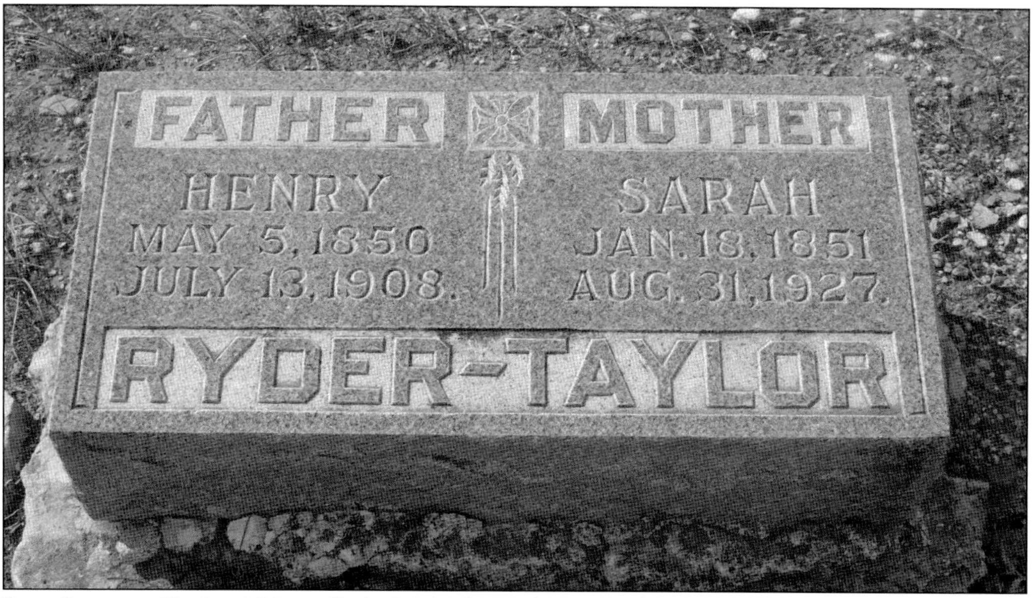

From Leicester, England, Henry Ryder-Taylor began his journalism career with the *London Telegraph* and a desk next to Charles Dickens. Before coming to San Antonio, he worked in Mexico City, St. Louis, and New York. He spent 20 years with the *San Antonio Daily Light*. He collaborated with O. Henry on the latter's *Rolling Stone* magazine in Austin. The *Light* staff affectionately referred to him as the "Old Guard." [8]

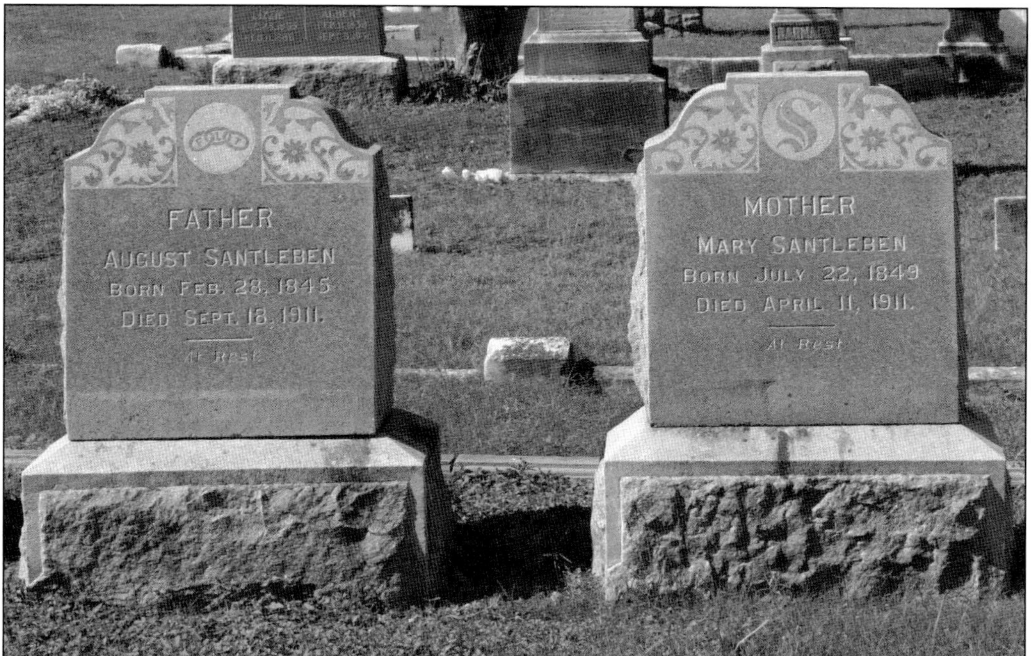

At age 14, August Santleben served as the youngest mailman in the country, traveling between Castroville and Bandera. With the Civil War, he fled to Mexico and joined the Union 1st Texas Cavalry. After that war, he established a stage line between San Antonio and Monterrey, and eventually a freighting business, for which he is best known. [22]

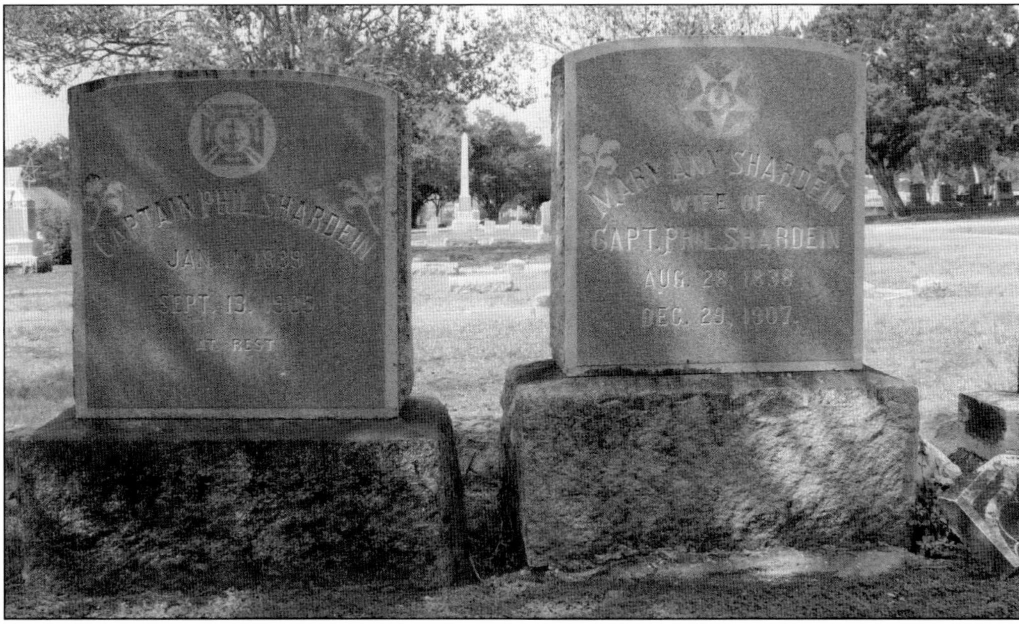

Capt. Philip Shardein was chief of police in San Antonio from 1879 to 1893. His service spanned much of the Bryan Callaghan era, an era of machine politics. However, during this time, the police department was expanded and modernized. After serving as chief of police, Shardein went into real estate. In 1896, he was appointed to the board of managers for the Southwestern Hospital for the Insane. [11]

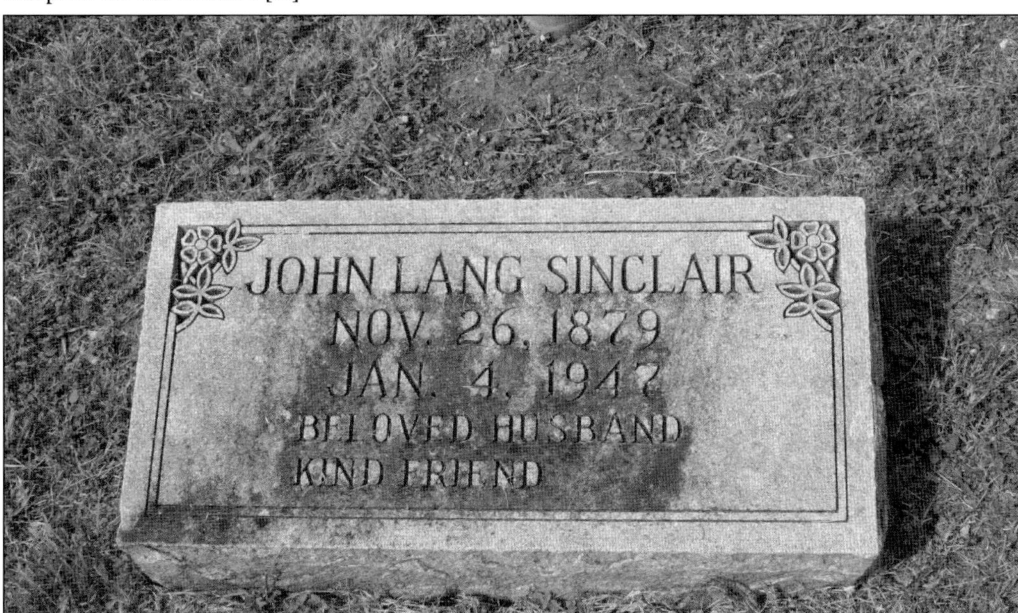

Born in 1879, John Lang Sinclair entered the University of Texas in 1899. In 1903, he was asked to write a school song, which became "The Eyes of Texas," first performed at the Hancock Opera House. Sinclair graduated in 1904 and returned to his family's dairy farm in Bexar County. Later, in 1923, he moved to New York and worked in a tax and investment service until his death in 1945. [11]

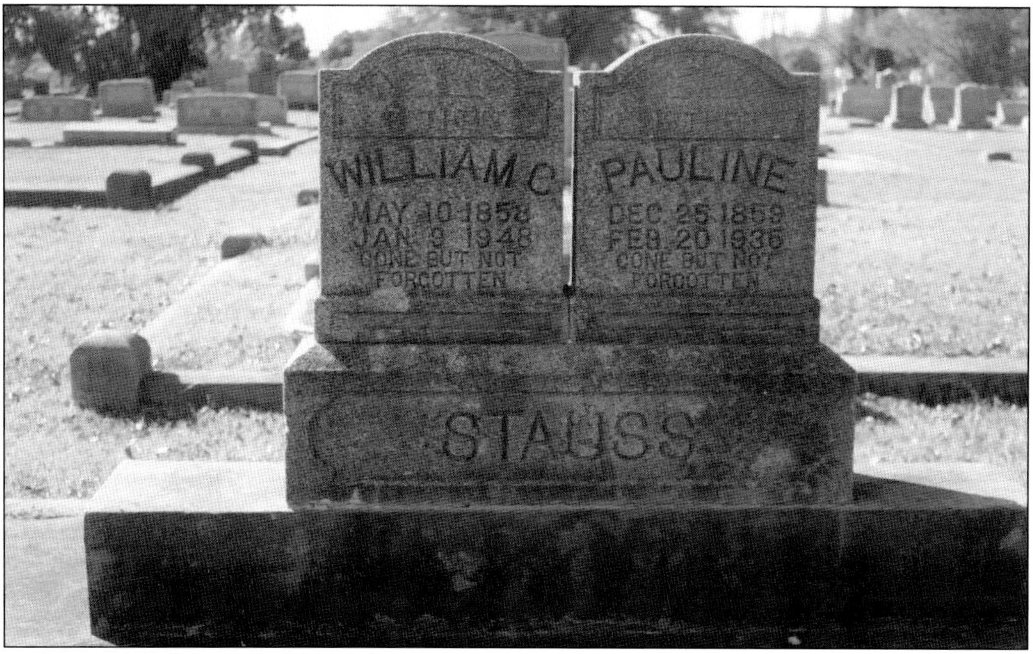

Pauline and William Stauss lived almost all their lives in Bexar County until moving to Bayside, Refugio County, probably to be near their son Fred J. Stauss who lived close by in Woodsboro. Pauline was a member of the Brunhilde Lodge, Hermann Sons, Woodmen Circle, and St. John's Lutheran Church. William was a member of Hermonia Lodge No. 1. [12]

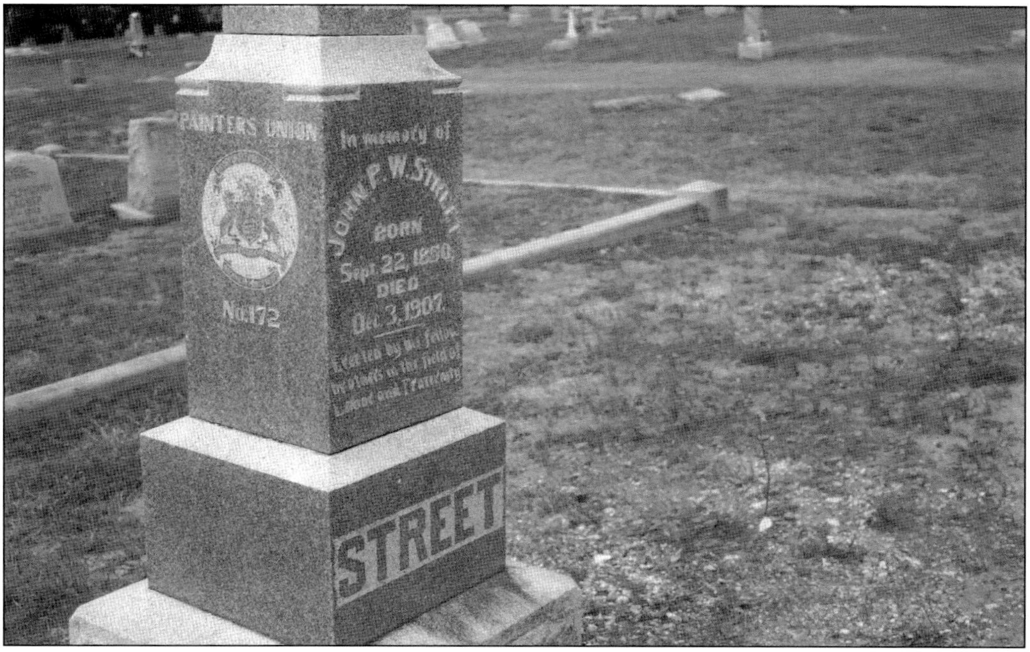

Virginia-born John P.W. Street Sr. appears in 1870 as a hotel clerk in Gallipolis, Ohio. In 1880, he was in St. Louis and married Bessie. John was a paper hanger. By 1883, the family moved to San Antonio, where he continued to work as a paper hanger. When he passed in 1907, fellow Painters Union No. 172 members erected a very nice monument to him. [8]

Born in 1848, George R. Stumberg studied at the German-English school and then finished his education in New York. He then entered his father's Stumberg General Store on South Alamo Street, which became the leading merchandise store in the city, especially among farmers, and a community center. He was an organizer of the National Bank of Commerce. In 1873, he married Dora Rossi, daughter of a pioneer stonemason. [11]

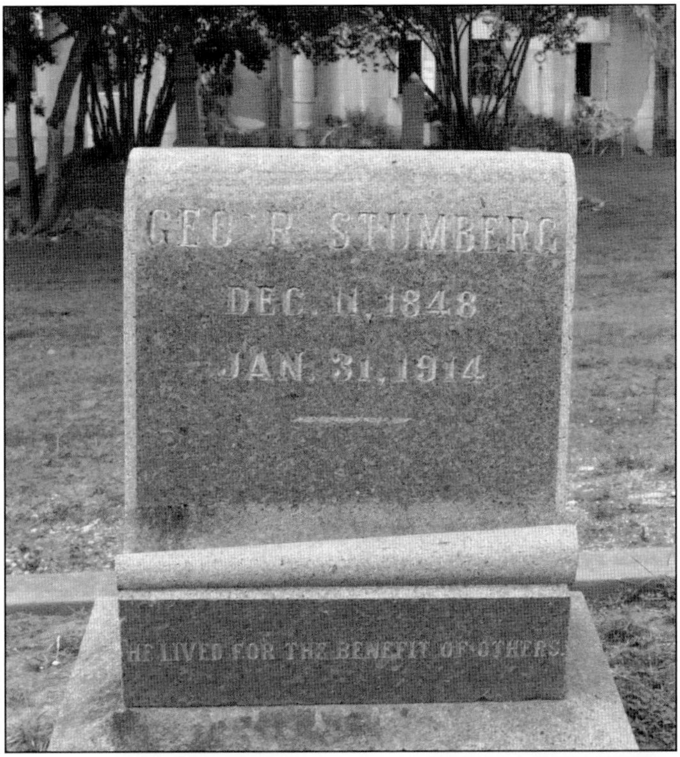

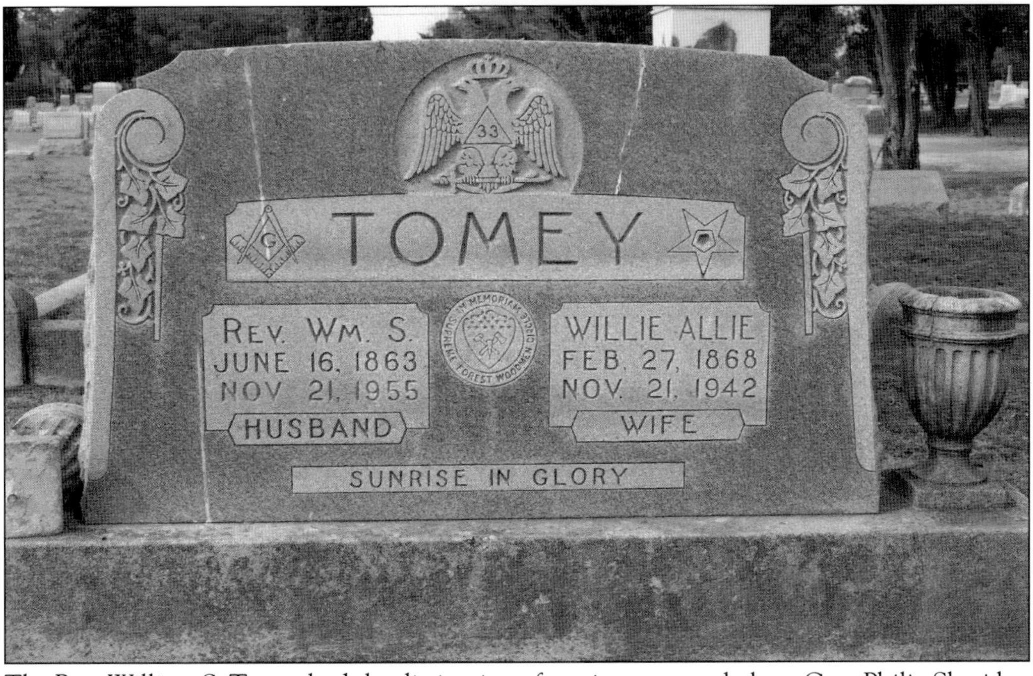

The Rev. William S. Tomey had the distinction of serving as an orderly to Gen. Philip Sheridan at Jefferson Barracks, Missouri, while he served in the 3rd US Cavalry. For many years beginning in 1893, he served as a minister in the Methodist Church. A 33rd-degree Mason, he attended 82 of 83 semiannual reunions at the Scottish Rite Temple. [31]

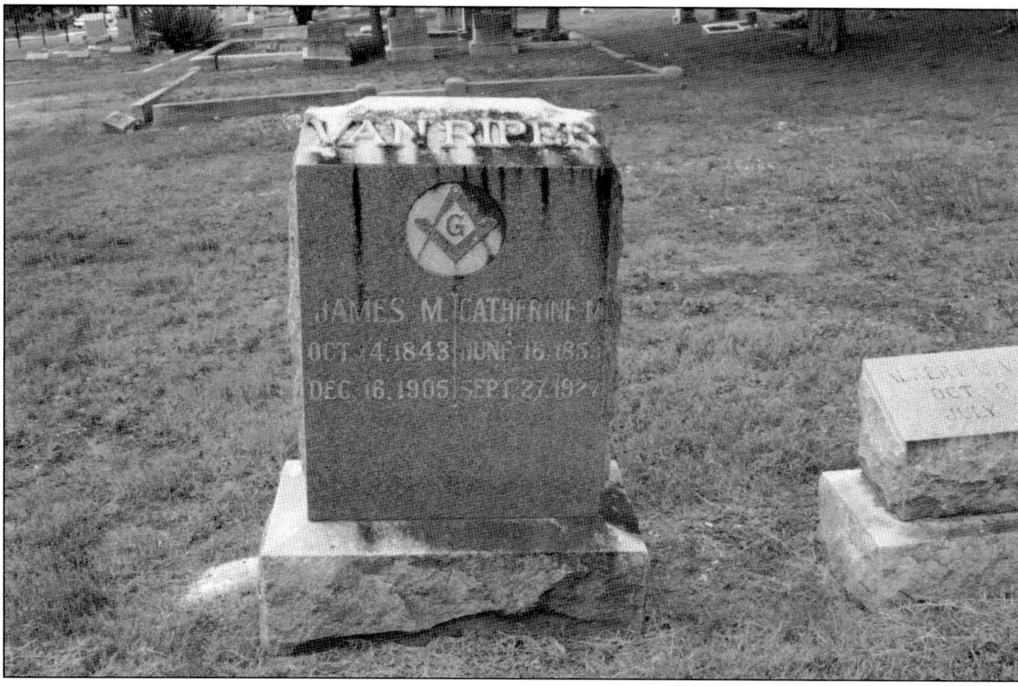

A New York boy, James M. Van Riper moved with his family to California where he herded sheep. In 1858, they settled near San Antonio. When the Civil War came, the young man joined the Confederacy's 21st Texas Cavalry. In 1870, Van Riper was appointed deputy sheriff of Bexar County and, later, a deputy US marshal. He served as city marshal (chief of police) from 1901 until 1903 and again in 1905. [11]

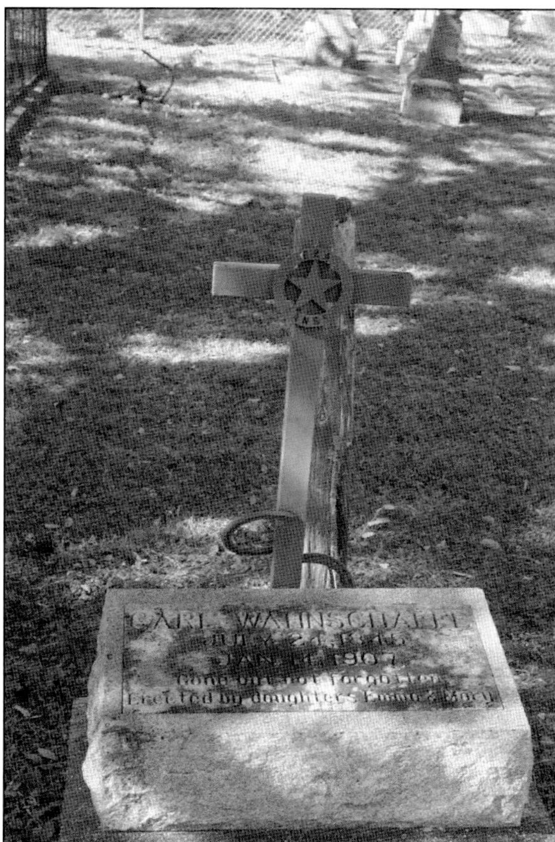

This simple stone, placed by two of his four daughters, marks the grave of Carl Wahnschaffe. The medal cross and star note the fact that for a while he served as a Texas Ranger. While he is buried here, his wife, Fredericka, is buried in the Old Lutheran Cemetery. She was a member of the Louisa Schuetze Lodge of Hermann Sons' Sisters, St. John's Lutheran Church, and Ladies' Aid Society. [28]

Amelia Wallace was laid to rest in the Hermann Sons Cemetery in June 1912. Her parents were Benjamin Berry and Annie Marie Simon of Germany. She died in Schertz. Just two years before, she had lived at 520 Monterey Street and had her home burglarized. The shells covering the grave are a Southern custom found throughout the region in African American, German, Anglo, and Hispanic cemeteries. [12]

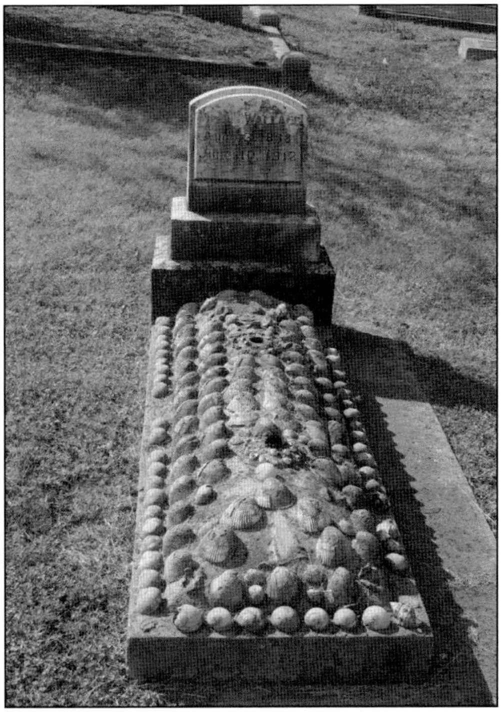

With cemeteries comes the need for monument makers. By 1883, Michael C. Brennan and Joseph Dellmare were established as marble dealers at 238 Houston Street at the corner of Navarro Street. By 1885, Joseph Bukiski had replaced Brennan, and the marble dealers were at Avenue C between Houston and Travis Streets. [4]

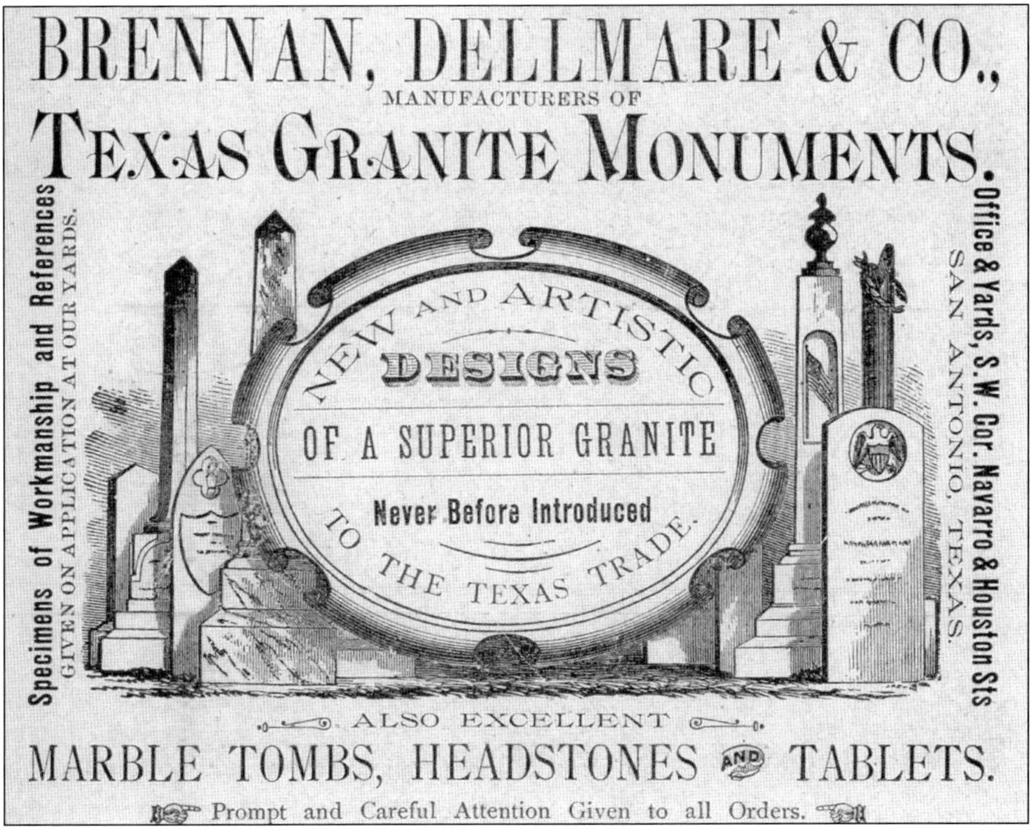

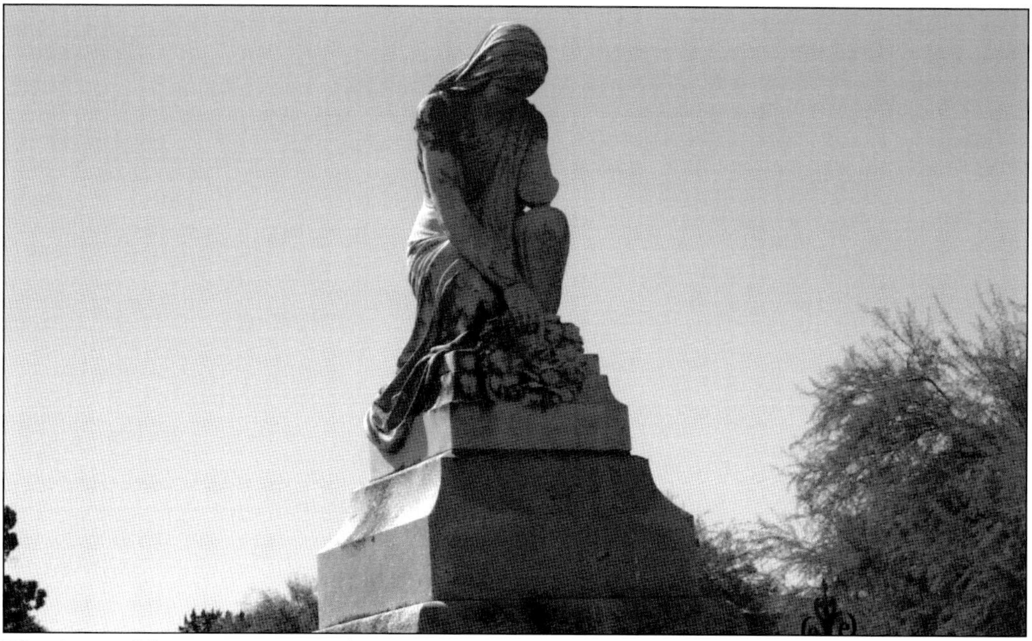

This beautiful statue sits atop the monument to Otto Zirkel, born in Dresden, Germany, on November 26, 1856. At age 14, he came to the United States, first going to Chicago, where he learned the granite business. Arriving here in 1885, he established a small granite works, which, by the time of his death in 1924, was a major business with 20 employees. He was a member of the Hackberry Methodist Church. [22]

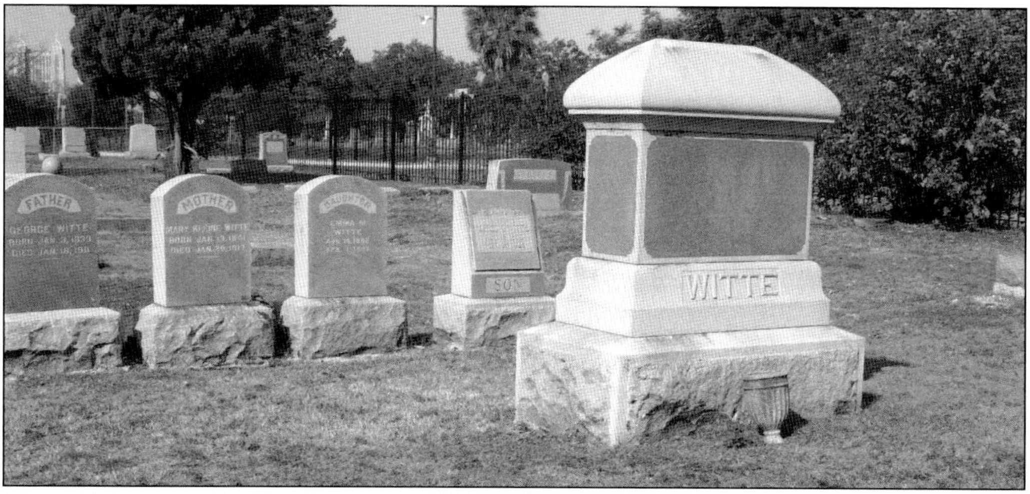

George Witte arrived in San Antonio in 1855. By that time, he had already had an eventful life. As a young man, he had traveled from Green Bay, Wisconsin, to the goldfields of California. From there he traveled to Australia in search of gold and then to South America and Mexico. Once in San Antonio, he bought large tracts of land mostly in the business section, which he developed over time. George's son, Alfred George Witte, grew up in San Antonio. The first 25 years of his business life were spent in New York, where he met and married Margaret Gray, daughter of Scotsman Thomas and Irishwoman Kate of New York. Upon returning to San Antonio, he engaged in real estate and financial matters, amassing a fortune. Upon his death, he left the city a large sum guaranteeing the construction of what is now the Witte Museum. [31]

Six

Small Cemeteries

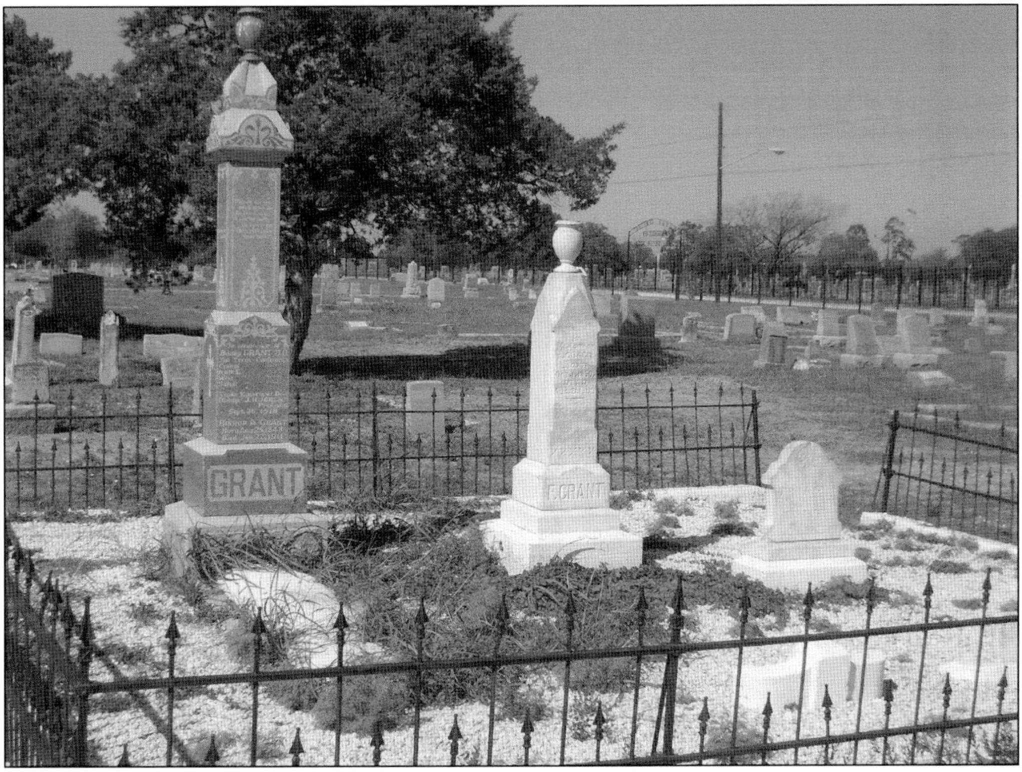

This is the family of Abram S. Grant, a bishop of the African Methodist Episcopal Church. Bishop Grant was born a slave in Florida. Educated after the Civil War, he moved to Texas in 1878, ministering to churches in Austin and San Antonio. He became bishop in 1888 and served in the West and Midwest. He passed away in 1911 in Kansas, but was returned to San Antonio, reuniting his family. [27]

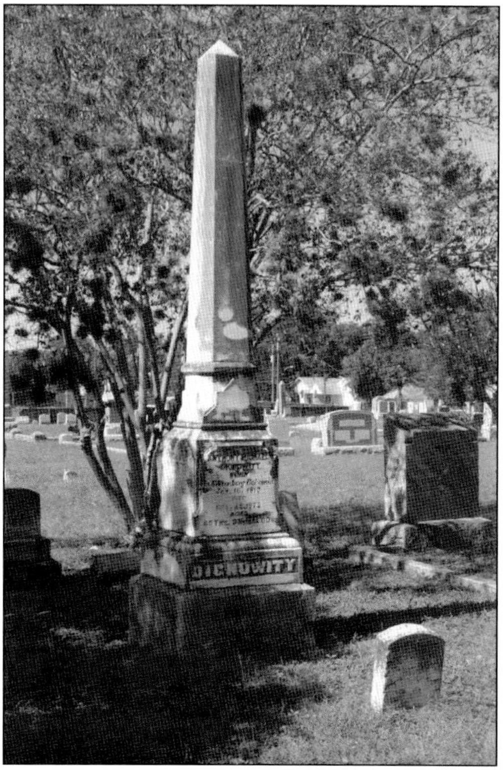

Anthony Michael Dignowity and his family were among the first Czechs to settle in Texas. Raised in Bohemia and trained as a mechanical engineer, he became involved in an unsuccessful revolution and fled his homeland. In Mississippi and Ohio, he studied medicine, first practicing in Indian Territory. He volunteered for the Mexican-American War in 1846 and was stationed in San Antonio. Because of the need for doctors on the frontier, he stayed. A staunch Unionist, when the Civil War began, he left his family in Texas and fled the state.

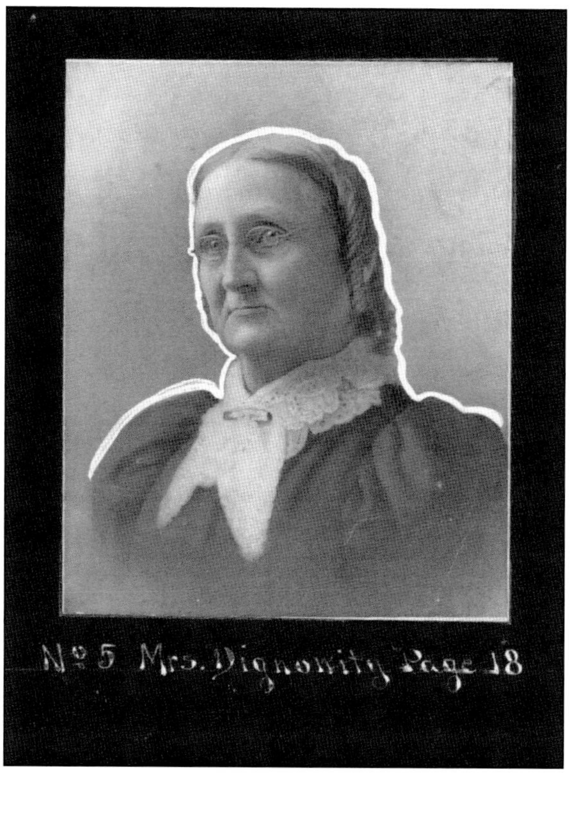

Amanda (McCann) Dignowity was born in County Tyrone, Ireland. Her family came to America, moving about the country for several years. In 1840, they settled in Arkansas where she met Dr. Dignowity, and they married. After the Mexican-American War, she and her children traveled to San Antonio by boat and mule train. She assisted Dr. Dignowity in his practice. Later described by Mary Maverick in her memoirs, Amanda was especially noted for her work during the cholera epidemic. (Courtesy of the Photograph Collection of the Texana and Genealogy Department of the San Antonio Public Library.) [7]

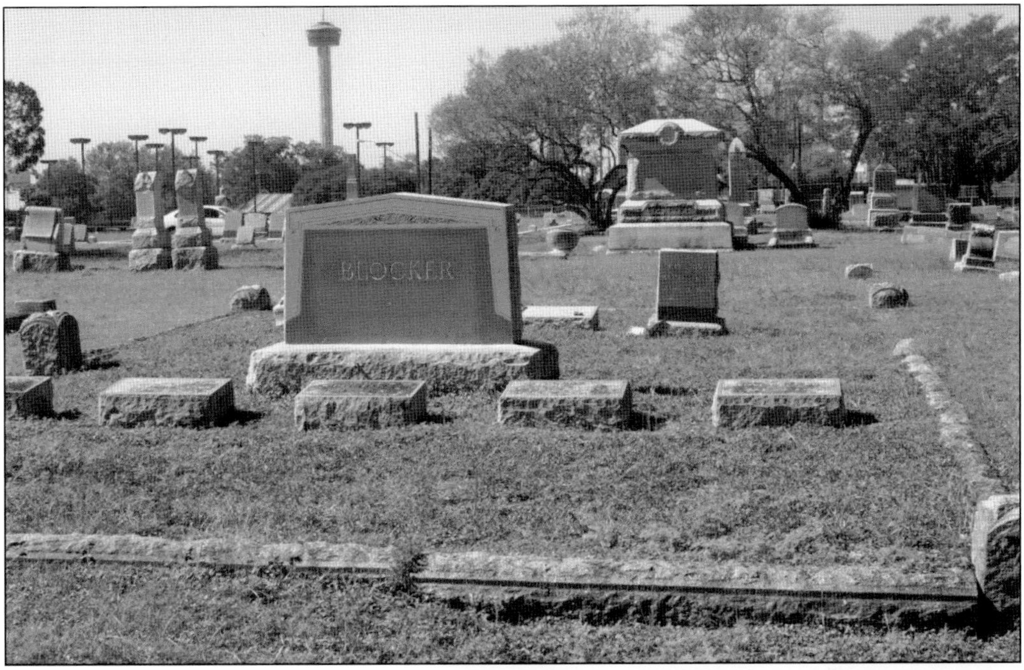

Abner Pickens Blocker was a trail driver who delivered the first herd of cattle to the famous XIT Ranch, also giving the ranch its name and brand. In 1877, he helped herd 3,000 head of cattle to Wyoming. During his career as a trail driver, he drove cattle herds to Kansas, Colorado, Montana, and as far as Canada. In 1912, he began working for the Texas Cattle Raisers Association. [7]

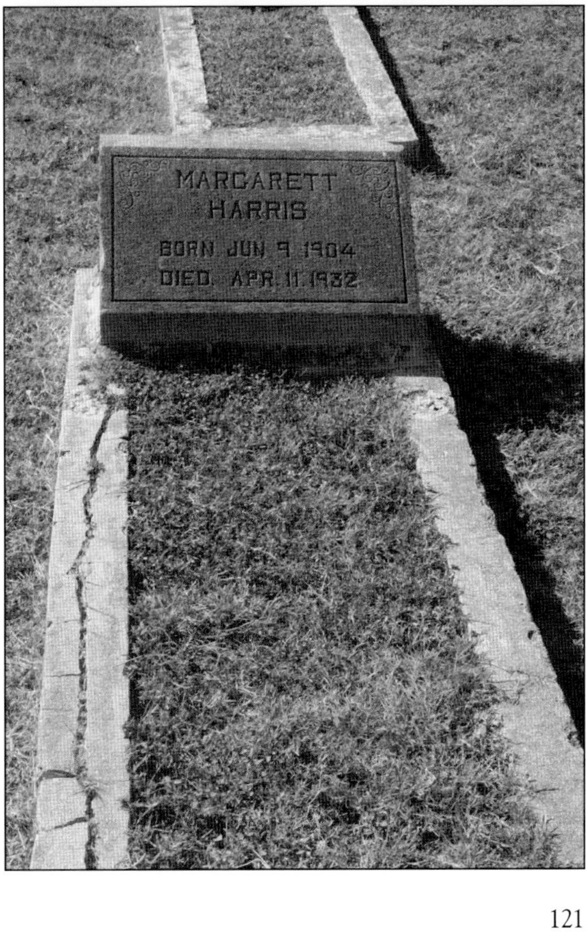

Margarett Harris was only 28 when she died of appendicitis. Her father, Thomas, was from Victoria, and her mother, Vannie, was from Brenham. Margarett worked as a domestic. [26]

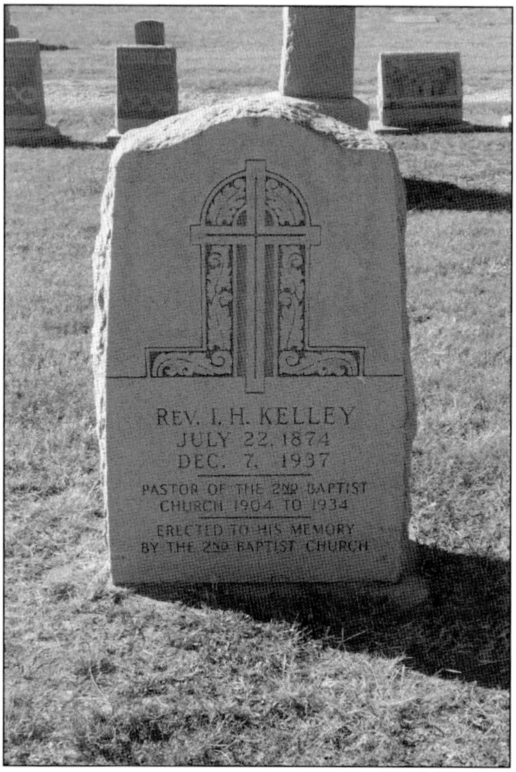

The Rev. Isaiah H. Kelley served as pastor of Second Baptist Church from 1904 to 1934. Reverend Kelley was born in Halletsville, attended local schools, and graduated from Guadalupe College in Seguin. At Second Baptist, a new building was constructed and completed by 1912. He was active statewide and nationally in the Baptist Church. He was a member of the Beacon Light Masonic Lodge and St. Elmo Knights of Pythias. [26]

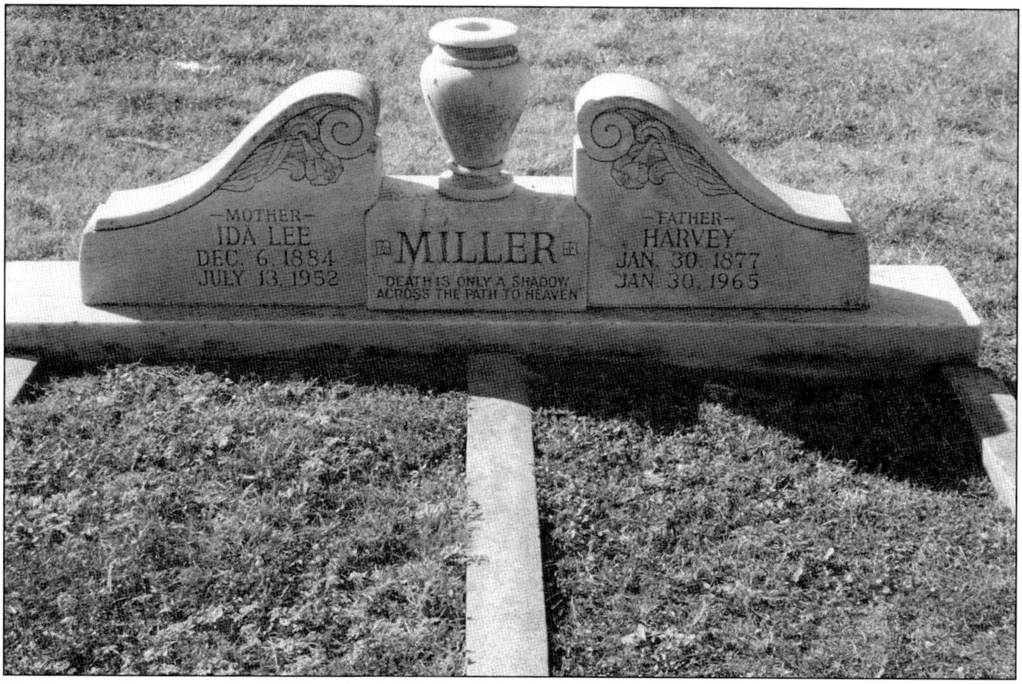

Ida Lee and Harvey Miller lived at 1020 Morales Street. Harvey was a porter for the Missouri Pacific Railroad, and Ida was a housewife. The message on the stone is enlightening: "Death is only a shadow / across the path to heaven." [3]

Charity E. Moore said she was born in Arkansas in April 1842. Her father was from Ohio, and her mother was from Tennessee. She died in 1919 of acute indigestion from "improper food," according to her death certificate. She was a cook for John Herndon, which explains the inscription: "God be with you / till we meet again / Faithful friend of / Mrs. John Herndon / James / for 30 years." [27]

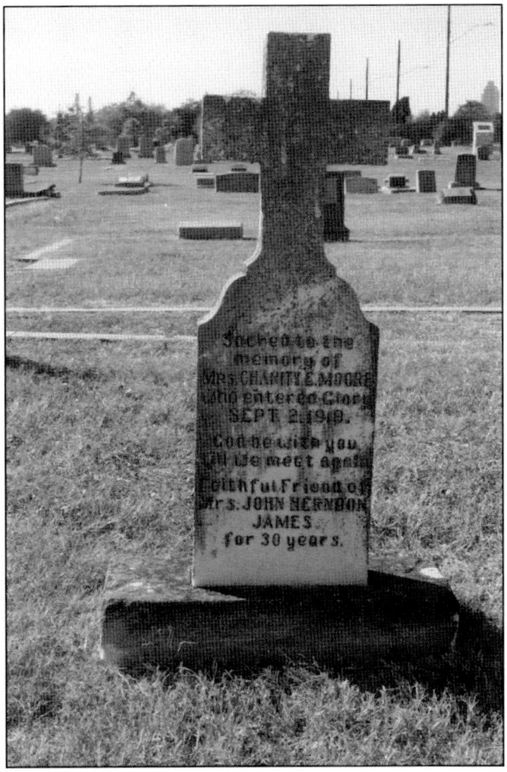

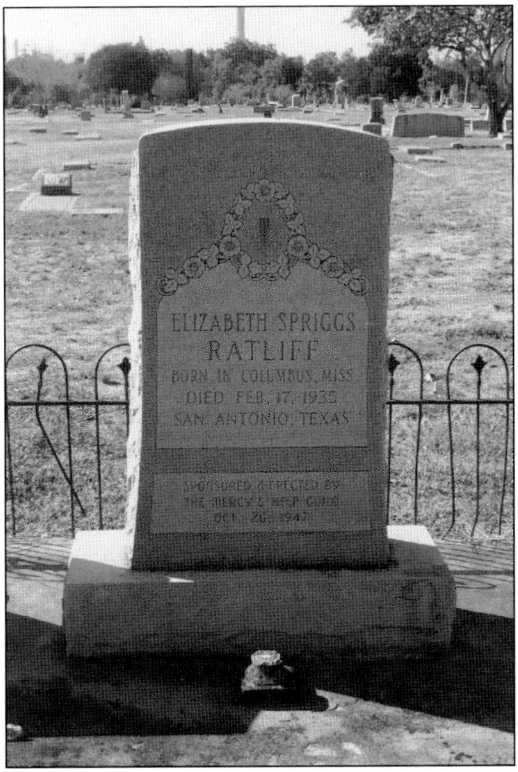

Elizabeth Spriggs Ratliff was born in Columbus, Mississippi. Her husband, John, was a janitor in an office building. Elizabeth worked as a dressmaker for a private family in 1910. Later, she was listed as a missionary for the Methodist Episcopal Church, as a member of St. Paul Methodist Episcopal Church. [26]

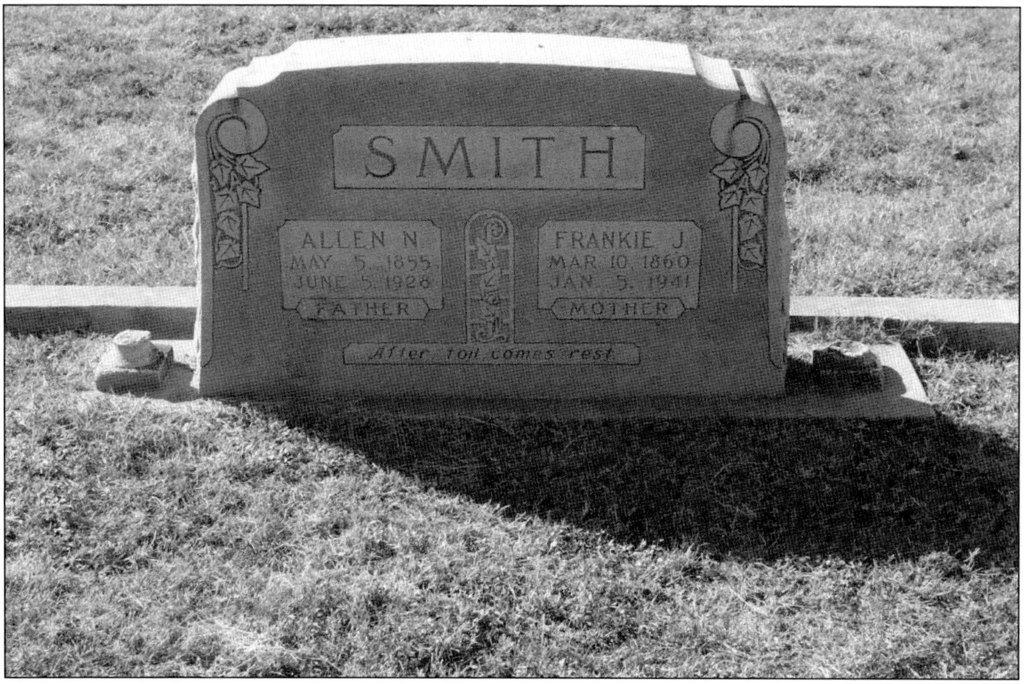

Allen N. Smith owned his own wagon for hauling. Frances, or "Frankie," worked as a laundress for private families. Born in Gonzales, Frankie died of influenza at age 40. The inscription on the gravestone is quite appropriate for these hard working people: "After toil comes rest." [27]

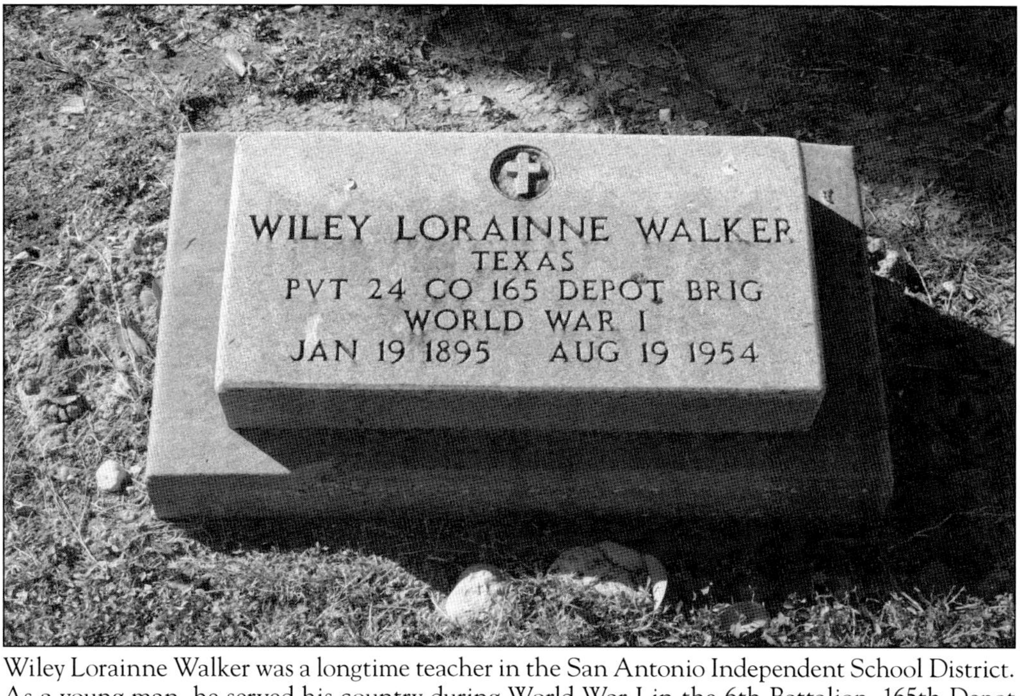

Wiley Lorainne Walker was a longtime teacher in the San Antonio Independent School District. As a young man, he served his country during World War I in the 6th Battalion, 165th Depot Brigade. He was a member of the American Legion, Fred Brock Post No. 828, and Phi Beta Sigma fraternity. [26]

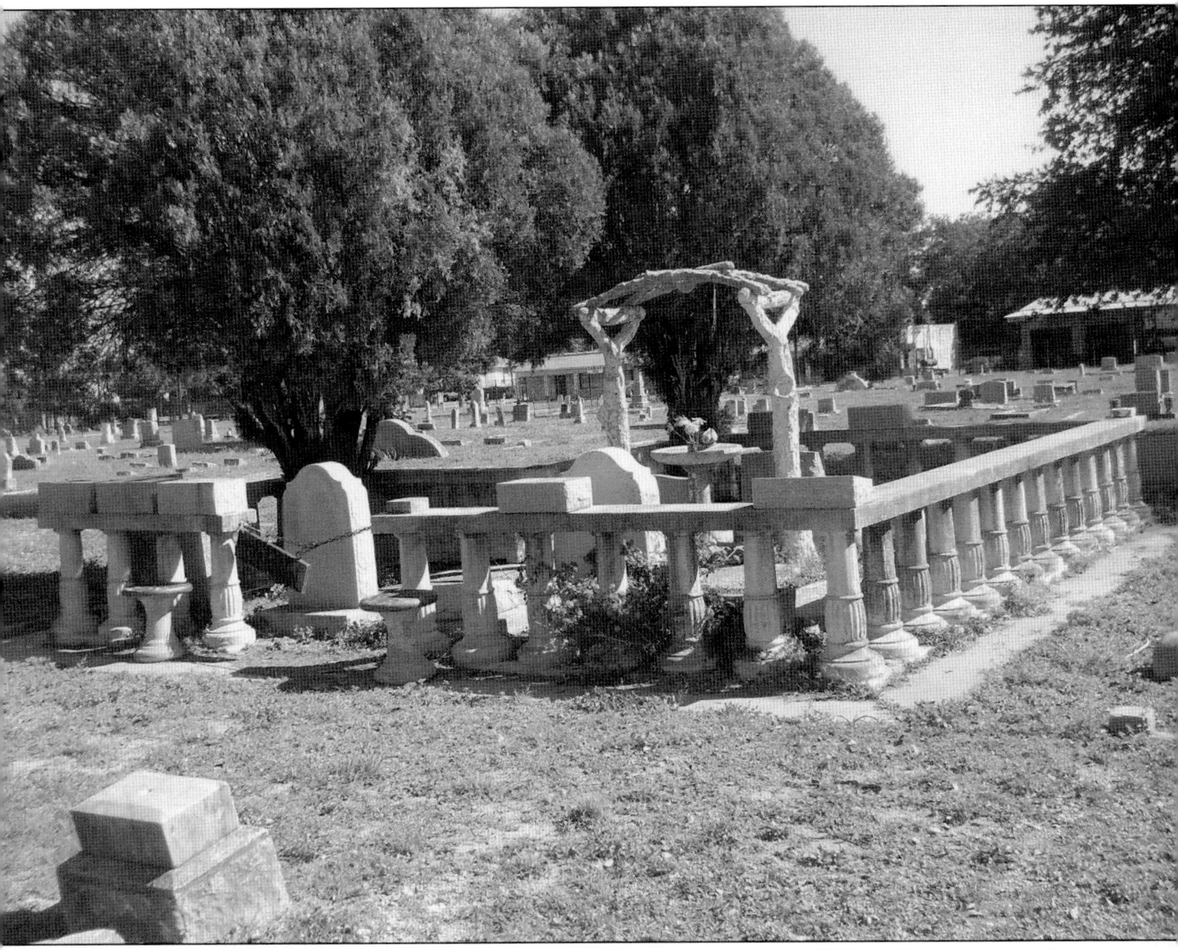

The Wrenn family lot is an impressive one. James Wrenn was born in 1870 in Texas, as were his parents. He had worked as a laborer and warehouseman, though he was retired when he died. Grace Joseph Wrenn, James's wife, was born in 1873 and was a housewife. Their son Joseph lived next door in 1920 and was a chauffeur for a lumber company. [3]

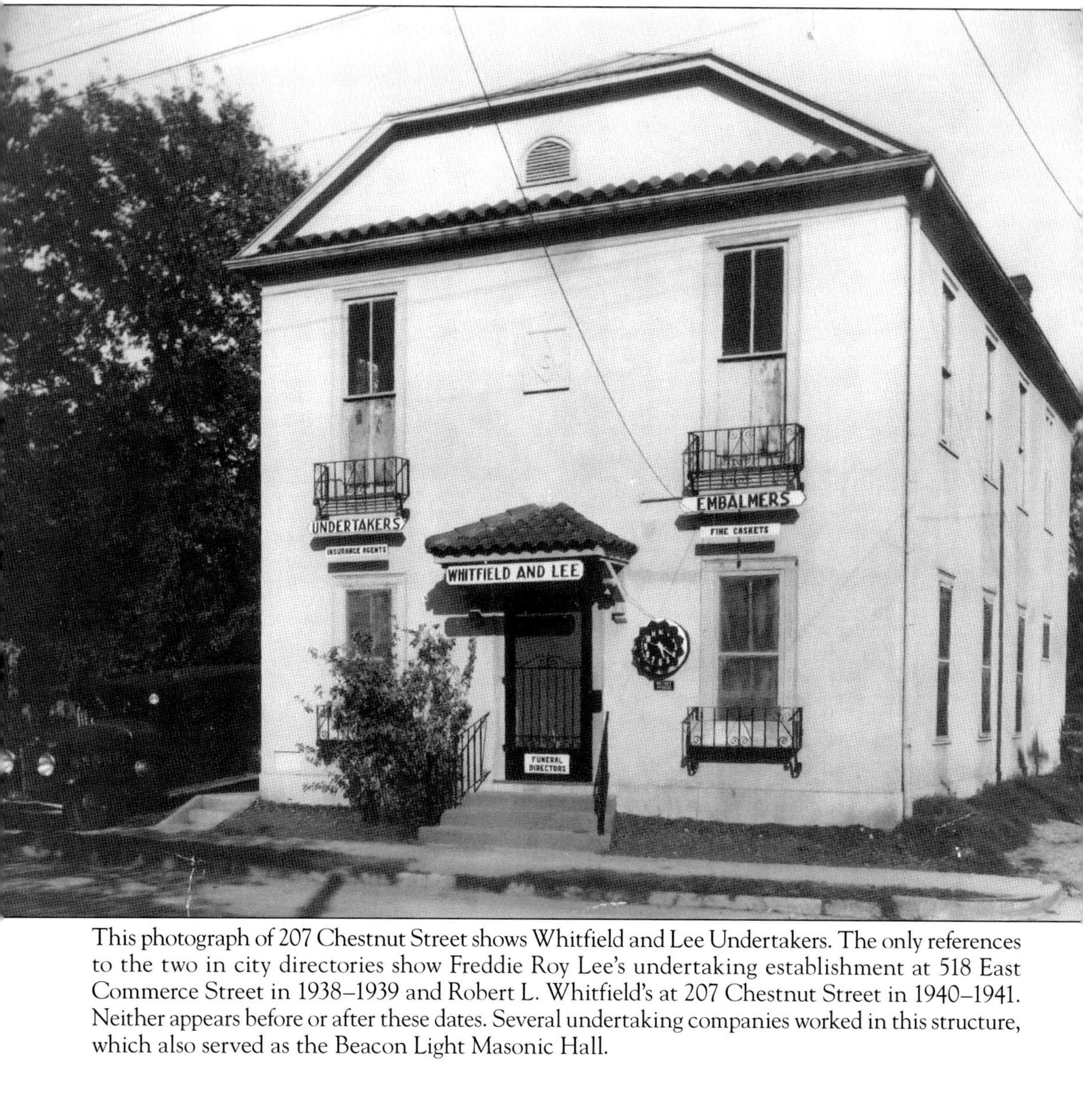

This photograph of 207 Chestnut Street shows Whitfield and Lee Undertakers. The only references to the two in city directories show Freddie Roy Lee's undertaking establishment at 518 East Commerce Street in 1938–1939 and Robert L. Whitfield's at 207 Chestnut Street in 1940–1941. Neither appears before or after these dates. Several undertaking companies worked in this structure, which also served as the Beacon Light Masonic Hall.

Bibliography

Art Work of San Antonio. Chicago, IL: W.H. Parish Publishing Co., 1894.

Barnes, Charles Merritt. *Combats and Conquests of Immortal Heroes*. San Antonio, TX: Guessaz & Ferlet Company, 1910.

Benevolent and Protective Order of Elks, San Antonio Lodge No. 216. San Antonio, TX: 1906.

The Eastside Cemetery District: Where San Antonio History Lives. 1991.

Jules A. Appler's General Directory of the City of San Antonio, 1898. San Antonio, TX: Appler, 1898.

Men of Affairs of San Antonio. c. 1912.

Morrison & Fourmey's General Directory of the City of San Antonio, 1883–84. Galveston, TX: Clark & Courts.

Parisot, Pierre F. and C.J. Smith. *History of the Catholic Church in the Diocese of San Antonio*. San Antonio, TX: Carrico and Bowen, 1897.

Photograph Collection of the Texana and Genealogy Department of the San Antonio Public Library.

San Antonio Parks and Recreation Department Historical Collection.

Six Historical "Colored People's" Cemeteries in San Antonio, Texas. San Antonio, TX: The African American Genealogical and Historical Society of San Antonio, 1997.

Theatre Archives of the Texana and Genealogy Department of the San Antonio Public Library.

Discover Thousands of Local History Books Featuring Millions of Vintage Images

Arcadia Publishing, the leading local history publisher in the United States, is committed to making history accessible and meaningful through publishing books that celebrate and preserve the heritage of America's people and places.

Find more books like this at
www.arcadiapublishing.com

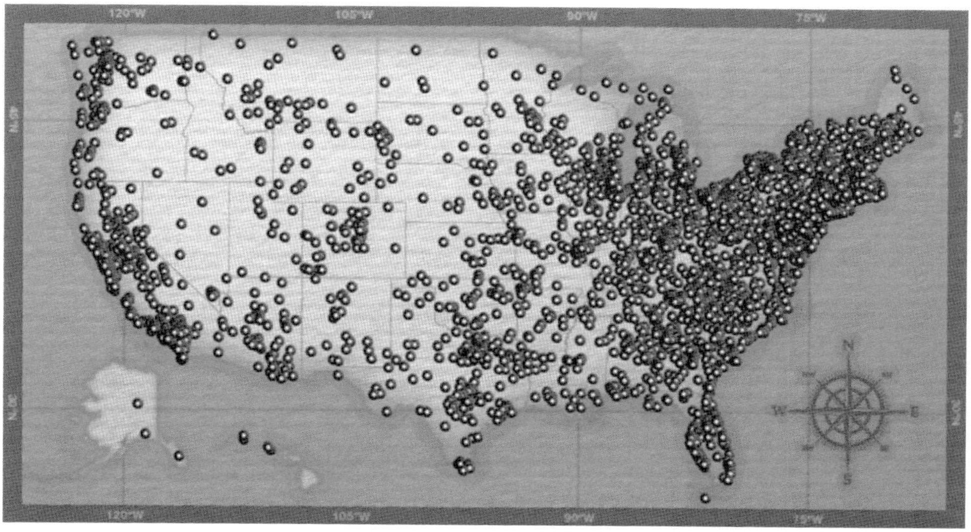

Search for your hometown history, your old stomping grounds, and even your favorite sports team.

Consistent with our mission to preserve history on a local level, this book was printed in South Carolina on American-made paper and manufactured entirely in the United States. Products carrying the accredited Forest Stewardship Council (FSC) label are printed on 100 percent FSC-certified paper.

MADE IN THE USA